Advance Pr

Phantoms of a Beleaguered Republic

"This nuanced interrogation of competing conceptions of American government—a Deep State based on a dense administrative apparatus transcending party and presidential administrations, and a unitary executive charting a direct relationship between president and people—combines theoretical clarity with uncommon learning. Written with cool reason, yet urgently, about a profound political conundrum, the book's quest for common ground offers a valuable act of democratic guardianship."

Ira Katznelson, Ruggles Professor of Political Science and History, Columbia University

"This pathbreaking book elucidates the competing, interconnected pulls of the 'unitary executive' and the 'Deep State' in American political development. By training on their juncture, *Phantoms* unravels the implications of these powerful ideas for how our federal government functions—and its profound and wrenching dysfunctions."

Daphna Renan, Peter B. Munroe and Mary J. Munroe Professor of Law, Harvard Law School

"*Phantoms* is a compelling account of a regime in distress. The authors deliver stunning insights into the excruciating stresses between presidential ambitions to singular executive power and a deep state capable of good governance but prone to hubris. Their conclusion that avoiding the complete loss of the value of depth requires systematic reimagining of institutional designs and relationships deserves the attention of all friends of the American republic."

Brian J. Cook, author of *The Fourth Branch: Reconstructing the Administrative State for the Commercial Republic*

"Skowronek, Dearborn, and King offer a brilliant analysis of the confrontation between 'the Deep State' and the unitary executive. Frictions between the president and the federal bureaucracy came to a head under Trump, but they predated his presidency and will remain a hallmark of American politics."

Margaret Weir, Wilson Professor of International and Public Affairs and Political Science, Brown University

"This book shows how Donald Trump's attacks on the 'deep state' laid bare a profound tension that pre-dated Trump and will survive him."

Rogers M. Smith, Christopher H. Browne Distinguished Professor of Political Science, University of Pennsylvania

"Taking seriously arguments too often reduced to partisan caricature, this book masterfully traces the historical tension between bureaucratic accountability and independent expertise. In so doing the authors tee up a new agenda for the study of executive governance – and write a field guide for presidents hoping to close the gap between good politics and enlightened administration."

Andrew Rudalevige, Thomas Brackett Reed Professor of Government, Bowdoin College

"In the best study of the Trump administration's executive actions to date, *Phantoms of the Beleaguered Republic* makes clear that Trump's war on expertise is more than a cult of personality; it is a reckoning in the long struggle to command a large and complex state that determines how fundamental American values are interpreted and enforced."

Sidney M. Milkis, White Burkett Miller Professor of Governance and Foreign Affairs, University of Virginia

"Blending grand historical sweep with meticulous political analysis, this is a wise and illuminating look at the deep roots of our contemporary predicament. From the perpetual tension between the 'Deep State' and the 'unitary executive,' Skowronek, Dearborn, and King fashion an important new interpretation of American political development."

Robert C. Lieberman, Krieger-Eisenhower Professor of Political Science, Johns Hopkins University

Phantoms of a Beleaguered Republic

The Deep State
and the Unitary Executive

New, Expanded Edition

STEPHEN SKOWRONEK,
JOHN A. DEARBORN, AND DESMOND KING

OXFORD
UNIVERSITY PRESS

OXFORD
UNIVERSITY PRESS

Oxford University Press is a department of the University of Oxford. It furthers the University's objective of excellence in research, scholarship, and education by publishing worldwide. Oxford is a registered trade mark of Oxford University Press in the UK and certain other countries.

Published in the United States of America by Oxford University Press
198 Madison Avenue, New York, NY 10016, United States of America.

© Oxford University Press 2021

First issued as an Oxford University Press paperback 2022

Library of Congress Cataloging-in-Publication Data
Names: Skowronek, Stephen, author. | Dearborn, John A., author. |
King, Desmond S., author.
Title: Phantoms of a beleaguered republic : the deep state and the unitary executive /
Stephen Skowronek, John A. Dearborn, Desmond King.
Other titles: Deep state and the unitary executive
Description: New York, NY : Oxford University Press, 2021. |
Includes bibliographical references and index.
Identifiers: LCCN 2020026314 (print) | LCCN 2020026315 (ebook) |
ISBN 9780197543085 (hardback) | ISBN 9780197656945 (paperback) |
ISBN 9780197543108 (epub) | ISBN 9780197543115
Subjects: LCSH: Trump, Donald, 1946—Influence. | Conspiracies—United States. |
United States—Politics and government—2017– | United States—Politics and
government—21st century. | Executive power—United States. |
Authoritarianism—United States.
Classification: LCC E912 .S59 2021 (print) | LCC E912 (ebook) | DDC 973.933092—dc23
LC record available at https://lccn.loc.gov/2020026314
LC ebook record available at https://lccn.loc.gov/2020026315

DOI: 10.1093/oso/9780197543085.001.0001

1 3 5 7 9 8 6 4 2

Paperback printed by Marquis, Canada

For Susan, Laura, and Sam

Contents

Contents

Preface

Early commentaries tended to detach the Trump presidency from the rest of presidential history. It was "not normal"; it was an "aberration"; it was *sui generis*. Thinking about it that way was oddly comforting. Attention focused on the man, not the governing arrangements that made him possible. But presidents are not aliens. They are home-grown products of our institutions. Rather than cabin Trump's performance, we have tried in this book to open it up to a more systemic inquiry, to treat it as a significant commentary on the state of the state in America.

The project began as coffee-table conversation in Oxford during the winter of 2019. King hosted Skowronek, on sabbatical at the Rothermere American Institute, to a weekly lunch at Nuffield College, and before long they settled into a discussion of what President Trump's assault on the "Deep State" might have to tell us about state formation and problems of institutional design in American government. They decided to write an article together that would examine the competing design ideas on display during the Trump years and how they interacted in practice. Of particular interest was how claims about a unitary executive had forced to the fore questions about the value of depth in the modern American state.

In the spring of 2019, King and Skowronek brought to Oxford a wide-ranging group of scholars for two days of intense conversation about the Trump presidency. The paper that emerged from this conference underwent significant changes over the course of subsequent transatlantic conversations, and it soon became clear that the article format was inadequate to the range of issues that seemed pertinent to our topic. That is when Yale's Dearborn joined the project. With his collaboration, conceptual exposition and empirical investigation sorted intuitions into chapters, and the project transformed itself into a book.

By May 2020—with the coronavirus lockdown concentrating the mind on a state seemingly at odds with itself—we had a complete manuscript. Oxford University Press generously allowed us more than the usual leeway to update what we had written while the book was in production, so until late August we were able to keep current with late-breaking developments. The text was locked in with an election looming. Some of the issues we had taken up seemed to intensify under that pressure. Others, newly emergent—like presidential interventions at the US Postal Service and the US Census Bureau—suggested patterns similar to those we identify here. Our intent has been to frame these contests, historically and analytically, clarifying thereby the stakes raised for the organization and deployment of state power in twenty-first century America.

We are grateful for the support we received in Oxford from the Rothermere American Institute's Winant Fund and Nuffield College's Mellon Fund. We acknowledge as well support at Yale from the Center for the Study of Representative Institutions at the MacMillan Center and from the Institution for Social and Policy Studies.

At the Oxford conference, the contributions of Nigel Bowles, Corey Brettschneider, Gareth Davies, Samuel DeCanio, Janina Dill, Gary Gerstle, Ursula Hackett, Richard Johnson, Hal Jones, Trevor McCriskin, Sidney Milkis, Gillian Peele, Andrew Rudalevige, Dara Strolovitch, Peter Trubowitz, and Stephen Tuck were stimulating and significant influences upon our thinking. Along the way, we benefited from extensive discussions with others, many of them offering helpful readings of chapters and drafts. We are grateful to Brian Cook, Blake Emerson, Daniel Galvin, Jack Greenberg, Stephanie Higginson, Andrea Katz, Christina Kinane, Didi Kuo, Frances Lee, David Lewis, David Mayhew, Sidney Milkis, Bruce Miroff, Karen Orren, Daphna Renan, Noah Rosenblum,

Andrew Rudalevige, Adam Sheingate, Calvin TerBeek, Ian Turner, Benjamin Waldman, and Margaret Weir.

At Oxford University Press, David McBride has been an enthusiastic and constructive editor whose support for the book has been invaluable. Emily Mackenzie and Jeremy Toynbee expertly guided the book through the production process. We are also grateful to the four anonymous referees whose comments prompted lengthy discussions among the authors and an important reworking of the text. We are unlikely to have appeased all the readers' queries but believe we have clarified our aims and content immeasurably in response to their prompts.

Foreword for the Paperback Edition

The publication of a paperback edition of *Phantoms of a Beleaguered Republic* affords an opportunity to reflect on the book's themes, to consider some of the commentary, and to scout events that have occurred since the volume first appeared. Our new Afterword takes up issues surrounding the 2020 election and ascendance of Joe Biden. In this Foreword, we revisit the broad ground of our analysis, the better to address readers who are looking beyond the Trump presidency.

By the time we started work on this book, much had already been said about Donald Trump's wanton disregard of the fundamentals of good government. We began with something different and more troubling in mind. As we saw it, fundamentals had been set at cross purposes long before Trump. We wanted to show how, over preceding decades, common sense understandings of good government had grown muddled and contradictory. *Phantoms* calls attention to the political and institutional arrangements that made Trumpism possible. These arrangements not only preceded him; they survived him. We looked at Trump's use of these arrangements to shed new light on the wayward course of presidential democracy in America.

Presidents mobilize the electorate, and they manage the executive branch. These are the rudiments of presidential democracy. The expectation, clear if often only implicit, is that these two activities will complement one another. But that is the nub of the problem: they don't align naturally.

The relationship between political mobilization and executive branch management is constructed and expressed institutionally. Presidential democracies rely on these constructions to prevent the incumbent's two assignments from collapsing in on one another and to maintain instead a salutary balance between popular rule and responsible government. But arrangements vary widely from one place to another and from one period to the next. Some perform better than others. Some prove downright toxic.

Although the spectrum of possible arrangements is quite broad, the original construction of the American presidency is an instructive outlier. Far from proposing a positive relationship between political mobilization and executive branch management, the Convention that created the presidential office sought to head off any such connection. When Article II of the Constitution vested presidents with "the executive power" and secured their independence from Congress, it immediately stipulated an indirect selection system. The exercise of executive power was to be detached from political factions, interested cabals, and popular enthusiasms. The notion of a politicized chief executive was abhorrent to the framers of the Constitution. They saw the threat that politicization would pose to a steady administration of the laws and, beyond that, to the delicate balances struck throughout the constitutional system. To safeguard the governmental commitments entrusted to national administration, the Constitution prescribed management *without* mobilization.

That initial apprehension of a politicized presidency and its potential to wreak havoc on government has come to resonate in contemporary America with newfound clarity. Nonetheless, the framers' formula for fending off these prospects was a nonstarter. Presidential power could not be detached from popular politics. The connection was made immediately; it steadily expanded its influence on government; it became fundamental. Over time, a series of alternative arrangements accommodated political mobilization around the presidency, and with popular leadership added to the president's job description, bringing mobilization into some constructive relationship with executive branch management became an ongoing project. Getting that relationship right remains the abiding problem of presidential democracy in America today.

Phantoms reminds us that our entire constitutional system has, from the very beginning, turned on exactly how, from one period to the next, national political mobilization and executive branch management were brought to bear on one another. Locating the Trump presidency in the long history of these constructions, it identifies an especially troubling shift in the relationship during the 1970s. By the time Trump arrived on the scene, presidential selection and presidential power had been realigned in ways that abetted both candidate-centered political mobilizations and the efforts of the victors to run the executive branch as a direct extension of their own personal following. Trump seized upon that potential, and in doing so, he exposed in full the perversity of the recent drift of affairs. In his hands, management became indistinguishable from mobilization, their virulent fusion nearly hollowing the government out.   TRUMP: mgmt = mobiliz.

Earlier constructions of presidential democracy in America had guarded against this outcome. The historic solution was to couple acknowledgment of a more prominent and political role for presidents as national leaders with a relaxation of the separation of powers and with stronger provisions for inter-branch collaboration in control over the executive branch. These serial rearrangements pushed ever-farther afield of the original constitutional design, but they echoed the sentiments of the founding generation in one particular: all of them shared a staunch republican aversion to presidential populism. For much of the nineteenth century, presidential control of the executive branch was mediated through the organs of a sprawling, decentralized party system. In the twentieth century, reformers "deepened" the state itself. Insulating administrative offices and institutionalizing the presidential office with professional advisers and specialized expertise offered additional hedges against unilateral impositions.

The pattern in recent decades has been quite different. As local party organizations lost their grip on the presidency, candidates for the office were freer to fashion political followings of their own. At the same time, a new formalism took hold, stiffening the separation of powers and, with it, the claims of incumbents to direct and exclusive control over "the executive power." The result is an odd combination of familiar elements. Unlike the original scheme for separating powers, this new arrangement promotes the president's politicization of the executive branch, and unlike latter-day improvisations concocted to control a politicized presidency, the new arrangement is hostile to power sharing. With separation joined to politicization, fundamentals have fused in a uniquely volatile and divisive arrangement.

Between 2016 and 2021, the dynamics inherent in this new arrangement were expressed more vividly than ever before. Trump showed us the strong affinity between the emergence of personal parties and insistence upon a "unitary executive." He also showed us how that amalgam amplifies tensions between the chief executive and the executive branch, fueling presidential efforts to strip away administrative insulation. But that was not all. Trump's attempt to "deconstruct" the executive branch commands our attention because it purported to defend fundamentals. His assault on the "Deep State"—on resistance to his preferences from within the executive branch—was waged in the name of constitutional authority and popular will.

As our text details, the Deep State and the unitary executive are conjectures, extrapolations from the notoriously complicated design of American government. We call them "phantom twins" because they haunt the shadows of the Constitution and draw each other out from its ambiguities. Willful insistence on a unitary executive, hierarchically controlled by the president, is bound to provoke resistance from administrative operatives, not least because Congress has endowed administrators with formidable resources with which to fend off rule by fiat. And resistance to presidential control is just as certain to elicit outrage from the "chief" executive, sharpening claims on behalf of electoral warrants, executive branch unity, and administrative subordination. This is a conundrum which the Constitution alone cannot resolve. It is ingrained in the structure itself, in tensions between the separation of powers, on the one hand, and checks and balances, on the other. If our history is any guide, the best way to address it is through innovations that bridge the divisions in that frame and promote inter-branch collaboration.

One astute reader of our book noted that each of the phantoms unleashed on American government during the Trump years has an attractive empirical counterpart.[1] The specter of a "Deep State" plays upon fears of power that cannot be called to account, but the "depth" derived from the articulation and insulation of administrative instruments is a real and valuable attribute of the state. Depth underwrites competence and professionalism, continuity and consistency, consultation and collaboration. The "unitary executive" has a doppelganger as well. It can be found in all those informal arrangements that sought in earlier times to instill greater "unity" in governmental operations at large. Unity *in the executive*, a notion derived from the constitutional principle of the separation of powers, locates good government in the president's personal responsibility and individual accountability to the people. By contrast, previous arrangements sought unity *in inter-branch relations* and located good government in collective responsibility for the government's commitments. The handiwork of early twentieth-century Progressives is especially telling in this regard. They sought at once to join more closely what the Constitution had separated (president and Congress) and to separate more firmly what the Constitution had joined (presidential power and public administration).

Several readers have said that our book turns out in the end to be a defense of administrative depth against the threat of a unitary executive.[2] Fair enough. Americans are suspicious of bureaucrats, and they idealize strong presidents. That leaves the governmental assets harbored by administrative depth underappreciated and vulnerable. *Phantoms* capitalized on an ironic effect of President Trump's aggressive assaults on depth. Those assaults served, inadvertently, to push the government's administrative assets to the fore. Drawing that dynamic out, we were able to bring the value of depth more fully into view.

But our analysis would hardly have been credible if we had simply ignored the baggage that depth carries in its train. Control of bureaucracy is a real and persistent problem, and we had no interest in covering it up. In the course of our inquiry, we observed stiff bureaucratic resistance to the president, some of it verging on outright subversion. Our objective was to reckon candidly with the values and risks at stake on both sides. We sampled the action at a wide variety of different sites. We examined the claims of the president and those of his administrative targets. We assessed a system under pressure, when the norms and distinctions that support its basic operating principles are most sorely tested.

All told, the threat posed by arbitrary impositions to the values protected by depth proved to be real, and it seemed to far outweigh the risks of protecting those values. The bureaucratic subterfuge we encountered was neutralized repeatedly and in short order. We could not say the same for the president's tempestuous intrusions. Tightening the president's grip on the executive branch may seem the straightforward answer to the problems posed by administrative depth, but this is one of those commonsense notions of good government complicated by the Trump administration. Happily, there is an alternative tradition to draw on, one that credits experimentation with more collective solutions. A little creativity and institutional improvisation might go a long way toward meeting the challenges posed by depth without risking the conceits of unitary command and control.[3]

Still, some readers may object that Trump's rendition of a unitary executive was so over the top that it does a disservice to the idea.[4] Along these lines, a leading advocate of the unitary theory has dismissed Trump as an "oddball" and suggested that we made too much of his efforts to strip away depth.[5] We will assess the effectiveness of Trump's efforts a bit more fully in our Afterword. Suffice it to say here, we look at the matter differently. Trump's assault on the executive branch had a leading theory of the fundamentals of good government to drawn on. A phalanx of lawyers, judges, and constitutional scholars had been advancing this theory for years and, in the process, facilitating presidential efforts to deepen their control over the executive branch. Time and again, officials in the White House and the Justice Department repaired to this theory to justify Trump's actions. Nuance no longer shades its implications. During the Trump administration, we observed the unitary executive in practice. The meaning of the idea was revealed by its active deployment in the pursuit of presidential power.

The Deep State charge figured prominently here. It sharpened the political edges of the unitary theory, weaponizing its largely formal, constitutional argumentation. When Trump stigmatized protections for administrative depth as impediments to the will of the people who had put him in office, he joined a formal claim to singular authority in the executive branch to a political mandate and plebiscitary prerogative. The effect was to transform the Constitution into a vehicle for promoting exactly what it had originally been designed to prevent. Formalism became an instrument for advancing a personal, populist, charismatic presidency. The notion that the Constitution resists power of that kind was met with a disarming response from Trump's mobilized base: "Get over it," they said. "Elections have consequences."

Trump may be an oddball, but the problem posed by Trumpism is institutional. To bracket this presidency as an aberration is to lose sight of just how effectively it pulled forward and drew together disturbing patterns in recent development. Commentators have been warning for decades of the risks of political mobilization through personal parties. Trumpism was no anomaly in that regard. It was the clearest manifestation yet of mobilization through a personal party, and it emphatically confirmed concerns long expressed about that line of development. This was an "extreme" case, to be sure. But Trump elaborated the pattern. In doing so, he told us as much about what is askew in current institutional arrangements as he did about himself.

Developments on the management side have presented themselves a bit differently. The decades-long drumbeat of agitation for a "unitary executive" has been sharply critical of current arrangements. The rhetorical thrust of the reform drive has been to return to the government's founding principles, to correct the errors that have accumulated in the organization of the executive branch, and to realign administrative control around the intent of the Constitution's framers. To that end, advocates have riveted attention on the categorical wording of Article II's "vesting clause." But for anyone attuned to how mobilization bears on management, this plea to return to basics will surely sound odd. The framers' attempt to resolve that critical relationship was a conspicuous failure. Management without mobilization was dead on arrival. That left subsequent generations to reconsider the matter by their own lights. Two centuries of institutional improvisation sought to compensate for the limitations of the framers' formula, and the various solutions reformers came up with were all more-or-less direct critiques of the original constitutional set up.

The point here speaks directly to the current confusion over fundamentals. It deflates our long, tortured debates about the "vesting clause" by calling attention to what immediately follows upon it in the text of Article II, Section 1. That oddly roundabout selection system, chosen after repeated consideration of alternatives, was an integral part of the original deal. When the Constitution separated powers, it vested "the executive power" in an officer who would be only obliquely connected to a popular following. Holding popular leadership at bay was the Constitution's way of binding the president to the national interest and to his duty to faithfully execute the law. Keeping faith with the Constitution after the collapse of that strategy and the rise of popular leadership has always been a matter of improvising alternative means to those ends. In other words, short of retrieving the idea of a depoliticized presidency, "originalists" are left with what is, at best, a partial rendering of the initial meaning, and it turns out that the skewed image offered compounds the underlying problem.

The framers wanted a strong presidency, but they were equally concerned to prevent the executive power from becoming the strong arm of one man's personal following. If we want to retrieve something of original meaning, we might begin there, for we have now seen the framers' nightmare become reality. The selection system has changed radically since the vesting clause was written. That makes an abrupt turn back to the "plain words" of that clause misleading, if not flat-out dangerous. In effect, it sends the fundamentals of presidential democracy crashing into each other. The Trump administration made that mismatch plain. Invoking the framers' words to justify the takeover of administration by a politicized presidency is a historical sleight-of-hand. Capturing "all" the executive power for the president, after a long history of expanding that power through pragmatic, power-sharing arrangements, is a political bait-and-switch. In effect, these are formulas for Trumpism.

What stands out in the end is the intimate, if paradoxical connection between the bizarre spectacle of the Trump presidency and the initial problem from which it sprang. The Trump administration was the full embodiment of a liability in the separation of powers that the framers of the Constitution sought to head off with their selection system. Now, after a succession of efforts to overcome the limitations in that original solution, we have turned full circle and stand face to face with the original concern. The historical inversion is stark. The Trump presidency was the mirror image of management without mobilization. It was mobilization all the way down, all governance values submerged in presidential partisanship.

Every time reformers strengthened the presidency, they reconstructed the relationship between political mobilization and government management. Now that the dysfunctions of the current arrangement have been exposed, we would do well to reconstruct it again. Our history tells us that management and mobilization work best when both rest on collective footings and when each is altered with an eye to its bearing on the other. *Phantoms* stops short of detailing how exactly to do that today, but it does indicate that the pathologies of a unitary executive are best addressed holistically and pragmatically. That means breaking our preoccupation with the Constitution's formal division of powers and, in particular, with the vesting clause. It means focusing more attention on the informal arrangements that surround the presidency, in particular, on the organization of our political parties and the configuration of the selection system. It means building back to a less personal presidency and a more collective understanding of political responsibility for the affairs of state. The hope therein is that the fundamentals can be realigned once more, that the strains that have put them at cross purposes can still be eased, that the lost art of promoting interbranch cooperation can be recovered and a common sense of good government reestablished.

PART I

THE DEEP STATE AND THE UNITARY EXECUTIVE

1

Push Comes to Shove

The Trump presidency conjured the Deep State whenever it met resistance from the institutions it was charged to oversee. Positing the operation of a shadow government that thwarts presidential authority and popular will, the epithet played to long-standing fears of power that cannot be called to account. The term "deep state" once referred to power arrangements in Turkey and Egypt where the military monitored the political leadership and conditioned its control.[1] Current usage retains those allusions to a clandestine, self-anointed band of guardians, but it casts the net wider. In Trump's America, the Deep State came to stand for cadres of administrators operating throughout the executive branch who put their own interests and ideology ahead of the preferences of the nation's "chief" executive. It envisaged a duly elected leader hindered in the pursuit of his political priorities by an entrenched officialdom and their extensive support networks. In a polity predisposed to be wary of the state, the specter of a Deep State is a national nightmare. Perhaps more to the point, it's a nightmare that conjures relief in the form of a strongman on top.

The differences between government in the United States and government in Turkey are substantial, and talk of a Deep State in America is apt to be waved off on that basis as political hyperbole.[2] But exaggerated as Trump's image may be, cursory dismissal of his charge is a mistake. Consider the now-famous op-ed published anonymously in the *New York Times* in September 2018. A Trump administration insider sought to assure an anxious nation that senior officials "in and around the White House" were "working diligently from within to frustrate parts of [the president's] agenda and his worst inclinations." The op-ed assumed broad public sup-port for such work, and more than that, it located guardian values where one would least expect to find them, among the high-level political appointees who are thought to serve the president's interests most directly. "Anonymous" voiced determination at the very top to "insulate" government policy from personal "whims" and to "thwart" ill-considered directives. "Resistance" of this sort was defended proudly, the pushback essential to "preserve our democratic institutions." In this telling, the nightmare scenario is not administrative interference with presidential will but a leader with an inflated sense of his own authority who disregards the "adults in the room."[3]

"Anonymous" disavowed any "deep state" conspiracy, prefer-ring instead to describe such actions as "the work of the steady state."[4] But the distinction is by no means transparent. On the face of it, that official's sense of duty seemed to encapsulate pretty well the president's suspicions about the entire operation. At issue is a widening disparity between what the state's managers have to offer and what the chief executive expects of them, between the value of a steady state and presidential demands for administrative subordi-nation and political responsiveness.

These divergent notions of good order suggest a stripped-down ver-sion of Trump's proposition, one that reckons with the reality of what he was up against while holding his provocative subtext in abeyance. Put simply, the American state *is* "deep." Depth, particularly depth added through the expansion of administrative and advisory instruments, is one of the most conspicuous byproducts of political development in the twentieth century. One may well reject the Deep State charge as a politically contrived fantasy and still acknowledge this state's depth. All that is needed for that is a glance at an organization chart.

Depth is, first and foremost, a function of public sector penetra-tion into all aspects of national life. It is a reflection of the enormous resources now committed to social regulation and national secu-rity. Trump's assault on the Deep State was an attempt to disrupt the current arrangement of those activities. The objective, at least in part, was to recast commitments the government supports or to dislodge them altogether. Fair to say, that is what presidents do.[5] All of them disrupt prior arrangements and attempt to recast the government's commitments, and those ambitions inevitably put "steady state" managers under pressure. We say off-handedly that each president creates an "administration" of his own, without much thought as to what that might entail. In this "administration," as in every other, the critical question is how far down the disruption reaches, how deeply it cuts.

That question points to other aspects of depth. It is apparent, for instance, that this state's administrative instruments are not just far reaching but densely articulated as well. Operating units from the White House to the customs house are variously organized according to set purposes, and they are elaborately impacted by roles and duties, rules and procedures, norms and protocols. More than the vertical distance from top to bottom, depth refers also to the insulation that, by degrees, circumscribes authority at all levels and protects it from arbitrary decisions and impositions. Any intermediation that depersonalizes control or elevates official duties over incumbent predilections deepens the state.

No doubt, depth of this sort makes it more difficult to redirect the executive branch from on high. Resistance is ingrained and likely to appear in many different guises. But ease of redirection is only one of many values at issue in the organization of state power. Depth helps to check the rationale for redirection and to vet plans before they are implemented. It can foster stability and continuity, anchoring a government in which commitments are carried forward and changed only upon due deliberation. Deepening the state can ensure that accountability is more broadly shared and that discretion is widely supervised. It can provide for multiple lines of communication among institutions—bottom-up and side-to-side, as well as top-down.[6] Depth can, in short, make it more likely that political leadership serves the public's purposes.

No less obvious is this state's depth in human resources. The American state is steeped in technical know-how and operational experience. It draws on a vast reservoir of professional expertise, managerial skill, and institutional memory. Authority today is not just legal and political; it is also knowledge-based. The roles and rules and norms and procedures that insulate administrative instruments and promote varied lines of communication have gone some way toward accommodating knowledge-based authority within the legal and political framework of American government, but depth in knowledge finds its firmest footings outside the state, with others who have a stake in it.

These connections—to universities, professional societies, think tanks, news media, and the like—are extensive. The bonds they forge are cultural and reputational. They anchor the decisions administrators make, they buttress the advice that they bring to their principals, and they amplify their voice, carrying it far beyond the formal boundaries of the government. All this is very much at issue in the Deep State charge. So too is the "sedimented" knowledge that managers acquire and accumulate over time about how the government works.[7] Whether they use that knowledge solely on behalf of best practices, or, as the Deep State charge alleges, in pursuit of more self-serving ambitions, it too is a factor of undeniable significance.

We will look more closely at indicators of depth in the next chapter, but enough has been said to turn back to the presidency. By any historical reckoning, the expansion of national administrative capacities has been a boon for America's chief executive. The concentration of decision-making power in national administration has, in effect, turned American government into a presidency-centered government.[8] By directing administrative agents, presidents harness enormous power across the whole range of state activity. They can change policy unilaterally. A Congress that is skeptical of the president's preferences, or just too cumbersome in its deliberations to act decisively on them, is now easier to circumvent. On occasion, administrators have gone even further in advancing presidential preferences. In the Iran-Contra affair, for instance, officials at the National Security Council defied a policy set by Congress, hatching a rogue scheme of their own that they thought comported with President Reagan's agenda.[9]

It has been clear for some time that the depth acquired by the American state has been testing a variety of institutional relationships basic to its constitutional frame. No less plain is that the issues posed by depth are not all the same. President Trump's charge of a Deep State conspiracy can be added to the list. It points to stress building on another relationship. While most of the commentary on the modern presidency focuses on the power that has accrued to incumbents through the expansion of national administrative capacities, Trump's complaint has been about administrative resistance to the authority of the president and the mediation of the public interest through political networks operated by his subordinates.

He is not alone in that. In subtle but profound ways, distinctly administrative forms of authority and influence condition a president's hold over "the executive power." Depth has always been something of a sore point for them. Determined to run administrations of their own, incumbents are institutionally inclined to devalue depth and to eye it suspiciously. The irritation on this point has been intensifying in recent years because, as the power of the executive branch has grown, governing the nation through administrative control rather than legislative direction has swelled into a live and attractive prospect. In the last decades of the twentieth century, the most remarkable change in the executive branch came not from the extension of new commitments and services to the nation but from the proliferation of political managers at the top.[10] With more assistants, more deputies, and more deputy assistants, the administration of presidents began to bear down more heavily on the permanent government. The United States stands out among modern democracies on this dimension, its thicket of political supervisors hinting at aspirations for control that remain unresolved and increasingly contested.[11]

Presidential impatience with administrative resistance and conditions on their control of the executive branch has flared repeatedly in recent years. Eyebrows were raised when President George W. Bush summarily dismissed a clutch of US attorneys.[12] President Barack Obama, a onetime critic of Bush's aggressive assertions of presidential power, prosecuted "leakers" of embarrassing information under the Espionage Act and set about to monitor and compel testimony from their collaborators in the press.[13] President Trump came to power in a long line of incumbents determined to clamp down on administrators, to cut deeper into the executive branch and stiffen specifically presidential claims over its work.

Trump wanted direct, hierarchical, and exclusive control over the government's administrative resources. In other words, he wanted a "unitary executive."[14] Trump was not the first president to invoke unitary claims. Constitutional advocacy and presidential actions favoring the unitary executive have been growing more elaborate for years. Nonetheless, Trump's arguments stood out. They penetrated to the heart of the matter.

Trump linked presidential assertions of personal authority over the operations of the executive branch, candidly and unambiguously, to hostility to its depth. His two propositions—the unitary executive and the Deep State—riddled American government. They pitted the chief executive *against* the executive branch, and they deployed the Constitution to dislodge anything within the president's domain that limited his authority or conditioned responsiveness to his directives. In this usage, the "Deep State" became a blanket indictment of long-standing arrangements of administrative power. When Trump declared a Deep State conspiracy, he stigmatized depth as a scourge to be eradicated root and branch, a feature of American government inimical to its democratic values and without any redeeming value of its own. With that, he sharpened the case for a unitary executive. The wager seemed to be that the suspicions Americans harbor toward bureaucrats would overcome any reluctance they might have to embrace a purer form of presidentialism.

Presidents have been forcing this contest into the open for years, and now that "push has come to shove," the rest of us might want to do some more serious thinking of our own about the value of depth in the organization of a state and where it fits into the larger scheme of American government. If nothing else, Trump raised the stakes of the lawyer's brief for a unitary executive. What was once a talking point for advocates of presidential power was put on full view. Its implications for the development of American government and politics are no longer just matters of speculation. They were displayed in headlines every day. In this book, we pause to take stock.

Phantom twins: The Deep State is a political allegation. The unitary executive is a constitutional inference. Both are abstractions, conjectures, what we will here call phantoms. Much has been written of late about each of these ideas, and many have scored them as unwarranted exaggerations. But the relationship between the two propositions is seldom noticed. The potency of these ideas is unleashed in their interaction. The alleged problem and the inferred solution hang together in a mutually constitutive package. Phantom twins, they draw each other out.

We light on these phantom twins to reflect on the issues they are wrestling to the fore. The unitary executive measures depth as insulation or distance from presidential authority and discredits it on that basis. But efforts to strip away depth expose as well the sweeping character of presidential demands for executive branch unity. They call attention to just how far the working assumptions of American government depart from a unitary design. One effect of Trump's assault on the executive branch, then, has been to display this state's depth in full. Another has been to reveal the risks of unitary control and to remind us of why all this depth was added in the first place. A third has been to draw out all manner of

administrative resistance, the reasonable, the shocking, and everything in between.

The contest, as Trump framed it, opens a new window into the
long, muddled history of American state formation.[15] In the first
part of this book, we take advantage of the opportunity to revisit
the backstory. Like other points of stress within modern American
government, the tensions at the root of this contest are built into
the constitutional frame of this state. They are ingrained in the relationship between the separation of powers, on the one hand, and
checks and balances, on the other. Throughout American history,
politicians found ways to finesse the maddening ambiguities in that
structure—ambiguities about how administrative management is
to be organized, about how the public interest is to be divined, and
about how political accountability is to be secured. Time and again,
the underlying constitutional questions were dealt with pragmatically and submerged in novel power-sharing arrangements. But for
a while now, and for reasons scholars still do not fully understand,
the spirit of accommodation that served the republic so well has
broken down, and improvisation has been fueling confrontation.
Our historical survey suggests that recent adaptations have driven
us into a corner. These age-old problems of state design and democratic legitimacy are now harder to negotiate away, and the issues
they present are getting blown out of all proportion.

Certain questions are sure to be debated for years to come. Do
the various manifestations of this state's depth add up to a Deep
State conspiracy? Does Article II of the Constitution authorize a
unilateral assault on it?

We address these questions in the course of our analysis. They
are unavoidable. But we have not set out to prosecute a case. That
much should be clear from our insistence on a distinction between
depth as an attribute of this state and the Deep State as an *a priori*
indictment of it. Our interests lie in the juncture itself, in why the
ever-present ambiguities of administrative power in the American
constitutional system suddenly got framed as a battle between

the Deep State and the unitary executive, and in the competing values thrust forward in that contest. This is an important moment because ideas of great consequence for the future shape of the American state revealed their significance in practice. Institutional actors seized upon the central questions at issue and ran with them. Trump and "the Resistance" supplied their own answers, politically, on the fly, by their own wits, and for their own ends. Delicate distinctions—between administrative protocol and rogue action, between presidential direction and arbitrary imposition—melted away in the process. The political scientists and constitutional theorists who have been debating these issues for decades are now racing to keep up with the implications of their arguments, and the underlying structural ambiguities find us at the mercy of the political contingencies.

We have focused our attention accordingly, confident that these political enactments are our best guide to what is at stake in an otherwise abstract and disembodied spectacle. In the second part of the book, we sample from the myriad conflicts that flared during the Trump years, taking snapshots of the various configurations of authority presented at different sites and over different issues. We survey some of the most high-profile cases, examining the ground claimed by the administrators who resisted the chief executive and how deeply the president cut into it.

The results of our sampling are a mixed bag. Overall, neither side comes off particularly well. Instead of endorsing a side, we recommend paying closer attention to a system now at odds with itself, a state out of kilter and no longer certain of its own assumptions.[16] Our reckoning with depth brings to light a polity driven to wit's end by two wildly different conceptions of what constitutes good government and bad.

The American people have been enlisted in an eerie face-off, one all the more nightmarish for the way the competing specters play off one another. On one side is a Deep State conspiracy that threatens to thwart the will of the people and undercut the constitutional authority of the leader they elected. On the other side is a raw personalization of presidential power, one that a theory of the unitary executive has gussied up and allowed to run roughshod over reason and the rule of law. These, we submit, are the phantom twins of a beleaguered republic. Each threat implicates the other. Our thesis is that the Deep State and the unitary executive are two sides of the same syndrome, that the contest they frame speaks to basic issues of governance long suppressed, and that two distinct conceptions of authority are now drawing each other out to no good effect. We are interested in the developments that have unleashed the phantom twins. Our worry is that, left untamed, they will continue to pull American government apart.

2

Weak State, Strong State, Deep State

The American state defies easy characterization. Scholars have wrestled for decades with the conceptual challenges it poses. If nothing else, the intrusion of this new term—the Deep State—stirs the pot. It throws together issues previously dealt with only here and there, and it forces to the fore long-simmering questions about constitutional design, institutional development, and political accountability. With talk of the Deep State roiling national politics, that hoary academic puzzle is no longer arcane. At a time when we are being pressed to reconsider the kind of state we want, gaining a clearer view of the state we have acquires irresistible urgency.

The neglect of depth in prior assessments of this state may be surprising given its many obvious manifestations. Other concerns have consumed the lion's share of attention. Hitherto, debates about the American state have turned on questions of strength and weakness, questions that tend to draw out its most anomalous features. Issues springing more directly from depth have gotten caught up in, and squeezed out of, a discussion that has revolved around American exceptionalism. The agitation over the Deep State breaks that frame. It suggests a more direct confrontation with issues that all states face. In this chapter, we reconfigure that old conversation around current controversies.

A weak state? Several *a priori* qualities of "stateness" have set America apart as a comparatively "weak" state.[1] Let's consider three.

The most significant is structural: the constitutional system of checks and balances fragments authority, dispersing power and fracturing the unified, hierarchical lines of control associated with "strong" states.[2] Setting aside for a moment presidential agitation for a strong, "unitary executive," the republican frame of "separate institutions sharing power" situates the administrative arm of American government in the crosshairs of three independent and discordant authorities.[3] Collectively, these "branches" pull at the state's managers from different directions. By preventing any of them from taking matters into their own hands, this design also makes it difficult to settle on a coherent course of action or to direct the whole. That is bound to frustrate political leaders. Squaring the Constitution with a robust conception of national political leadership has been a problem from the start.

Less noticed is how weaknesses of this sort might contribute to depth. The value of central direction in a divided structure is apt to be acknowledged as a matter of give and take. Congress and the Court may endorse a stronger leadership role for the president, but they are also likely to try to keep pace with it. To the extent that they aim to protect their own claims on management as presidents advance theirs, they will deepen the state with offices and rules that continue to defy simple hierarchical designs. The claims of the chief executive need not be denied outright. Control over the executive branch has remained conditional and opaque even as provisions for overhead management have multiplied. Congress can protect administrative authority from personal impositions by preserving a measure of collaborative decision making, or by lacing administration with alternative lines of access and communication, or by underwriting its insulation and independence, but, one way or another, the legislature is likely to accommodate new demands for central direction in ways that are hedged and that remain ambiguous, even as the power of the executive branch grows.

A second, related feature often associated with weakness is political: as the divided structure of this government renders the position of administrators uncertain, it adds leverage to interests on the outside. Scholars have long been attuned to the external support networks arrayed behind administrative agencies, but, like the fragmentation of authority at the center, the pervasive influence of civil society in administrative affairs has traditionally been associated with the dispersion and dissipation of this state's power. An earlier generation of analysts focused attention on the problem of "capture," whereby agencies are controlled by the interests they are supposed to regulate.[4] Lateral ties between congressional committees and the various administrative bureaus, and through them to the interests served, were said to create impermeable communities of interest, "iron triangles" that exacerbated problems of overhead management and central direction.[5]

Interest capture is an allegation that retains considerable currency. It is, in fact, one of the leading arguments for a unitary executive, hierarchically organized and subordinated to the president's control.[6] But presidential empowerment is not the only possible response. When Congress and the Court addressed this problem in the 1970s, their impulse was not to strengthen the presidency or stiffen the executive hierarchy; it was, rather, to open interest access to administrative decision making more widely and to distribute influence more broadly. To counter the risks of "capture," they elaborated upon the pluralist notion that the public interest is best served by the direct participation of all interested parties.[7]

Here again it might be useful to distinguish *depth* from *weakness*. Administrative power in America does not easily conform to tight hierarchical lines of control, but it has sunk its roots deep into the nation it serves. Presidents may chafe at the connections forged through administration to the society, the culture, the economy, and the wider world, but those connections are not weak.[8] They are formidable, and many of the formative effects are lost on the notion of capture. When President Eisenhower warned of the emergence of a "military-industrial complex,"[9] he was observing something more than the scattered, clientelistic relationships characteristic of America's "interest-group liberalism."[10] His concern was not with the dissipation of this state's power but with its concentration in informal networks that wield pervasive influence. After the financial crisis of 2008, similar concerns were raised about the Federal

Reserve Board, in particular about its tight relationship to the banking community and its close-minded thinking about the social impact of the nation's financial policies.[11] A "complex" like that, powerful enough to steer its own course at home and abroad, is unquestionably significant, but its significance is lost on conventional understandings of strength and weakness.

Just before Donald Trump was elected to the presidency, commentators were beginning to apply the term "Deep State" to America in precisely these ways. The reference at that time was to the interpenetration of government institutions and private economic power—"big money" and "big oil."[12] Influence of that sort is one of the most serious problems posed by depth, but the question that was raised in the 1970s is no less pertinent today: is a strong state design, one with tighter presidential controls, the best solution?[13]

We know from past experience that this is not the only conceivable response to interest control, and the temptation to adopt it rests on heroic assumptions about what presidents themselves represent in politics today.[14] Indeed, one reason legislators in the 1970s pulled back from further empowering the presidency was their belief that the president was as susceptible as Congress to special-interest influence.[15] To say the least, the interpenetration of government institutions and private economic power has not spared the presidency.[16]

Demographics have offered a third template portraying the American state as weak. Those who staff the state in America are a remarkably representative lot, reflective of the great diversity of the nation they serve.[17] They are hard to distinguish by social rank or common background. There is nothing in America comparable to the historic influence of "Oxbridge" on British government or the *Grandes écoles* on the French.[18] If the governing class in America is associated with any one group, it is with the lawyers, professionals who move freely across a porous, public-private divide and who can be counted upon to litigate virtually every question of state authority. All told, America's governing class is unlikely to think with a single mind, much less to act in concert upon some common interest of its own.

But here too a preoccupation with *a priori* indicators of strength has obscured the complications of depth and impeded a clear view of the current state of affairs. It may be comparatively harder for American administrators to cultivate a common *esprit de corps*, but it happens nonetheless.[19] Bonds of professionalism and government service and shared understandings of agency purpose run deep through the foreign service, the national security establishment, and the law enforcement apparatus. More often than not, these attributes are touted as essential features of good government. Their exemplars are held up in the political culture as the best of the American spirit, and all the more so because their personal backgrounds are so diverse.

Few institutions of government are more widely respected by the American public today than the military.[20] Presidential authority is undisputed in that domain, but this is also the arena in which public servants are held in highest esteem and where training and expertise are likely to command the widest respect. The president is sure to win in a face-off with the military brass, but as political scientist Richard Neustadt noted long ago, a showdown that pits constitutional authority against military credentials can be politically costly for presidents.[21] When the military becomes anxious about its professional reputation, when its sense of integrity is besieged, when the gap between the president's assessment of a situation and its own becomes manifest, so too do the political complications of depth.[22]

There is, to be sure, a difference between administrators using their authority to try to persuade principals of the wisdom or folly of a particular course of action and administrators developing capacities to undermine the authority of those principals. But both entail a good deal of depth, and instances in which that distinction has been blurred are not unheard of in America's past. Perhaps the most notorious personification of a Deep State threat in America is J. Edgar Hoover, the entrepreneurial director of the FBI, who, through administrative acumen and a careful cultivation of professional reputation, built a fiefdom powerful enough to intimidate elected politicians, even presidents.[23] A more subtle but increasingly prominent contributor to this blurring is the dissemination of the authority of government administrators through the wider political culture. For example, the nation's news media now routinely enlist retired military, law enforcement, and foreign service officers to provide running commentary on presidential choices and governmental decision making. In the process, they extend the influence of the administrative class far beyond the confines of the executive branch of government and inject it directly into national political debates.[24]

Or consider an entirely different angle: although America's bureaucracy is relatively representative, the creation of a permanent administrative staff introduces a measure of depth into state operations all of its own accord, and presidential politics is routinely caught up in the complications that follow. Just as surely as civil service protections insulate public servants from the everyday pressures of politics and cultivate a storehouse of knowledge and expertise, they also extend the tenure of unelected decision makers and leave them exposed to changes in political leadership. The competing values of continuity and change become evident every time the presidency switches control from one party to another. As the new "administration" seeks to redirect the use of executive power, it charges headlong into career administrators who promulgated policies under prior mandates. Sometimes this tension is expressed in presidential efforts to marginalize whole departments, as President Nixon did early on with the State Department.[25] On an even grander scale, consider the implications of "big bang" moments of rapid state expansion: the government growth spurt that occurred during the long period of liberal dominance in the 1930s and 1940s ensconced a generation of placeholders that politicians in the more conservative 1950s came to eye suspiciously as a fifth column of left-wing subversives.

The policy breakthroughs of the 1960s and 1970s brought another round of rapid expansion. National programmatic power penetrated even more deeply into American life, and political contestation over control of administrative power ramped up precipitously. Since then, adjustment and recalibration have become more elusive. The seeds of the current contest between the Deep State and the unitary executive were planted in the 1970s.

A strong state? Objections to characterization of America as a "weak state" are not hard to come by, but hitherto, issues of depth have figured no more prominently in the demur than in the assertion. The leading attempt to dispel "the myth of the 'weak' American state" begins by pointing to the manifest power of American government at home and abroad. It uses these measurable strengths to question the analytic value of abstract, *a priori* qualities of stateness derived from a few European cases, and in doing so, it calls attention to the pejorative connotations of the word "weak," as these seem to idealize a more imposing, allegedly "stronger" organizational design.[26] This is all quite useful in evaluating demands for a unitary executive.

The follow-up, however, switches the analytic ground altogether. Arguments for strength tend to sideline the design standards used to identify weaknesses and to show that the American state has drawn its considerable potency from other sources entirely. Scholarship along these lines has brought to light a state that was often invisible, its effects "submerged," its strength experienced only indirectly.[27] Developmentally speaking, some of this state's most forceful and consequential actions were "out of sight" to most Americans.[28] Strength was more often apparent at the periphery than at the center.[29] It came less from hierarchical command and control than from "infrastructural" powers that were deployed instrumentally and in conjunction with the interests they served.[30] Public and private power fused in horizontal relationships that afforded flexible responses to situations as they presented themselves.[31] Strength was felt less immediately by those who enjoyed the full rights of citizenship than by those who did not.[32]

These assessments shift the focus onto performance measures of state strength. At issue is the capacity to mobilize public resources and deploy government power for collective purposes. The American state may have been unassuming, but it was remarkably adept at the release of social energy.[33] Law operated in America as an extension of the nation's political ambitions, an instrument of self-rule, not a threat to it. Strength of this sort is not strictly constitutional. Nor is it necessarily a consistent feature or constantly present in all spheres of state activity. It materializes when it is needed. The uniquely pragmatic disposition of the American polity made the state as strong as it had to be in the circumstances it confronted.[34] Its leading attributes were utility, ingenuity, accessibility, adaptability, responsiveness, and broad political footings.

Important as a corrective to traditional characterizations of America as a "weak" state, this case for a "strong" American state now seems rather quaint. On inspection, it too is a brief for American exceptionalism. And because it does not challenge the case for weakness directly—because it brings entirely different criteria to bear—both assessments can be maintained at the same time. The conundrum, as one study puts it, is that "the federal state is administratively weak but normatively strong."[35] All told, the weak-state/strong-state "debate" has turned less on a substantive disagreement than on a distinction between organization and operation. The point is that a state that appears weak on paper can be quite strong in practice, and conversely, that a strong state design says little about actual capabilities.

The debate in America today is different. It is, in fact, about something else: *depth*. In confronting depth, Americans are grappling with a state that has grown far less exceptional and far more visible. The most pressing reason to revive scholarly discussion of the state in America is that, for the first time, everyone else is talking about it quite candidly. There has been nothing esoteric or inscrutable about the state in Trump's America. The phenomenon became unavoidable. The president pushed it front and center.

America's long history of pragmatic improvisation and institutional bricolage certainly has a lot to tell us about how this state acquired depth,[36] but the confrontation between the Deep State and the unitary executive has shifted the focus rather abruptly back to structure and the formal organization of authority. Those knotty issues of constitutional design—the separations, the checks, the devolution and dispersion of power, the complicated provisions for political accountability and democratic legitimacy—are now the critical points of contention. Whatever might be said of the free-wheeling spirit of innovation that brought us to this point, the current mood is decidedly formalistic, bogged down in debates about the proper distribution of authority. Everyone today is trying to get right with the framers, as if the only way to figure out what to do now is to try to divine what they really meant. Issues once taken in stride now seem ponderous and hard to finesse.

Of special note is how this confrontation with depth pries open the weak/strong dichotomy. On one side, it reveals something other than weakness in the divisions of power embedded within the basic constitutional frame. On the other, it brings to the fore a much starker alternative: the strong-state design implicit in a unitary executive. Distance from the president now carries the stigma of a Deep State threat, and hierarchical command and control presents itself as the antidote. Presidentialism promises to elevate democracy over bureaucracy, to cut deep through the clientelistic networks of interest-group liberalism, and to combat administrative subterfuge. When viewed against the many problems associated with depth, a strong state like that appears as safe haven.

A Deep State? If talk of the "Deep State" can be credited with pulling together a scattered set of issues and reconfiguring an old debate, it is not without some serious drawbacks of its own. The sheer variety of the issues we have just brought to light should indicate the problem. The modern American state exhibits depth in many different aspects, and they are only loosely bound together. The concept of the Deep State is rhetorically loaded precisely because it is prone to indiscriminate applications.

The issues that can be pulled under the umbrella of the Deep State are so different one to the next that more seems lost on the concept than gained. It can refer to rogue administrators who take advantage of their position to resist or subvert lawful authority, but it may also refer to embattled administrators seeking protection in the law from whimsical decisions made on high. It can speak to entrepreneurial administrators who leverage their knowledge and expertise to guide those nominally in charge, or to administrative clients who seek to secure their own special interests, or to administrators with a reputation as "straight shooters" who parlay their knowledge of government on the inside into authority as political commentators on the issues of the day.

Rather than add something specific to our understanding of American government and politics, the Deep State seems beset by false equivalences. Administrators may, in fact, act on their own biases. They may resist directives that threaten their interests, their power, or their political preferences. But there are many other bases for administrative resistance: the request may be legally proscribed; it may violate established rules and procedures; it may be an affront to norms of best practice; it may be half baked and in need of further reflection and refinement; it may be impractical, unlikely to solve the problem it purports to address or perhaps even make the problem worse. Often it will be difficult to draw bright-line distinctions among these motives. The political potency of the broad-brush charge of a Deep State conspiracy lies in blurring these distinctions. The indictment stigmatizes everything that is not under the president's direct control, lumping the potential value of depth together with its potential liabilities.

Americans may just now be taking full measure of the governing arrangements they have created over the long course of their political development, but that is all the more reason to be wary of phantoms. The reality to be confronted is the state per se; the opportunity at hand, to sharpen our understanding of the American formation in all its different dimensions. Strong or weak, states are complicated organizations with varied purposes, competing priorities, far-flung agents, disjoint operations, and extensive social ties. Though their authority is plenary, they have many moving parts, and their operations are seldom all of a piece. Even in those designed to maximize efficiency in action and to facilitate top-down direction, transaction costs run high. Simply put, the concept of "the state" should convey enough depth all by itself to render "the Deep State" indistinct and redundant. The obfuscation inherent in the new term is evident in the pushback from the administrators targeted by it. The alternatives they propose do not deny depth; instead, they celebrate its desirable effects. By altering the modifier, they give the very same properties a positive spin: the "steady state"; the "dedicated state."[37]

The true test of a state is how it handles issues associated with its depth—how it taps the capacities afforded, counters the attendant liabilities, and balances the various values it seeks to realize. American government has been dealing with such issues all along, and consistent with the various and sundry nature of these issues, it has done so in a variety of different ways. But these issues have grown more contentious, and we now find them jumbled together in an encompassing new term, as if they *are* all of a piece. The Deep State bids to alter our perceptions of the challenges posed by depth and the appropriate remedies. It commands our attention as a political premise, significant for the support it lends to a more full-throated presidentialism.

3

The Unitary Executive

Whether or not the varied and disparate expressions of this state's depth add up to a "Deep State" conspiracy, they do have one feature in common: they are all an affront to a "unitary executive." The unitary executive is another provocative proposition with political currency in contemporary discourse. It too is a plausible conjecture, and it too is casting a long shadow over modern American government. As with the concept of the Deep State, a great deal can be pulled under the umbrella of a unitary executive, so long as the rubric is not scrutinized too closely.

As we have suggested, the Deep State and the unitary executive are not just two abstractions that share some interesting properties. Together the two propositions construct a politics all their own. They draw each other out and tear at one another. Exposing basic ambiguities of constitutional design, their interaction throws the entire system off kilter.

Presidents use the theory of the unitary executive to cut through the insulation that shields administration from their direct control. Instinctively intolerant of depth, they can advance the case for unitary control by conjuring a "Deep State" threat to their constitutional authority. Intimidating as that is to those on the receiving end, the effort to clamp down rouses all their available defenses. When public servants resist what they see as arbitrary impositions—when they call upon the resources that shield them from hierarchical command and control—they reveal just how deep this state is. In the second half of this book, we examine this contest in action and assess the prospects for maintaining depth in the face of bellicose assertions of executive branch unity.

Trump as unitarian: Although Donald Trump lost the popular vote in 2016, his election packed a wallop. Part of it was the shock that comes from defying expectations;[1] part of it, the wildcard character of the victory. Trump was a loner. A critic of the party that nominated him, he had built a following all his own. His message to the faithful was that the federal government was "rigged" and "corrupt" to its core. Not only did his insurgency signal an intent to cut deep, his critique of the government steeled him against any resistance he might encounter from within. Little wonder the theory of the unitary executive held special attraction for him. It was, in a purely instrumental sense, all but irresistible.

Coming to power with no prior experience in government, Trump embraced the unitary theory like a businessman whose tax adviser has just alerted him to an advantageous loophole in the code: "It's a thing called Article II. . . . It gives me all of these rights at a level that nobody has ever seen before."[2] These are not the words of a constitutional theorist, but as a rule, presidents are not scholars. They latch onto ideas that are useful to them. Trump sharpened the political edges of this one. The formulations may have been crude—"I have an Article II, where I have the right to do whatever I want as president"—but, for their targets, the message was unmistakable.[3]

President Trump surrounded himself with ardent unitarians and turned their theory into a touchstone of his administration. His bond with the Republican Party rested in good measure on the alliance he forged early on with the conservative legal movement, seedbed of the theory: "We're going to have great judges, conservative, all picked by [the] Federalist Society."[4] Brett Kavanaugh, a Federalist Society member and Trump's second pick to the Supreme Court, was known as a stalwart advocate of the president's exclusive hold over the executive power. He was an avowed critic of the Court's defense of the constitutionality of the Office of Independent Counsel, he was a skeptic of independent regulatory commissions, and he was wary of the courts' authority to order the president to disclose information in response to a subpoena sought by a subordinate official in the executive branch.[5] Neomi Rao, Trump's replacement for Kavanaugh on the DC Circuit Court of Appeals and likewise a Federalist Society member, initially served as Trump's administrator for the Office of Information and Regulatory Affairs. She advocated for the strong arm of presidential control over the executive branch on both democratic and constitutional grounds: "Elections should truly have consequences for administration; otherwise we will have an unconstitutional fourth branch of government."[6]

John Dowd, the president's legal adviser, explicated the unitary theory to his client, assuring him that the president alone runs the executive branch and that controversial actions (such as the removal of the FBI director) were well within the boundaries of his constitutional authority.[7] Marc Kasowitz, another attorney hired by the president to deal with allegations of collusion with Russia in the 2016 presidential election, turned the same argument into a thinly veiled threat to shut down any investigation into presidential conduct: "The President . . . possesses the indisputable authority to direct that any executive branch investigation be open or closed because the Constitution provides for a unitary executive with all executive power resting with the President."[8] William Barr, Trump's second attorney general, wrote a memo prior to his appointment assuring the president that "he alone is the executive branch."[9] In a dispute over the constitutionality of the administrative structure of the Consumer Financial Protection Bureau, Trump's solicitor general, Noel Francisco, argued that an agency with a single director who had any independence from the chief executive was a threat to presidentially directed policy: "It is for such reasons that the framers adopted a strong, unitary executive. . . . Vesting such power in a single person not answerable to the president represents a stark departure from the Constitution's framework."[10] Prominent proponents of the theory outside of government, in the wider legal community, enlisted it to defend

Trump against accusers from within. John Yoo, a law professor who served in the Office of Legal Counsel in the administration of George W. Bush and who would later offer informal legal advice to the Trump White House, took aim at the official who blew the whistle on Trump's dealings with Ukraine: the framers "vested 'the executive power' in the president, which they understood to include the power over national security and foreign affairs." Therefore, "the intelligence community works for the president, not the other way around."[11]

We are all familiar with political criticisms of "big" government, of concentrated power, and of bureaucracy. The unitary executive is something different. The claim is not that there is too much power in the executive branch but rather that not enough of it is under the president's direct control. The idea is that presidents should be able to deploy the executive power for their own purposes, with accountability only to the people who put them in the office. By denying administration any integrity of its own, the assertion of a unitary executive magnifies the personal, populist, charismatic character of presidential power. It converts the widely recognized authority of the president to supervise the executive branch into a power of command and control.[12] Under its auspices, the transfer of "the executive power" from one incumbent to another—long associated with the creation of a "new administration"—swells into a warrant for remaking the executive branch wholesale, in the new incumbent's image.

President Trump's articulation of a Deep State threat was his signal contribution to the theory of the unitary executive. It turned rage over "rogue bureaucrats" into an invaluable political asset in the assertion of unitary control.[13] Anticipating "the destruction of the deep state," the president boasted, "I think it'll be one of my great achievements."[14] In that, he echoed his former chief strategist Steve Bannon, who proposed that the "deconstruction of the administrative state" become the political project of the Trump presidency.[15] Neither Trump nor Bannon wanted to get rid of the executive branch. The objective was to strip away its depth, to deny administrators authority and to subordinate them to the president.

Actors within and outside the executive branch responded in kind, staking out a diametrically opposed view of good government and the place of administrators in the modern American state. They asserted their distance from the leader. They recognized direction from a variety of different principals and claimed for themselves the intermediation of their assorted instructions. They portrayed unilateral impositions as a threat to the rule of law and to the public—as opposed to the president's—interest. Media surrogates took up the contending arguments and prompted the nation to choose sides. "President Trump is right," declared one opinion piece. "The deep state is alive and well," made up of "patriotic public servants" who "have somehow remembered that their duty is to protect the interests, not of a particular leader, but of the American people."[16] "Thank God for the Deep State," exclaimed former acting CIA director John McLaughlin at a panel that featured other retired CIA and FBI officials.[17] James Comey, the FBI director summarily dismissed from his post by Trump, parried the Deep State charge with his own spin on the idea:

> [Trump's claim] is both dead wrong and dead right. . . . There's no Deep State looking to bring down elected officials and political leaders that represents some deep-seated center of power. . . . But it's true in a way that should cause Americans to sleep better at night. There's a culture in the military, in the intelligence agencies, and in law enforcement that's rooted in the rule of law and reverence for the Constitution. It's very deeply rooted and, thank God, I think it would take generations to destroy.[18]

For those in the Comey camp, the Deep State is not about administrative sabotage or rogue resistance to the will of the people. It is about protecting the national commitments lodged in the executive branch from individual whims, personal interests, and partisan hacks. It is about the integrity of public administration, about a state in which officials pledge loyalty to the Constitution, not to the president.

Text and context: But fealty to the Constitution is the very point at issue. The "unitary executive" is itself a constitutional claim. It is a proposition derived from the opening sentence of Article II: "The executive Power shall be vested in a President of the United States of America." In contrast to the vesting clause in Article I, where the legislative purview of Congress is limited to powers "herein granted," the wording in Article II is unqualified. A modest interpretation of this difference credits the original debate over whether or not the constitutional head of state should share responsibilities with some type of executive council. It may be that Article II's vesting clause was just announcing a rejection of that widely recognized and oft-discussed option and empowering a single person to exercise the powers that follow in the rest of Article II.[19] The theory of the unitary executive advances a much stronger claim, one that finds in the vesting clause itself a general grant of power.

The assertion is that Article II does not vest "*some* of the executive power" in the president, or even the preponderance of the executive power in the president. It vests "*all* of the executive power" in the president.[20] The key contention for our purposes is that all the powers lodged in the executive branch are exercised at the sufferance of the president, that the Constitution sanctions an administrative domain run directly, hierarchically, and exclusively through the chief executive officer, and that, if need be, the president can exercise the powers of his agents personally.[21]

That proposition has provoked a heated, rich, and discriminating debate. It has produced a large literature discussing the merits of these claims, how and where to draw boundaries around them, and what "the executive power" entails.[22] But the thrust of the theory is plain. It slices through depth, extends hierarchical control, and stamps administration with the will of the president. It pushes against authority in administrative intermediation, it has little use for alternative modes of administrative control, and it stigmatizes a long history of practice. All this makes it a handy proposition for incumbents who face any sort of resistance from within.

Though presidents have advanced claims consistent with a unitary executive all along the way,[23] elaboration of the theory did not begin in earnest until the 1970s and 1980s. This belated surge of intellectual interest in the idea is notable on several counts, and we will have occasion to revisit the implications repeatedly. Perhaps the most obvious point to be made about context is that the theory was elaborated on the heels of the major expansion of the national government that began in the mid-1960s. The theory offered a timely principle for the reassertion of order and control at a juncture at which administrative power was reaching into national life more deeply than ever before and swelling to consume the lion's share of governing. Anchoring the principle of unitary control in a close reading of the constitutional text, the theory provided a way of sorting through past practice and correcting prior "mistakes" in arranging administrative instruments. It promised to reorganize operations on the basis of fidelity and consistency with the Constitution's original meaning.

More subtle is how the theory altered the approach to presidential direction taken in the 1930s and 1940s, the previous period of rapid administrative expansion. The development of the Executive Office of the President in those years certainly strengthened the presidency, but it did so by seeking to integrate presidential direction more thoroughly into governmental operations at large. The thrust of those earlier reforms was to "institutionalize" the presidency, to regularize its engagement with other institutions by staking out common ground for central direction and mutual adjustment. Overhead management and advice relied on specifically administrative values—expertise and professional judgment—to broaden the credibility of presidential initiatives and facilitate their receptivity to those on the receiving end. The unitary theory altered those terms of control. Reaching back to the vesting clause, it sidelined arguments for central direction based on knowledge and expertise and pulled forward a conception that was more detached, solitary, personal, and subjective. The president was not just the "chief" executive; he "alone" was the executive branch. Any problems posed by the proliferation of administrative instruments and the penetration of administrative power were to be resolved, not through give and take within the "institutional presidency," but individually and unilaterally, by presidents themselves.[24] Given the enormous concentration of governing power in administration that had occurred in the interim, this shift drew from the Constitution a strong-state design for a presidential democracy.

Presidential democracy and republican government: Equally notable is the political argument implicit in the theory's constitutional reasoning. We heard it in Rao's remark about the significance of elections. It has become an especially prominent part of the theory in the Trump era. In resisting Trump, FBI director Comey claimed to be protecting the interests of the American people against the personal interests of the president, but as Trump saw it, Comey's resistance was a plot to overturn the will of the American people expressed in the 2016 election. Attorney General William Barr agreed: "the idea of resisting a democratically elected president" was "where the shredding of our norms and our institutions is occurring."[25] So, while the legal argument for the unitary executive draws formalistically from Article II's vesting clause, the political argument for it draws on a decidedly plebiscitary understanding of accountability in American government.[26]

The unitary theory rests political responsibility for administering the national commitments that have accumulated in the executive branch on a single person, the one who is selected in a nationwide referendum. It equates good government with presidential administration. Anything less than complete control over administration by the president risks an obfuscation of responsibility, clouding the judgments on presidential performance that "the people" get to deliver retrospectively in the next quadrennial election. Notwithstanding the theory's insistence that a unitary executive was the original idea, this political rationale seems strikingly contemporary. Indeed, in presenting the framers as unalloyed democrats, the theory strains to explain why their Constitution kept the expression of popular will in presidential elections indirect and why it confounded exclusivity in the exercise of administrative responsibilities with so much power sharing.

The American Constitution may be roundly criticized for its democratic deficits and its propensity toward blame shifting, and the expansion of administrative capacities in later decades may well have magnified the potency of those criticisms, but simply reading these problems out of the Constitution creates problems of its own. By making "administration" the exclusive province of the president, the unitary theory gives pride of place to the separation of powers. In doing so, it truncates the purview of checks and balances, arguably the Constitution's most novel innovation, and it obscures in the process the different theory of accountability that checks and balances make available.

The alternative to the unitary executive that can be teased out of the Constitution—call it the republican theory—rests on the conjoint operations that offset its institutional division of primary responsibilities.[27] Bring those into view, and accountability in national affairs appears to be more collective than singular, and the division of responsibilities looks like a prod to cooperation among all three branches in the management of the whole. This conception of good government is consistent with a reading of the "take care" clause, in which presidents are charged to enforce court rulings and congressional statutes "faithfully," regardless of their views of the substantive merits.[28] It is reinforced by Congress's Article I authority to set all rules and regulations "necessary and proper" for the execution of its mandates. The Constitution involves others in all aspects of "administration": for example, in appointments and oversight, in defining the terms and conditions of tenure, in arranging inferior offices and specifying their duties.

A state organized along republican lines would likely develop collaborative arrangements for administrative control. It would rely on institutions that mediate what the Constitution separates and invite crisscrossing channels of communication with administration among branches that are otherwise divided and juxtaposed. In a republic, the public interest would be something distilled, not unilaterally declared. A state like that is apt to remain organizationally "weak," in the sense that lines of empowerment and accountability will grow complicated and compromised, but it is also, for that very reason, likely to tolerate, even foster, a considerable amount of depth. A republic will sacrifice a good measure of unity in the executive to set political support for the administration of government on an inter-branch footing.

Conversely, the unitary theory advances a strong state design hostile to depth. It dismisses the idea of "separate institutions sharing power" as "mushy thinking."[29] It takes aim at republican safeguards for collective control and rests accountability instead in the president alone. The unitary executive is the phantom menace of the republic. It moves against administrative insulation, administrative neutrality, administrative intermediation, and administrative independence. It conceives of administration not as common ground but as the president's domain.

The great advantage of the unitary theory is that, as a political proposition, it is far more straightforward than the republican theory. And increasingly so. The extended drama of presidential elections in modern America punctuates the point by touting every canvass as the most significant in our lifetimes and by building to a critical moment of national decision and apparent resolution. As Trump's unitarians never tired of reminding us, elections have consequences.

On a plain reading of the text, however, the republican theory seems no less plausible than the unitary theory, and that has become our dilemma. Legal scholars have expended a lot of energy trying to convince us that the Constitution is of one mind on the matter, but its framers were a contentious bunch,[30] and the arguments on both sides suggest otherwise. Most likely, the framers thought they could have it both ways. The current push for clarity indicates nothing so much as the heightened stakes of resolution at a time when so much power has been concentrated in administration that control of the bureaucracy is tantamount to control of the government's entire operation.

It is undeniable that the Constitution leaves the presidents of our day politically and personally exposed in their responsibilities, often uncomfortably so. They have strong incentives to reach deep into the federal bureaucracy, to try to align executive branch operations more closely with their own preferences, and to do so as quickly and thoroughly as possible.[31] Their interest in clear lines of authority makes them natural and strong advocates of a unitary executive, and, as a practical matter, they can be expected to press for powers consistent with the theory.[32]

Contemporary responses to the structural ambiguities have been clouded further by a thick political overlay. Again, the promulgation of the unitary theory in the 1970s and 1980s suggests the point, for it coincided with the gestation of a conservative insurgency. The rhetoric of the insurgency was anti-government, with particular hostility directed at the commitments and responsibilities assumed by the federal government during the "social revolution." The theory gestated in the conservative legal movement and in the Federalist Society. Its cutting edge has been sharpened during Republican administrations. Its most explicit and aggressive advocates were the Reagan administration, the George W. Bush administration, and the Trump administration. The political biases in the theory are unmistakable.

These political biases should not, however, be exaggerated.

Republican administrations do not shrink the government. To achieve their policy aims, Republican presidents are no less reliant on administrative capacities than are Democratic presidents. They do not hesitate to augment those capacities that advance their policy priorities. Trump's administration proved no exception.[33] More to the point, Democratic presidents, if less hostile to administrative expansion in principle, have themselves shown an increased determination to clamp down on administrators and to fashion a unitary executive in practice. Jimmy Carter, who rose to power in the post-Watergate years on conspicuous displays of shedding the trappings of the "imperial presidency,"[34] had complaints of his own about "disloyal" officials within his administration.[35] He was obsessed with rooting out what he perceived to be organizational inefficiencies in the executive branch and replacing them with more hierarchical arrangements. Carter's civil service reform reorganized personnel management to increase presidential control, and by easing restrictions on top-level career officers, it enticed them into closer collaboration with their political supervisors.[36] When, in reaction to the excesses of the Nixon administration, Congress seriously considered bolstering the independence of the Department of Justice, the Carter administration scuttled the move.[37] Carter also introduced regulatory review, the central oversight of agency rule making that Ronald Reagan made famous.[38] Bill Clinton had an opportunity to dismantle regulatory review in deference to the authority of the individual agencies, but he preferred instead to strengthen the operation in ways that pushed hard against the distinction between presidential oversight and presidential command.[39] Elena Kagan, a leading advocate of "presidential administration" from the Clinton years, was appointed to the Supreme Court by Barack Obama. Democratic presidents, committed as they are to the social revolution and to an even more extensive federal government, have seized upon the idea of executive hierarchy and unity because it helps them pursue their political agendas administratively.[40] Presidents of both parties share an interest in immediate action on their policy and ideological commitments, and for that, the idea of an executive branch unified under presidential control has bipartisan attraction.[41]

A glaring mismatch: The Constitution's framers knew that when the public selects the chief executive officer, incumbents are apt to bolster their constitutional claims on executive power with other authority assumed to follow more directly from their election. They saw quite plainly that a president's political ties to his followers might compete with his constitutional stewardship of the commitments of the whole. The problem, from a republican point of view, is that when "the executive power" is vested in a single individual and the selection is by public choice, the government's commitments are likely to be treated as a direct extension of the interests of a presidential party.

Extrapolating the consequences, Alexander Hamilton warned that presidential elections are apt to foment "a disgraceful and ruinous mutability in the administration of the government."[42] That prospect struck at the heart of the federal project. The framers were driven to Philadelphia in no small part to counter what they saw as frightening political volatility in the governments of the several states. They sought a "steady administration" of the laws.[43] Presidents, animated one to the next by popular mandates to "reverse and undo" the work of their predecessors, threatened to overwhelm the priority they assigned to stable and continuous operations.[44]

This points to a glaring wrinkle in the theory of the unitary executive: it joins an originalist argument for an expansive reading of the vesting clause to selection procedures that have been radically altered in the course of time. The original selection procedure (which follows immediately upon the vesting clause in Article II) stands out as exhibit number one for the view that the framers were looking to have it both ways. What they came up with was unwieldy, equivocal, and unworkable; nevertheless, there is no mistaking the danger they perceived and sought to head off.

One way to minimize the disruptions of popular rule was to give the president a long term in office and to set no term limits. Another way was to try, so far as possible, to detach selection from power, to keep presidential prerogatives anchored in the Constitution and not electoral politics, and to favor individuals who mirrored the interests of the whole nation. That is why the popular connection in presidential elections was originally indirect, and why candidate appeals and national campaigns make no appearance in the document. The selection was to be made in discrete locales by specially chosen electors who would vote for two people without distinguishing which they preferred for president. The wager was that these electors would not waste their votes on candidates narrowly committed to their own interests and would look instead for figures widely known to be safe, contenders of national repute who were unlikely to threaten anyone's interests. The model incumbent was George Washington. If no such figure emerged, the fallback was selection by the House of Representatives, where claims on executive power could be brokered.[45]

Originally, the Constitution conditioned presidential empowerment on assurances that presidential elections would not exacerbate national divisions by carrying them into government and politicizing the entire operation. The selection procedure was not designed to put a strong political leader in the presidency. But it did comport well with the framers' notion of what a unitary executive might achieve: stability, national resolve, and efficient action in the general interest.

The near-immediate rise of national campaigns, organized opposition, and contested elections made short work of that solution. Whatever the constitutional case for the unitary executive, it is an argument that has long been shorn of the political foundations provided to support it. If the objective is to recapture the wisdom of the framers, mixing contemporary presidential politics with an expansive reading of the vesting clause should raise a red flag. Consistency would tie constitutional support for a unitary executive to an office that is radically depoliticized and resistant to any hint of insurgency, all partiality filtered out through selection mechanisms that elicit a diffuse sense of the interests of the nation at large.

By the same token, the rise of a direct, plebiscitary democracy would seem to call for different arrangements altogether, arrangements capable of inducing mutual trust and institutional

cooperation in some other way. Short of that, the unitary executive becomes exactly what the framers most feared, a formula for
maximum disruption. It is prone to imposing decisions at will, to
marginalizing dissent, and to radicalizing opposition. As national
administration expands its reach and partisanship becomes more
presidential,[46] these effects become more visible and consequential.
Power hierarchically controlled, thoroughly politicized and concentrated in the executive, is a constitutional nightmare, a bitter denouement for a beleaguered republic.

4

Republican Remedies

For nearly two hundred years, the pattern of state development in America was decidedly mixed. Improvisations exploited the ambiguities in the constitutional design, and the resulting arrangements indicated nothing so much as an abiding determination to have it both ways. Support for the idea of a unitary executive can be found in a persistent string of vigorous assertions of presidential control over the executive branch.[1] These were aided and abetted by the development of a more presidency-centered democracy. But this is only half the story. All along the way, the republican impulse to temper unitary pretensions remained strong.

This push and pull between presidentialism and republicanism is apparent into the 1970s. Its most remarkable feature is the succession of informal institutional and organizational devices invented to recast working relationships between constitutionally separated branches. Playing fast and loose with the written text, these extra-constitutional contrivances created several distinctive "systems" of government. Each settlement was quite different from its predecessor, and each marked a profound change in the operations of the national government at large. But at every stage, a more powerful presidency was corralled into novel arrangements that reaffirmed commitments to collaborative decision making and collective responsibility.[2]

Presidents bought into these republican remedies, and, at times, actively promoted them, because each adaptation was, in effect, bolstering their leadership position. Institutional improvisations grew progressively more conducive to executive power and presidential democracy. Given this long history of accommodation, it was perhaps only a matter of time before presidents grew impatient with these partnership agreements and the conditions and constraints they placed on their executive powers. By the 1970s, the signs were clear that partnership had run its course. In the decades since, collaborative arrangements have given way to a constitutional face-off. The strong arm of presidential control over administration presents itself today not only as a more practical and straightforward alternative to republican depth and deliberation but also, and quite astoundingly, as the only formula consistent with the Constitution.

Party remedies: During the nineteenth century, the institutional reconciliation of these competing models of state organization was achieved mainly through changes in the selection system and the development of party government. Jefferson, the first president to come into office on a transfer of power from one party to another, was also the first to grasp the partisan implications of unity in the executive. He moved quickly, unleashing a multi-front assault on the depth that had accumulated in the executive branch after twelve years of Federalist dominance.

Nowhere were Jefferson's efforts to cut through the received order and redirect the executive branch more clearly on display than in the administration of justice, an arena of intervention that has sparked considerable controversy in the politics of our day.[3] Convinced that the law enforcement apparatus carried over from the Adams administration was neither blind nor neutral, Jefferson identified federal attorneys and federal marshals as intolerable impediments to fairness for his followers. He acted immediately to replace them all.[4]

What makes Jefferson's presidency remarkable, however, is that even as he reached deep into the executive branch to fashion his own administration, he also relaxed the separation of powers with extensive outreach to Congress. He went out of his way to promote inter-branch cooperation, and he actively facilitated the development of new forms of collective responsibility over national affairs.

Jefferson brought Congress into his orbit through "conference, consultation, and free discussion," and once the House leadership got atop the machinery he had created to solicit their support, they found that they themselves were "in a position to control the whole executive administration."[5]

Even more striking was the Jeffersonian move beyond the default position assigned to Congress in the original selection system. Enacting the 12th Amendment, and through it, opening the door to the specification of a national party ticket, the Jeffersonians consolidated the position of their party caucus in Congress as the first mover in the electoral process. The framers had spent a lot of time figuring out a way to get Congress out of the business of presidential elections. The constitutional separation of powers turned in no small measure on securing an alternative to selection by the legislature. But the Jeffersonians were less interested in separation than in collaboration, and they did not hesitate to fiddle with the framers' design to achieve their objectives. The congressional party caucus not only selected the national candidates, it also coordinated the actions of the local electors. Soon the caucus was "King," the nomination of candidates by the congressional party and its instructions to local electors reconfiguring accountability from top to bottom.[6] The effects of congressional control of presidential nominations reverberated throughout the constitutional system. It tugged at the executive hierarchy, leaving the presidents of the late-Jeffersonian era in charge of administrators who were openly competing for congressional favor. The operation of the caucus "was such as always to imply and on occasion to make explicit executive subordination to congressional President-makers."[7]

In the second transfer of partisan control over government, claims on behalf of a unitary executive ratcheted up precipitously, and presidential hostility to depth was put on full display. Andrew Jackson asserted presidential authority over all policy affecting the executive branch.[8] At the climactic moment, he ignored a congressional proclamation of faith in the National Bank as the national depository and ordered his treasury secretary to remove the federal funds. When the secretary balked, claiming that he had a responsibility to Congress and that he would be hard-pressed to account to it for such an action, Jackson dismissed him. Then, in a public pronouncement of his intention to remove the deposits, Jackson claimed that his authority to act had been augmented by an electoral mandate delivered by his followers in his recent bid for reelection.[9]

Jackson's assertions of political power and institutional prerogative did not go uncontested, either by the Court or by his proto-Whig opponents.[10] Even as his followers gained the upper hand and expunged a congressional censure of his actions from the record, his unilateralism divided the nation politically and fostered the development of alternative means of ensuring institutional collaboration and shared responsibility. A far more elaborate system of nomination and election took hold in the wake of the Jackson presidency, this one too relaxing the separation of powers.[11]

By the middle of the nineteenth century, national networks of local party machines had recalibrated the operation of all the formal institutions of government. More independent of those institutions than the parties of the Jeffersonian era, these organizations worked bottom-up to fashion a new, loosely knit system of collective control. In time, their leaders became known as the "bosses." They selected presidential candidates in national party conventions, and the nominees relied on their mobilizing capacities to win in competitive elections. The typical president of the nineteenth century came into office as a "dark horse" candidate, the compromise choice of the party convention. They were often little more than faceless representatives of the coalition behind them. In this arrangement the president was "bound to the party which by its efforts had placed him in the White House."[12]

James Polk's famous declaration "I intend to be *myself* president of the U.S." was daring precisely because it defied his unassuming rise as a ninth-ballot nominee.[13] It invoked the personal character of presidential power at a time when personalities were being submerged in organizations. As it turned out, Polk's statement of intent proved hard to square with the pledge that had carried him into office: the promise to do "equal and exact justice" to every faction of his party.[14] To complete the community of interests forged by state-based parties, presidents like Polk were expected to offer up the largesse of the executive branch to the organization that had elected them, and consequently they spent a good deal of their time trying to avoid the alienation of one faction or the other in dispersing it. The presidency of the nineteenth century was undoubtedly strengthened by its organized political base, but because these organizations operated independently of candidates and incumbents, and because they colonized all the government's political institutions, they fostered more interdependence than independence.[15]

The tight connection forged between party mobilization and governmental management in the nineteenth century thoroughly politicized administration. Presidents routinely swept the administrative offices clean to make way for a new class of partisan job seekers. By the same token, however, the "spoils system" elevated the collective (unity in the national party) and suppressed the personal (unity in the figure of the president). It integrated the presidency into the far-flung interests of the fast-sprawling nation, but kept the power of the executive branch dispersed. It assumed a chief executive officer with little more to do than service other centers of power, and the primary service on offer was that of a loyal office broker.

Administrative remedies: By the turn of the twentieth century, Progressive reformers were determined to break the stranglehold that the spoils system held over the executive branch. They wanted to expand the administrative capacities of the national government and to raise the political profile of presidents. These efforts drew support from factions in both parties. Theodore Roosevelt pushed the cause along by articulating a "stewardship" theory of the presidency, one that would give the president broad authority to act in the national interest. Woodrow Wilson advanced the case as well, modeling an enlarged role for the president in setting the national agenda and impressing a positive program of action on the legislature. For its part, Congress passed the Budget and Accounting Act of 1921. This statute endorsed the subordination of agency budget requests to presidential priorities, explicitly accepting a leading role for the president in both agenda setting and policy development.[16] Arguably, the Court did even more to strengthen the president's hand in this period. Its decision in *Myers* (1926) confirmed the broad power of presidents to remove executive branch officers, and its *Curtiss-Wright* (1936) decision advanced the president as the "sole organ" of American foreign policy.

But though the Progressives pushed vigorously for a more presidency-centered government, they most assuredly did not push for a unitary executive. The overarching themes of America's administrative expansion reflected the Progressives' reaction against the partisan practices of the nineteenth century. The president's national political profile rose in this period in conjunction with a drive to reverse the politicization of administration, to render it nonpartisan, to insulate it and instill it with an integrity of its own. Progressive modifications to the presidential job description emphasized political leadership and agenda setting over purely executive action. They turned the presidency into policy central, a coordinating hub that could orchestrate the work of other institutions into a grand concert of action on the nation's problems.[17]

If the first priority in progressive reform was to get politicians in different institutions to agree upon a set of policy solutions, the second was to give professional civil servants the discretion to figure out the best way to implement them. When the Progressives promoted "separation," it was to put greater distance between administration and politics. When the Progressives promoted unity, it was to forge closer, more collaborative relations between president and Congress. Neither idea prioritized unity in the executive.[18]

The keynotes of the Progressives' administrative expansion were political neutrality, administrative competence, and inter-branch coordination around professional expertise. Under those formulas, the state piled on layers of depth, and top-down intrusions were correspondingly limited. Progressives enshrined their faith in non-partisan administration in civil service protections for the government workforce and in a proliferation of independent regulatory commissions. Even the removal power in *Myers* was crafted subtly to respect the insulation of a permanent civil service.

Franklin Roosevelt is the standout case of this era not only because he contributed mightily to administrative expansion on these terms, but also because he ventured the most aggressive claims of the first half of the twentieth century on behalf of a redesign along the lines of a unitary executive. In one test, he removed a recalcitrant member of the Federal Trade Commission, who was serving a fixed term set by Congress.[19] Later, he presented Congress with a comprehensive plan for reorganizing the executive branch to concentrate power and accountability in the presidential office. His plan would, among other things, have abolished the Civil Service Commission to tighten presidential control over personnel, it would have moved the independent regulatory commissions into the regular executive departments and reconfigured their policy-making and administrative functions into bureaus, and it would have brought most of the responsibilities of Congress's independent auditing agency—the General Accounting Office—directly under presidential authority.[20]

Notably, however, these forays were rebuffed. Between them, the Court and the Congress reaffirmed all the forms of administrative insulation that Roosevelt had threatened with unitary controls— the Civil Service Commission, fixed terms of appointment, independent agencies, and independent audits. The president's reorganization plan was defeated. Following up, the Hatch Act bolstered the separation of politics from administration and headed off the construction of new political machines operated directly out of presidential offices. The insistence on shared responsibility and collective control remained remarkably robust.

It is telling in this regard that today's unitarians challenge the common characterization of the New Deal settlement as a pivotal turn toward a presidency-centered government, seeing instead aggressive congressional encroachments on the president's domain.[21] But the congressional response to FDR is better seen as another ingenious accommodation, another invitation to coordinate and collaborate. After his reorganization bill was defeated, a compromise found its way into law. This one gave the president limited authority to reorganize the executive branch on his own initiative and increased presidential oversight of the now-sprawling national bureaucracies. Roosevelt used that authority to create a new Executive Office of the President (EOP). The EOP anchored central direction and coordination in technical expertise and professional judgment. It did not personalize the presidency; it "institutionalized" it. Eventually, the Bureau of the Budget, the Council of Economic Advisers, and the National Security Council surrounded the chief executive with the kind of "neutral" competence and advice that Congress could abide and employ in its own work.[22] Not content with that, Congress then reasserted the role of others in administrative oversight. The Administrative Procedure Act of 1946 regularized the active participation of the courts in the review of agency decisions, and the Legislative Reorganization Act of 1946 bolstered Congress's own capacities for what it called "continuous watchfulness" over administration.[23]

Well into the twentieth century, American government was still having it both ways. Presidents were becoming more formidable players, but Congress and the Court ensured that administration would remain a collaborative game. Mutual buy-in to administrative expansion preserved republican commitments by turning presidential leadership into a matter of bargaining and persuasion,[24] and the integrity of the administrative sphere became a kind of public good around which the different branches could cooperate.

When, in the 1950s, the Court rebuked President Truman for an overblown assertion of constitutional prerogative, it reasserted these precepts. The Constitution, Justice Robert Jackson wrote, "contemplates that practice will integrate the dispersed powers into a workable government. It enjoins upon its branches separateness but interdependence, autonomy but reciprocity."[25]

Roots of a beleaguered republic: Developments since the 1970s, however, have steadily elevated "separateness" and "autonomy" over "interdependence" and "reciprocity." One reason refers us back to the major expansion of national administrative capacities that occurred in the 1960s and 1970s. With so much more of the actual governing shifted into the executive branch, presidents found that they had at least as much to gain by asserting control independently, through administrative direction, as through further collaboration with Congress in the interest of enacting new legislation. In these circumstances, there arose, in the words of a staffer for Bill Clinton, "a broader way of thinking about the Presidency . . . not just what you can do legislatively, but the full panoply of what you can do with the office."[26]

Of course, the primary obstacle to a change in leadership strategy from the legislative orientation of the twentieth century to the administrative orientation of today was all the depth that administration had acquired during the long period of progressive collaboration. With the prospects for governing through direct control of administration growing more attractive, the "semi-permanent bureaucrats and quasi autonomous agencies" that were only "nominally part of an 'executive branch'" became more than just an abiding annoyance to the chief executive. Pundits impatient with congressional deliberations saw that a president willing to "go to war within his own executive branch" in the pursuit of his "mandate" could redirect national affairs unilaterally, through personal control over administrative affairs.[27]

Part and parcel of this change in the calculus of governing was the fact that the recent administrative expansion had been driven in large part by a social revolution and democratization. With the last vestiges of localism, social hierarchy, and traditional rule uprooted, all issues became, in effect, national issues.[28] That made it more difficult to reach the political consensus needed for inter-branch collaboration and concerted action at the center. Stiff opposition to the Vietnam War compounded that problem, undermining prospects for reaching a consensus on foreign as well as domestic policy. The collaborative arrangements of republican rule had always rested, at bottom, on some modicum of agreement among officeholders about what the national government should be doing. As that common ground evaporated, divided government became the new normal, and as the likelihood of achievement through legislation became more remote, a new "political logic" took hold, one that "push[ed] the President toward the administrative sphere as the forum most readily available for translating his policy objectives into action."[29] All this made those knotty constitutional questions of control over administration harder to finesse, and inter-branch suspicions harder to contain.

The changing calculus of presidential leadership had a third dimension as well, for the nationalization of policy and power had profound effects on the selection system and the character of national party politics. The reformers of the 1970s rebelled against the old "transactional partisan organizations," in favor of "issue politics and programmatically distinct parties."[30] They saw parties not as state-based organizations banded together in loose coalitions but as "nationwide combinations" of interests with well-defined policy priorities. They wanted to "register the strength" of those interests "in the nation as whole."[31] A new breed of party leadership agitated against "pale pastels," in favor of "bold colors which make it unmistakably clear where we stand on all the issues troubling the people."[32]

Both the Democrats and the Republicans altered their selection procedures accordingly. The reforms of the 1970s diminished the mediating role of the party machinery and turned nominations over to candidate-based organizations that competed with one another in primaries and caucuses. Through these new procedures, presidents gained control over their own political organizations, and with a more independent base for political action to draw on, they personalized their claims to democratic legitimacy.[33] This new form of presidential democracy made incumbents more self-reliant politically, but presidential politics would not become more consensual as a result. As it stripped the national plebiscite of the organizational trappings of collective responsibility, the new selection system facilitated the emergence of a more ideological and polarized politics. Candidates were thrust into direct relationships with the nation's most intense policy demanders, concentrating the power of special interests within these new presidential parties.

These developments have a direct bearing on arguments for presidential administration. Part of the rationale for a firmer presidential hand is that hierarchical control over the executive branch will *diminish* the role of special interest networks in American government, that it will break the curse of interest capture and recover the promise of representing the interests of the nation as a whole.[34] The new reality, however, is that winning the presidency and implanting the campaign staff into the White House increases the prospect of running the executive branch as a direct extension of the particular interests mobilized behind the presidential party.

In fact, the new constitutional formalism embedded in the unitary theory pulled these various elements together into a virulent combination. The whole package—getting straight with the framers, correcting the mistakes of the past, drawing a hard line of separation between the responsibilities of the president and the Congress, rediscovering the full scope of "the executive power"—aligned the Constitution with presidentialism plain and simple. All that was needed to shift the template from governing collaboratively *through* the presidency to governing unilaterally *within* the presidency was a more expansive interpretation of the Constitution's vesting clause.[35] A generous reading of Article II allowed presidents to capitalize on party developments and administrative developments that were augmenting their power while at the same time sidelining the collective and collaborative stipulations that had previously made those developments acceptable to others. The rise of presidential parties coupled with the simultaneous elaboration of the unitary executive jettisoned the historic commitment to collaboration in administrative operations and replaced it with the impositions of personal devotees.

Each of these developments was prefigured in the Nixon presidency. Richard Nixon saw little to be gained through collaboration. He came to power in 1969 as a Republican facing a Congress controlled by the Democrats. Sitting atop a bureaucracy that his opponents had just recently expanded, he felt himself surrounded by institutions hostile to his priorities. From his perspective, the administrative state was a presumptuous impediment to his leadership.[36]

Nixon was wary of getting entrapped by the siren song of stability and continuity. The political officers he appointed to supervise the work of the agencies were prone to "go off and marry the natives."[37] He wanted to purge the state's ballast: "I don't believe that civil service is a good thing for the country."[38] Taking aim at that now-ingrained undertow of resistance, he clamped down on career administrators and ratcheted up his claims to control the executive branch. He upended the norms of neutral competence and cooperative management that had led Congress to support the creation of the EOP, and he recast those overhead agencies to impress his own preferences more directly. He reorganized the Bureau of the Budget as the Office of Management and Budget for tighter program supervision. He expanded the White House Office, strengthening the hold of his personal loyalists over the business of the federal government.[39] He pushed political operatives deeper into the administrative structure, creating a "counter-bureaucracy" to redirect the work of the agencies. He asserted wider authority to act unilaterally, impounding funds appropriated by Congress when their priorities ran contrary to his own.[40]

A new governing formula was foreshadowed by Nixon on the electoral front as well. When he ran for reelection in 1972, he asserted his distance from the regular Republican Party and organized a personal campaign though his "Committee to Re-Elect the President." By exploiting the national divisions emerging over social issues, he hoped to remake the party on his own terms and create a new majority in his own image.[41] Asked later where the boundaries of his expansive new conception of the presidency might lie, Nixon nodded to a form of accountability that was decidedly plebiscitary and retrospective: "a president has to come up before the electorate."[42]

What, then, of the traditional republican response to presidentialism? The 1970s was a pivotal decade, but it was not a decade of capitulation. In fact, it seemed at first that these intimations of a strong state, stripped down and hierarchically organized as a presidential democracy, might produce the characteristic compromise. As they had so many times before, other powers in the system pushed back. A remarkable string of improvisations and institutional inventions echoed the republican remedies of the past.

It soon became clear, however, that this round of presidential assertion and institutional reordering was not just more of the same. Despite some renewed overtures to collaboration, there was no revised partnership in the offing. Categorical changes in the underlying conditions of American government were working against negotiation of a new settlement. The resurgent Congress of the 1970s did not corral the presidency into a more collaborative posture. Instead, both sides doubled down on constitutional prerogatives. The emergent face-off drew out the most problematic features of the government's formal design.

Digging in: Congress reacted to the Nixon administration with a fierce determination to thwart presidentialism and reassert its own role in governmental affairs. No longer trusting the information provided by the president's budget office, Congress created a budget office of its own. It also devised its own budget process and committee structure to provide a specifically congressional plan for national action. Later in the decade, Congress went beyond a re-assertion of its own role. A "stunning rise in oversight" challenged presidential control of the executive branch more directly. In 1976, Congress created an inspector general (IG) in the Department of Health, Education, and Welfare (HEW), and in 1978, it placed IGs across the executive departments and agencies, granting them investigatory authority and responsibilities to report to Congress regularly.[43] The Ethics in Government Act of 1978 created independent prosecutors to check potential abuses of executive power.[44] Congress also put teeth into the whistleblower protections of President Carter's civil service reform proposal. To pry open that new channel of communication between administrators and lawmakers, it stipulated the rights of civil servants to petition Congress and forbade supervisors from preventing their subordinates from alerting Congress to wrongdoing.[45] Those protections were later expanded with the Whistleblower Protection Act of 1989, and a separate process for employees involved in national security matters was created by the Intelligence Community Whistleblower Protection Act of 1998.

These reforms defied the presidential hierarchy by lacing administration with alternative lines of communication and mechanisms of protection. Indeed, they identified the Congress more clearly than ever before as the principal promoter of a deeper state. A new era of collaboration and cooperation seemed, however, beyond reach. Explanations for new forms, like the Congressional Budget Office, indicated that Congress was digging in for a rocky and extended contest over control of the state. Senator Bill Brock (R-TN) warned against further reliance on the presidency in helping with the work of the Congress. He did not want to be placed "as we are today, at the disposal and the mercy of a huge and talented staff for which we have no counterpart to give us alternative suggestions."

Senator Hubert Humphrey (D-MN) agreed: Congress must "be in a position to act independently, to make our own choices, gather our own data, do our own analysis, and propose our own policy alternatives."[46]

In its IG initiative, Congress took aim at "central clearance," presidential control over the kind of information that executive branch officers would present to legislators. Though the 1978 act would ultimately carve out a workaround for presidential budget requests, it established a regular semi-annual reporting process for an IG to provide information directly to Congress, and it created a seven-day reporting option to flag abuses requiring urgent attention. The act specifically prohibited officials in the agencies from interfering with IG investigations, and it stipulated that IG reports be made public within sixty days.[47] The bill's sponsor in the House, Representative L. H. Fountain (D-NC), predicted that this would "turn out to be one of the most monumental laws ever passed." It would keep "Congress fully and currently informed."[48] For Fountain, who was representative of a Democratic majority during a Democratic administration, the problem was the presidency per se: "Presidents—not just this one—don't want Congress seeking out or getting information statutorily because they feel that it in some way infringes upon their rights."[49]

Coming in the wake of the Watergate scandal, the reforms of this decade momentarily threw the presidency back on its heels. But they had an additional, ironic, and, in the long run, more important effect: they stimulated earnest elaboration of a unitary theory of the executive. The reaction began in and around the Ford administration. As Dick Cheney, Donald Rumsfeld, and Antonin Scalia well knew, the first president to take office without having stood in a national election had only one line of defense, and it was strictly constitutional.[50] Strong proponents of presidential power, they urged Ford to double down, to match the resurgent Congress with more aggressive assertions of the separation of powers and stiff readings of the formal warrants lodged in Article II.

Consider in this regard the elaborate provisions for inter-branch consultation contained in the War Powers Resolution of 1973. These stipulations might have been read as a new partnership offer, a congressional invitation to more sustained collaboration and deliberation in the exercise of war power. But the Ford administration mocked the law at its first test, informing the congressional leadership of its intent to take military action in Cambodia only after the mission was over. Its justification was "the President's constitutional Executive power and his authority as Commander-in-Chief."[51] The IG plan for HEW drew pushback from the Ford administration as well. Representative Benjamin Rosenthal (D-NY) originally proposed an IG who would hold a single ten-year term and be removable only by impeachment. Ford's HEW Under Secretary Marjorie Lynch blasted this setup as a violation of executive branch hierarchy, as the IG "would not be directly responsible to the Secretary, or, in fact, to anyone in the executive branch of the Government." Ultimately, the HEW IG act provided for presidential removal.[52]

Ford's successor Jimmy Carter seemed an unlikely unitarian, but he went toe to toe with his Democratic Congress to assert and defend presidential control over administration. We have already mentioned his success in centralizing control through civil service reform and regulatory review and his resistance to congressional efforts to make the Department of Justice (DOJ) more independent. Congress's determination to create IGs across the executive branch evoked a similar institutional reaction. Objections to the 1978 act from the Carter DOJ were categorical: "the continuous oversight of Executive agencies contemplated by the [IG] bill is not a proper legislative function but is rather a serious distortion of our constitutional system."[53] The Department of Agriculture agreed, calling the bill's provision for direct reporting to Congress "an apparent violation of the 'separation of powers' doctrine."[54] Congress was having none of it. Hearing yet another complaint about IGs violating "basic Constitutional safeguards separating the executive and legislative branches of government," Representative Fountain shot back: "I thought we had just about eliminated that kind of argument as a result of everything that took place regarding Watergate."[55]

Ever since the 1970s, proponents of a unitary executive have been denouncing congressional overreach. They have pointed to restrictions on the president's reorganization authority, to inspectors general, to independent prosecutors, to whistleblower protections, to incessant investigations, and to "legislative vetoes," statutory provisions allowing one or both houses of Congress to nullify an executive action on its own authority. But there is little doubt who has gained the upper hand in these confrontations. In 1986, Ronald Reagan's Justice Department called for a "greater articulation in conflict situations of each branch's constitutional authority and legitimate interests." The DOJ report outlined a "comprehensive way of 'thinking clearly' about the separation of powers." Tellingly, it looked to "the differing formulations of the first sentences of Articles I–III," finding that "only Article II is an open-ended grant of power."[56]

Congress has found it harder to sustain actions that protect its institutional interests. Its resolve to protect itself, compromised long ago by the rise of political parties, has always been uncertain and politically contingent.[57] A significant faction of the president's party in Congress can be counted upon to indulge presidential claims on policy grounds, and presidential popularity can weaken the opposition. Congress's new budget procedures never had a chance to take hold. Reagan upended them at their first major test. For its part, the Court found some of Congress's most promising improvisations to be steps too far. In *INS v. Chadha* (1983) the justices signaled new interest of their own in sharpening the separation of powers. That ruling voided Congress's use of legislative vetoes, undercutting a key inducement to inter-branch accommodation. The statute for independent counsels also came under heavy fire as an unwarranted interference with the president's power to execute the law. In another victory for the unitarians, it was allowed to expire in 1999.[58]

Congress pushed back in the 1970s, but confrontation does not play to its strengths. Historically, republican remedies worked by first acknowledging a more powerful role for the presidency and then enlisting it in cooperative arrangements. The new institutional politics was different. Rather than submerge the ambiguities of the constitutional design, it accentuated them. Less cooperative than combative, it also put Congress in a tough spot. The hard-line response to the Nixon administration unwittingly fostered a theory of strict separation that would eventually leverage the president's considerable advantages. In this beleaguered republic, claims on behalf of a unitary executive steadily gained ground.[59]

PART II
PHANTOMS UNLEASHED

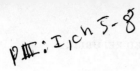

Introduction

Part II of this book intervenes at a tumultuous moment, with critical contests still in progress. What is clear at this point is that the face-off set in motion a half century ago has reached an inflection point. The Trump presidency has drawn it out. With resources on both sides fully deployed, the alternatives before us appear unmistakable. It is a time for reckoning.

To be sure, the courts have already pushed back on some of Trump's more outlandish claims.[1] The temptation, perhaps, is to think that the judiciary will sort all this out for us. But of all the illusions hovering over this episode, that may be the most fantastic. The answers we seek are not to be found in the Constitution. If they were, judges would have solved the problems posed by our state's depth long ago, and we would have avoided the current tumult. In no small measure, the resort to legalism and formalism is what has driven us to this point.

To state the obvious: the theory of the unitary executive is a lawyer's brief. It is not targeted to presidents, whose interests align nicely with its constitutional claims, but to the courts, where judges need to be convinced. Appointments to the bench have become an integral part of this campaign. Not only are presidents apt to look for nominees favorably disposed to their executive power, they are prone to use the ideas at their disposal to test the boundaries of that power, taking chances to find out how much more the courts will allow. Courts deal with these issues case by case, often resolving them after the president's actions have had their effect. The courts have, in fact, been on all sides of the unitary claims advanced by the Trump administration. Their remands and reversals invariably prompt assurances that our institutions are working and that the constitutional system is taking care of itself, but dismissing the most absurd claims sets a pretty low bar for effective government. The constitutional system is only as resilient as its practical working arrangements, and courts are not well equipped to re-engineer those.

Faith that answers to these questions must lie in the Constitution is one more symptom of the exhaustion of the political remedies on which we previously relied. If the past tells us anything about these issues, it is that the ambiguities of the Constitution are best resolved pragmatically and extra-constitutionally. Neither the nineteenth-century solution—turning national administration into an employment service for local party machines—nor the twentieth-century solution—separating administration from politics—did much more than wink and nod at the Constitution. More than anything else, the historic capacity of this state to submerge constitutional difficulties and to get on with the business of governing reflected a modicum of agreement on what that business was. Scrutiny of the Constitution is no substitute for that.

The influential Progressive economist John R. Commons advised that we look at the state as "officials-in-action."[2] Ambiguities of state design and constitutional structure are painfully abstract until officers engage them directly. Contending officials acting instrumentally personify the different operating assumptions and institutional predispositions in play. It is their engagements that reveal the dilemmas of state formation in America. That is where we focus our reckoning.

What we see are two different systems of administration working at cross purposes. Each is coherent enough unto itself, but it is forced in practice to contend uncertainly with its rival. Here, we have distilled schematically the dueling chains of association that make up these systems. Table II.1 points up the respective attractions and liabilities of each and suggests their relative strengths when pushed to confront one another.

Table II.1 Contending Systems of Administration

	Unitary	Republican
Design	hierarchical	insulated
Executive Power	personal	collaborative
Authority	direct	mediated
Constitutional Disposition	formalistic	pragmatic
Legitimacy	plebiscitary	prudential
Outlook on Depth	encumbrance	asset
Principal Liability	arbitrary imposition	bureaucratic subversion

The positive case for the unitary executive is that it maximizes the personal responsibility of presidents for the operations of the executive branch. The chief executive can be held singularly accountable both formally and electorally for the performance of his administration. The corresponding risks are that boundaries on presidential power become harder to maintain. Good government can become whatever the president says it is, the personalization of power over administration can devolve into arbitrary imposition, and consequential decisions can be made by whim, instinct, or partisan interest without regard for any larger public interest in regular order and due process. Presidential administrations, singly and in succession, then become an ironic perversion of original aspirations, a threat to the steady administration of the laws.

These trade-offs invert as administration deepens. The positive case for depth is that it steadies the state and maximizes the collective responsibility of the coordinate branches of government. When administrators respond to and mediate the interests of multiple principals, they extend the deliberative process and broaden protections for the public interest. The risk, however, is that all this administrative intermediation can blur the lines of control, thwart political direction, obfuscate responsibility, and devolve into subversion.

President Trump's intervention in the Navy's system of military justice affords a capsule summary of the murky field described by this typology. During his 2016 campaign, Trump complained that the American military was too restrained in its prosecution of the war on terror. Once in office, he acted on that view by intervening directly on behalf of service members accused of war crimes. In one case, he reversed the demotion of Chief Petty Officer Edward Gallagher, who had been acquitted of murder charges by a Navy tribunal but convicted for taking a trophy photo with a corpse.[3]

Trump's constitutional authority to take personal control of Gallagher's fate was never in question. The White House clarified its ground in no uncertain terms: "The President, as Commander-in-Chief, is ultimately responsible for ensuring that the law is enforced and when appropriate, that mercy is granted."[4] Nor is granting clemency to members of the armed services an unusual action for presidents. Most presidential pardons have been for troops accused of desertion or citizens who had avoided the draft. A day after his inauguration, Jimmy Carter granted unconditional pardons to those who had evaded military service during the Vietnam War.[5] Abraham Lincoln pardoned so many deserters during the Civil War that his attorney general, Edward Bates, told him that "he was unfit to be entrusted with the pardoning power."[6]

Trump's decision to intervene in Gallagher's case drew substantial pushback from within and outside the military. Reaching deep into the system of military justice to pluck out one particular offender cut hard against norms, especially because the president's action looked less like mercy for a guilty soldier than a pointed public endorsement of an alternative standard of military conduct. Secretary of the Navy Richard Spencer, who would eventually be fired over his role in the episode, characterized Trump's actions as a "shocking and unprecedented intervention in a low-level review." It was, Spencer thought, a reckless and capricious imposition by a president who "has very little understanding of what it means to be in the military, to fight ethically or to be governed by a uniform set of rules and practices." Resistance to the perceived imposition drew out the case for depth, for the integrity of a system that operates within the executive branch but at some distance from direct presidential control. "Normally," the Navy secretary said, "military justice works best when senior leadership stays far away."[7] Presidential contempt for the system, critics charged, posed a threat to the general morale of the armed services and the larger, group purposes of its proceedings. As the Navy pressed its review forward with an eye toward removing Gallagher's Trident pin and expelling him from the Navy SEALs, a juror from the earlier murder case argued that Gallagher's peers were better equipped than the president to make the appropriate judgments: "Let other SEALs decide if he deserves to be a SEAL."[8] Senate Minority Leader Chuck Schumer (D-NY) chimed in as well: "Good order, discipline and morale among the armed services must transcend politics."[9]

The president responded to the criticism with an appeal to his political base. He stigmatized the pushback as an administrative form of subversion. At a reelection rally, he told the crowd: "Just last week I stuck up for three great warriors against the deep state. . . . And so many people said, 'Sir, I don't think you should do that.' "[10] Before the inevitable denouement, all sense of the appropriate order of things had evaporated. As if to confirm the Deep State charge, Spencer defied a presidential tweet—"Navy will NOT be taking away Warfighter and Navy Seal Eddie Gallagher's Trident Pin"— and decided to press ahead with the demotion case.[11] Spencer said that he "recognized that the tweet revealed the president's intent," but that he "did not take it to be an official order, chiefly because every action taken by the president in the case so far had either been a verbal or written command."[12] The administrator's obfuscation was as transparent as the president's political imposition. The secretary of defense, Mark Esper, fired Spencer, ostensibly for failing to inform him of his attempts to work out some sort of compromise that would allow the standard Navy process to proceed.[13]

The Trump administration was riddled with controversies like these. The Gallagher affair was just one of those involving the military.[14] Others were spread far and wide. Rather than provide an exhaustive inventory, we offer a representative selection. We examine different, though not mutually exclusive, kinds of depth, each of which has locked horns with President Trump's demands for personal, hierarchical control over the executive branch. First, we consider depth in staff—the White House officials tasked to bridge the president's personal direction with the institutional presidency and the executive branch at large. Next, we look further at depth in norms—conventions that inform practical operations—focusing this time on the Federal Bureau of Investigation and the Department of Justice. Third, we examine depth in knowledge, including rules-based protections for knowledge-based authority, at the National Weather Service, the Environmental Protection Agency, the Department of Agriculture, and in the executive branch's response to the coronavirus pandemic. Fourth, we consider depth in appointment, examining how demands for executive branch unity elevate loyalty to the president above all other qualifications. Finally, we look to depth in oversight. We consider the resistance to unitary claims provided by whistleblowers and inspectors general, and we turn to Trump's impeachment in 2019, where the relationship between administrative depth and congressional power was clearest.

5

Depth in Staff

"The President needs help." This now-famous declaration animated the 1937 report of Franklin Roosevelt's Committee on
Administrative Management. Congress responded to that call in
the Reorganization Act of 1939, authorizing, among other things,
staff support for the president within the White House itself. These
"executive assistants" were to be the president's "direct aides," more
attentive to his immediate needs and interests than any other
officers of the executive branch.[1] They were to serve at his pleasure
and to promote his interests in the rest of the government. But staff
of any kind adds depth, and curiously enough, some of the most
brazen acts of internal resistance to President Trump's assertion of
unitary command and control came from these high-level helpers.

The White House staff "helps" the president by establishing
regular order in his consideration of national issues. It controls
access to the Oval Office, manages the workflow, and facilitates
responsible decision making. Even within the intimate setting of
the White House, intermediation of this kind conditions presidential action.[2] The President's Committee on Administrative
Management saw that clearly. It certainly intended the White
House staff to strengthen the personal hand and political control of
the president over the affairs of the executive branch, but the staff's
job, as described in the report, was much more than simply doing
the president's bidding:

> Their function would be, when any matter was presented to
> the President for action affecting any part of the administrative
> work of the Government, to assist him in obtaining quickly and

without delay *all pertinent information* possessed by any of the
executive departments so as *to guide him* in making his responsible decisions; and then when decisions have been made, to as-
sist him in seeing to it that every administrative department and
agency affected is promptly informed.[3]

Conceived in this way, the White House staff was part and parcel
of the committee's broader conception of an institutionalized presidency. The assumption was that information sharing and responsible action constituted common ground on which the personal
authority of the president could be integrated into the burgeoning
machinery of the executive branch. The efficiency of the staff lay
in making "a speedier clearance of the knowledge needed for executive decision." By keeping the president "in closer and easier
touch with the widespread affairs of administration," his closest
advisers could maximize the virtues of both depth and unity.[4] Staff
would improve communications upward from the departments
and agencies as well as downward from the president. The expectation was that presidents would find it in their interest to use the
resources concentrated in the executive branch to inform their
decisions, and that the staff would serve the president by bringing
those resources to bear on those decisions.

To be sure, this put the staff in a delicate position. They sat at the
interface between command and prudence, between the personal
and the collective, between the individual and the institutional.[5]
They were to act as honest brokers of information and expertise, but
they were not politically neutral. As members of the president's entourage, they were to see to it that the incumbent avoided mistakes,
but they were also expected at all times to advance his interests and
priorities.

The fact that staffers are normally part of the presidential party
adds further nuance, for they often represent collectively all the different wings of the president's electoral coalition. In this respect,
the political circumstances of the Trump administration posed

some serious impediments to unity in the executive. Representing the party "establishment" in the White House was the chief of staff, Reince Priebus, the former chair of the Republican National Committee. Representing the insurgent populist wing of the party that had crushed the establishment and propelled Trump into the White House was Steve Bannon in a newly created position of chief strategist. Setting up Priebus and Bannon as coequals on his staff, the new president began with an awkward political amalgam. The unity afforded in his person covered over sharply divergent approaches to administration and policy.[6]

Managing the president: The White House staff jostled for influence and favor throughout the president's first year. Trump bristled at their efforts to establish regular processes and to control the flow of information. The president saw management of that sort, quite correctly, as an impingement on his authority to act on his own instincts and to direct his subordinates at will. The institutional presidency turns political leadership toward deliberation and negotiation; the plebiscitary presidency turns it toward individual will and personal imposition. The tensions that boiled over on the issue of trade afford a brief, but sharp, illustration.

Trump came into office proclaiming free trade deals bad for America. His opposition to these agreements was, along with his opposition to immigration, a signature of his insurgent brand of politics. The president's position on trade stood in stark contrast to the line of policy charted by previous administrations of both parties, and in assembling a White House staff broadly representative of the coalition that put him in office, he tapped advisers with strong priors on both sides of the issue. The free trade camp, aligned with the Republican establishment, was led by a former president of Goldman Sachs, Gary Cohn. Trump appointed Cohn to be assistant to the president for economic policy. The pro-tariff position aligned with Trump's campaign commitments was represented by Peter Navarro, the deputy assistant to the president for trade. Navarro was a rare find, an economist who held protectionist views.[7]

As might be expected, the staff tried to turn the incipient policy dispute over trade into a question of proper management. As we will see in several different arenas, this contest between the Deep State and the unitary executive pivoted off concerns about process. The more the president's advisers enlisted regular processes to stave off unilateral action on Trump's preferred positions, the stronger his impulse became to shut down deliberations and to dictate decisions on his own authority. The enormity of the stakes for those on both sides of the trade dispute put these two systems of authority on a collision course. Mutual suspicions unleashed the phantom twins, and before long the staff was resorting to acts of outright sabotage.

During the first week of the Trump administration, the protectionist Navarro drafted a memo for the president announcing a peremptory withdrawal from the Trans-Pacific Partnership.[8] At the same time, staffers aligned with the "establishment" consensus on trade were attempting to put in place regular procedures for presidential decision making. The managers' use of process as a shield against the president's inclinations on trade did not go unnoticed by Navarro. "The Trump trade agenda does indeed remain severely hobbled by political forces within the West Wing," Navarro wrote in a letter to Trump. He complained about the machinations of the "Wall Street Wing," tying Cohn's support for established trade policies to powerful financial interests. He then linked the policy disagreement to attempts by the staff to define the channels through which information would flow to the president. Flagging the relationship between Cohn and Staff Secretary Rob Porter, Navarro wrote, "Any proposed executive action on trade that moves through the Staff Secretary process is highly vulnerable to dilution, delay or derailment."[9]

As if to underscore Navarro's point, Porter intervened to silence the adviser's alarm bell by preventing this letter from reaching the president: "I'm going to keep it on my desk, keep it in my files. Not going anywhere." Chief of Staff Reince Priebus proved sympathetic to Porter, and he initiated a broader campaign to stave off at-will presidential action. Regular order was just the tonic. "Decisions are not final—and therefore may not be implemented—until the staff secretary files a vetted decision memorandum signed by the President," Priebus declared. "On-the-fly decisions are strictly provisional."[10] It was a decidedly administrative rendition of good government: process impedes unilateral action; decisions must be circumspect.

When attempts at controlling information channels and decision-making processes failed to dampen the president's instincts on trade, the staffers became more aggressive. They reached deeper into the executive branch for allies, enlisting the authority of cabinet officers to help them impress their policy concerns on the president. As if following the President's Committee's charge to the staff to provide the president with "all pertinent information," Cohn planned to corner the president into listening to what the rest of the executive branch had to say. Working with Secretary of Defense James Mattis and Secretary of State Rex Tillerson, he arranged a meeting in which the president would be given an overview of the US role in the world and receive instruction on the damage that might be done by trade wars to America's alliances and to global stability. Their tutorial on the international order and policy interdependence occurred in "the Tank," a secure meeting room deep in the Pentagon that is normally used by the Joint Chiefs of Staff and that had impressed Trump on a previous visit.[11]

The meeting was a test of the strength of the institutional presidency in the face of an incumbent determined to set a new course on his own authority, a president confident in his instincts and indifferent to the old rules of the game. Expertise concentrated in the executive branch was meant to have a moderating effect, or at least to open a discussion. But Trump sensed a trap. Instead of impressing upon the president the importance of listening to others, the meeting was received as an impertinent challenge to his authority. Trump "appeared peeved by the schoolhouse vibe" and "allergic to the dynamic of his advisers talking at him."[12] Every attempt to "instruct" the president produced heated rebuttal and ridicule. Rather than broaden the president's thinking, the advisers stiffened it, their patronizing demeanor seeming to confirm his suspicions of deeply ingrained administrative biases. When Cohn explained that trade deals and trade deficits were "actually good for our economy," Trump exploded. "I don't want to hear that. . . . It's all bullshit."[13] Those involved in the meeting were thoroughly deflated. The staff "needed to educate, to teach, to help him understand the reason and basis for a lot of these things" and "change how he thinks," one senior official asserted. The meeting left the staff "dismayed and in shock when not only did it not have its intended effect, but he dug in his heels."[14]

Still, the staffers at the White House did not give up. When Trump decided that he wanted to announce a withdrawal from the North American Free Trade Agreement (NAFTA) on his 100th day in office, they again reached deep. Porter acted to alert the president to other interests implicated politically and administratively in established policy. He enlisted Secretary of Agriculture Sonny Perdue of Georgia to remind the president that agricultural exports for Trump-supporting farmers depended on NAFTA. The staff might have rested content at this point that it had done its job, that it had given the requisite "help" and had fully informed the president of the likely consequences of his intended actions. But when Trump ordered a draft withdrawal letter anyway, the staff grew downright insubordinate. Cohn responded by taking the letter off of Trump's desk: "If he's going to sign it, he's going to need another piece of paper." Porter agreed. "We'll slow-walk that one too," he pledged.[15]

This was not the end of the subversion. By August 2017, Trump decided he wanted to withdraw not only from NAFTA, but also from the US-Korea Free Trade Agreement (KORUS) and the World Trade Organization (WTO). "We've talked about this ad nauseam," he complained. "Just do it," he ordered. Soon the president had a letter terminating KORUS ready on his desk. But resistance to Trump over this particular agreement extended to other worries about the president's unwillingness to consider the bigger picture, in particular how a peremptory withdrawal might affect the American troop presence and the US missile detection systems in South Korea. Cohn again took the letter: "He's never going to see that document. Got to protect the country." "It's not what we did for the country," Cohn later reported. "It's what we saved him from doing."[16]

Confirming intuitions: The Deep State charge evokes images of rogue administrators within the permanent bureaucracy seeking to derail the president's policy agenda. But nowhere in the Trump administration was outright insubordination and administrative sabotage more glaring than under his own roof. The journalist Bob Woodward dubbed these episodes "no less than an administrative coup d'état, an undermining of the will of the president of the United States and his constitutional authority."[17] Reporting Bannon's view of the matter, Woodward noted, "The Deep State was not the problem.... It was the up-in-your-face state."[18] That resistance was all the more surprising since, unlike those in the permanent bureaucracy, staffers at this high level had no real authority of their own to fall back on. These truly were the president's minions. The disparity here between the power of the Deep State and power of the unitary executive was glaring, for, as a formal matter, these protectors of depth were completely defenseless. When push came to shove, the staff's only argument was prudence, and within months, prudence was shown the door.[19]

On the policy front, the brief period of staff resistance was not entirely without effect. Improvised, tactical, and doomed as it was, it did prevent peremptory withdrawal from the key trade agreements. But, with the rout of the resistance, tariff increases and a trade war with China ensued.[20] Recovering from his marginalization by establishment Republicans, Navarro was "able to leverage a close personal relationship with the president to gain more access" and a promotion to the position of assistant to the president.[21] Describing his part in fulfilling the president's trade agenda, Navarro made it clear that he viewed his role as finding a way to take action on Trump's instincts: "This is the president's vision. . . . My function, really, as an economist is to try to provide the underlying analytics that confirm his intuition. And his intuition is always right in these matters."[22] That sentiment was disputed by Cohn, who remained unrepentant after his resignation: "I don't think the tariffs helped us get to any different outcome. I think it has hurt the U.S."[23] The verdict remains out on the policy effects of Trump's trade war, but both farmers and manufacturers took serious hits as a result.[24]

Though the policy dispute was never far below the surface, this episode was also a clash of systems: the institutional and the personal; the deep and the unitary. When systems collide, neither comes off particularly well. We will have occasion to turn to other issues related to staff in Chapter 8, but this brief episode raises several points all on its own. First is the connection between the staff's sabotage and its perceptions of presidential recklessness. The phantom twins took flight when the president proved indifferent to pertinent information and hostile to norms of appropriate institutional behavior. The staff's brazenness seems to have been driven at least in part by incredulity, a refusal to credit authority perceived to be impulsive and seemingly irresponsible, even, perhaps especially, when it came from a president. Second is the close connection on display here between the unitary executive and the empowerment of a presidential party. As this episode illustrates, a broadly based party coalition does not comport well with a unitary executive. The struggle over trade was part of the transformation of the Republican Party into the "Trump Party," a party with the wherewithal to be what the president says it is and to govern according to his will.[25] Finally, there is the power of the presidential plebiscite itself, in particular the potential for a unitary executive empowered by an electoral mandate to disrupt established governing arrangements and reset the course. The president's personal approach to making trade policy may advise extreme caution about empowering a unitary executive, but it must be admitted that the results in this episode delivered handsomely on one of its chief selling points. The president insisted against all advice on a position that had carried him into office. He not only bucked the establishment wing of his party but also the interests of Wall Street and the farm sector. He sliced through dense networks of interest and power, even risking the ire of some of his most ardent supporters.

The coda to this story was as blurry as its climax was clear. Ultimately, Trump's key achievements on trade would owe less to snap decisions than to the good government values he had repudiated. The principal beneficiary of the staff shakeup was Robert Lighthizer, the US Trade Representative (USTR), whose Senate-confirmed job lay in the Executive Office of the President, a step removed from the White House staff. An old Washington hand, Lighthizer had once been characterized as a personification of the "iron triangle."[26] He was unusual among USTRs in that he espoused the "venerable history of protectionism," but unlike Bannon and Navarro, he combined a protectionist outlook with policy-making experience and the political connections to move the agenda forward on solid ground.[27] His skill set was impressive enough to command respect from both of the factions warring within the White House staff. Unsurprisingly, Navarro enthused that Lighthizer was the "finest U.S. trade representative we have had in our history."[28] More revealingly, Rob Porter, one of the principal White House saboteurs, recognized Lighthizer's authority as well: "Even those who disagree with his substantive approach respect Bob's deep legal knowledge and unwavering professionalism."[29] In negotiating a replacement for NAFTA, Lighthizer was able to bridge political divides and forge institutional cooperation. Ironically, the United States–Mexico–Canada agreement, one of the president's most significant victories, was the result of Lighthizer's willingness to compromise on Trump's proposal and to cultivate the support of Democrats in Congress and their allies in organized labor.[30] That same slow boring of hard boards produced a preliminary agreement on a trade deal with China.[31]

Lighthizer's successes shed some additional light on the staff's most desperate acts of defiance. They seem to confirm that the resistance within the White House was less about ultimate objectives than about steady hands—deference to process, commitment to negotiation and informed decision making. When it came to getting things done on trade, harnessing depth proved far more effective than assaulting it.

This was a lesson that eluded the president on the broader management front, as Trump continued to struggle with staff. The president couldn't seem to find exactly what he wanted from it. His steady reliance on family members, like his son-in-law Jared Kushner, suggested a conception of the office and its powers that was wholly personal, cutting against the institutional roles and skills that Roosevelt's committee had anticipated for staff. Kushner's authority—"Nobody has more influence in the White House than Jared"—proved far more durable than any of the many chiefs who attempted to run the Trump White House.[32] Priebus's replacement as chief of staff, the retired general John Kelly, was unconnected to intra-party disputes, so his attempts to try to impose order with a military style could credibly appear to be about the value of process itself. But this second attempt to ensure that presidential decision making was informed by some regular order fared only marginally better than the first. Kelly backed off as the president tired of the restraints. Trump turned next to Mick Mulvaney, but credited him only as "acting" chief of staff. Mulvaney assumed the post with no intention of following the route of his two predecessors. He made it clear that "his job is to manage the staff and not the president."[33] As media outlets dubbed the strategy, Mulvaney would "Let Trump be Trump."[34] After Mulvaney's ouster, Trump turned to a proven congressional ally and founding member of the House Freedom Caucus, Mark Meadows. Meadows did not want to "to redirect the president's impulses or change his ways" either. He was perceived as "an aide who tries to understand what the president wants, and looks to help him achieve it through any means possible."[35] For a unitary executive, that may be the only "help" that ultimately proves acceptable.

6
Depth in Norms

At bottom, the American state's depth rests on shared understandings of what constitutes appropriate political and institutional behavior. Norms that shield the work of administrators reflect an abiding, collective interest in preventing the operations of the executive branch from being overrun by personal interests and momentary political calculations. They are effective, however, only to the extent that all the relevant agents buy into them.[1] A unitary executive is likely to have little patience with norms that limit political control and shield collective interests. By the same token, administrators whose work is insulated by norms are well advised to exemplify them without blemish.

Nowhere in the executive branch do norms play a larger role than in law enforcement, where they figure prominently in public perception of the legitimacy of the entire operation. The Department of Justice (DOJ) and Federal Bureau of Investigation (FBI) depend on their reputations for even-handedness to retain trust and remain efficacious. Professional self-discipline and service to the rule of law afford a critical measure of insulation for the administration of justice; they hold political manipulation of prosecutions at bay and underwrite investigatory independence. But though these norms are deeply held, the arrangements that support them sit gingerly on the constitutional frame. That is precisely what makes the collective buy-in critical.

The Department of Justice was established in 1870 by voice votes in both houses of Congress. Enforcement of the Reconstruction program in the South was an immediate motive, but the initiative to create DOJ was also an early sign of what would become a general rethinking of the relationship between politics and administration, in particular about how to make administration internally upright while keeping it politically responsive. The statute establishing the department was written by Representative Thomas Jenckes (R-RI), a leader in the postwar campaigns for retrenchment and the creation of a permanent civil service.[2] The problem, as Jenckes and his fellow reformers saw it, was that the received practice of spreading law officers throughout the various departments undermined their independence, leading them to "give advice which seems to have been instigated by the heads of the Department."[3] The new arrangement was designed to create a department of committed professionals, one in which the lawyers would hold one another to account.[4]

These aspirations were not realized right away, for the DOJ could not consolidate its staff until it had a building of its own, something it obtained only in 1935.[5] More to the point, in important ways, the consolidation sharpened issues surrounding presidential power and the rule of law. The department depended not only on forging a strong *ésprit de corps* among legal practitioners but also on presidential support for professionalism and administrative integrity in law enforcement. Despite its strong association with blind justice, the DOJ has never been an independent agency. The Constitution gives the president the power to "execute the law." The DOJ is part of the regular executive establishment and subject to presidential direction. When Jenckes was questioned on this point, he tried to assure his colleagues that by deepening the pool of legal professionals, the new department would protect the rule of law, and, in fact, prevent it from devolving into the president's law.[6]

The merger within DOJ of these two different kinds of authority—constitutional and professional—was murky from the start. The idea seemed to be that "law officers would shift their political accountability from the various department heads to the Attorney General and the President, providing a mix of legal professionalism and political accountability."[7] But that left virtually everything to norms. Shared understandings might finesse the normative ambiguity, but clarity has never been the strength of this mixture, and the tensions implicit in it have never been entirely submerged. More often than not, presidents select political loyalists to head the DOJ.[8] President Kennedy selected his brother. Ronald Reagan started his second term by selecting a White House intimate and leading proponent of the unitary theory, Edwin Meese.

Even in the wake of the scandal that drove Richard Nixon from office and discredited presidential interference in law enforcement, efforts to insulate the DOJ and the FBI from White House political pressure were carried forward on faith and goodwill. Consider again the disposition of the Carter administration. It opposed the congressional push to make the DOJ an independent agency, but it endorsed post-Watergate interest in independence by strengthening that norm.[9] Carter's attorney general, Griffin Bell, advised that the "course best calculated . . . to inspire confidence in the faithful execution of the laws is for the President *to allow* the Attorney General freedom from undue influence." This approach, he suggested, would bolster public confidence that the AG and DOJ officials "are free to exercise their professional judgments." To that end, Bell issued instructions on contacts between the White House and the department. He stated that presidents would be "best served" by limiting their involvement with the DOJ and restricting communications between the Department and other White House officials. But what Bell asserted with one hand, he took back with the other: "in a Constitutional sense, the Attorney General remains responsible to the President, and the President to the public," and "true institutional independence is therefore impossible." Bell thought that there should "always be free and easy but confidential communications between the President and the Attorney General."[10] Subsequently, every administration has issued Bell-like memos limiting contacts between White House officials and the Department of Justice. None, however, explicitly binds the president.[11] The norm of independence has thus been left to hover ambiguously over the structure of the executive branch, two different conceptions of good government jumbled uneasily together.

Although the congressional reformers of the 1970s deferred to Bell on DOJ independence, they did create a ten-year term for the director of the FBI. That suggested a particularly strong legislative preference for independence in investigations. But Congress was also mindful—with good reason after the abuses of the J. Edgar Hoover years—of the risks of a rogue FBI director, so again independence was a norm more strongly implied than secured. Trying to have it both ways, Congress stated that the "purpose" of the ten-year term was "to achieve two complementary objectives. The first is to insulate the Director of the Federal Bureau of Investigation from undue pressure being exerted upon him from superiors in the Executive Branch. The second is to protect against an FBI Director becoming too independent and unresponsive."[12] Complementary or not, the latter concern meant that, notwithstanding the ten-year term, the director would remain at all times removable.

When push comes to shove, then, DOJ resistance to political imposition has little to fall back upon other than a shared respect for legal ethics and professional integrity.[13] That is not nothing. Violations of the norms will register within the larger legal community and, through it, to Congress and the general public. The protections afforded for DOJ and the FBI are sturdier than those available to, say, the White House staff. By the same token, however, political insulation and administrative discretion make DOJ a prime site both for resistance to the claims of a unitary executive and for presidential suspicions about a Deep State with interests of its own. When each side calls upon its own considerable resources to act out its suspicions of the other, the phantom twins take flight.

Investigatory independence: The collision in the Trump administration between norms of DOJ and FBI independence and presidential demands for personal deference and political control had origins predating the president's inauguration. In 2016, the Intelligence Community assessed that Russia was interfering in the presidential election to sow discord and, in their final analysis, to favor Trump's candidacy over that of Hillary Clinton. That determination would be confirmed repeatedly over the next few years, including by Trump's own senior intelligence officials, by a special counsel investigation, and unanimously by the Republican-controlled Senate Intelligence Committee. Moreover, after initial inquiries, the FBI had opened a cognate investigation, "Crossfire Hurricane," into whether there was any coordination between those Russian efforts and members of the Trump campaign. For his part, Trump received the revelation that Russia had sought to aid his victory as a challenge to his political legitimacy. He eyed the investigation suspiciously. The rudiments of a clash were in place even before he took office.

The fact that the FBI director, James Comey, was a holdover from the Obama administration fueled the conflict. Appointed to his ten-year term in 2013, Comey personified the tension between unity and depth, and all the more so, because he was a department stalwart with a history of deflecting presidential direction as a threat to the rule of law. For instance, when President George W. Bush sought reauthorization of the "Stellar Wind" surveillance program, Comey, serving briefly as acting attorney general, balked. Finding the program illegal as constituted, he enlisted support to block the president's initiative from then-FBI director Robert Mueller. When Bush told Comey that, as president, "I say what the law is for the executive branch," Comey offered a caveat: "You do, sir. But only I can say what the Justice Department can *certify* as lawful. And we can't here." More tellingly, Comey put norms to the test. Willing himself to resign over the surveillance program, Comey informed Bush that Mueller too was planning to resign rather than defer. Bush backed down. Meeting next with Mueller, the president said, "Tell Jim to do what needs to be done to get this to a place where Justice is comfortable."[14]

Score that for the power of norms. Obama had appointed Comey to succeed Mueller at FBI in part because he wanted to set himself apart from what he perceived to be the Bush administration's over-blown claims about a unitary executive. In announcing the appointment, he had quoted Comey on the importance of independence: "As Jim has said, 'We know that the rule of law sets this Nation apart and is its foundation.'"[15] Under the pressures of the 2016 campaign, however, the overlay of norms on structure scrambled the rules of appropriate behavior for everyone concerned, and before it was over, no one's motives remained above suspicion.

Ironically, the most explosive political intrusions came from Comey himself. His decision to make public statements about an FBI investigation into the use of a private email server by the Democratic candidate, Hillary Clinton, rocked the election, some say decisively.[16] Comey's actions went against a long-standing DOJ norm attuned to "election year sensitivities," which prioritized "safeguarding the Department's reputation for fairness, neutrality, and nonpartisanship."[17] But as Comey saw it, the interventions were necessary to protect perceptions that the bureau was *above* politics and not in cahoots with the current administration. Among Comey's concerns were President Obama, who was stating peremptorily that Clinton's careless use of email as secretary of state had not endangered national security, and Attorney General Loretta Lynch, who wanted to avoid the criminal connotations of opening "an investigation" and told the director to refer to his inquiry as just "a matter."[18] At the same time, the bureau feared that higher-ups in the Obama administration might seek political gain by leaking news of its investigation into the Trump campaign's contacts with Russians. In this instance too, Comey was at pains to avoid charges of political bias. But upholding norms and keeping the Russia investigation *out* of public view did little to limit his political exposure.[19]

If nothing else, Comey's gymnastics during the 2016 campaign demonstrated the precariousness of norms under pressure. The election's outcome sharpened the lines of conflict. The self-styled protector of administrative integrity and the newly elected unitarian insurgent had two entirely different conceptions of what constituted good government at DOJ. Acting on these assumptions, they drew out basic but long-finessed issues of state design, and ultimately, their collision shook the government's foundations. From the start, Comey tussled with Trump over the role of the FBI director and the relationship between administrative and political authority. Trump arranged a private dinner with the director in the early weeks of his presidency to make clear his expectations: "I need loyalty, I expect loyalty." Comey's not-so-subtle demur shifted the ground from administrative subordination to administrative intermediation: "You will always get honesty from me." At the time of this meeting, the bureau was still investigating Russian interference in the 2016 election, so sensitivities were heightened on both sides. The exchange signaled to Comey the president's indifference to investigatory independence, and far from gaining his objective, Trump's demand raised suspicions of obstruction. Comey sought to inoculate himself from any future challenge to his reputation and the FBI's autonomy by writing contemporaneous memos on each interaction he had with the president.[20]

Soon after the loyalty request, Trump broached a more direct order concerning a specific part of the Russia controversy. He asked Comey to go easy on his recently fired national security adviser, Michael Flynn. As Trump told Comey, "I hope you can see your way clear to letting this go, to letting Flynn go."[21] But since Flynn's pre-inauguration contacts with the Russian ambassador had made him a significant subject of the investigation, that request only made matters worse. As FBI deputy director Andrew McCabe saw it, Trump was inappropriately attempting to "manipulate the functions of government mainly for [his] own interests." Of course, the president saw the matter very differently. In line with the unitary view that the administrative realm is an arm of the presidency without any integrity of its own, Trump expressed outrage that Comey was "acting like his own branch of government." The final straw was the director's refusal to publicly declare that Trump himself was not under FBI investigation when, at the time, he was not.[22]

Comey exuded confidence in his reputation, in the insulation of the DOJ and the FBI, and in the wherewithal provided by that depth to resist subordination to the political interests of those above. But the prospect that these agencies might find themselves embroiled in the investigation of a president posed a severe test of that confidence, one that has long posed a constitutional conundrum.[23] Can the executive branch investigate the chief executive? Trump pressed that test forward when he fired the FBI director. In response to the public firestorm that ensued, he brushed the ten-year term aside: "I am the president. . . . I can fire anybody that I want."[24] Then, he went further. As if to impugn his own motives, he linked the firing to the Russia investigation, and he politicized his action as a response to all those who refused to acknowledge his election victory: "in fact when I decided to do it, I said to myself, I said, you know, this Russia thing with Trump and Russia is a made-up story, it's an excuse by the Democrats for having lost an election that they should have won."[25] That characterization drew the battle lines starkly. Trump deemed any deviation from executive branch unity a direct threat to his political legitimacy, and the FBI saw the clampdown as a direct threat to its official mission. Steve Bannon warned Trump of the consequences of provoking the Deep State: "You can fire Comey. You can't fire the FBI. The minute you fire him, the FBI as an institution, they have to destroy you and they will destroy you."[26]

Though Bannon's assessment of the relative strength of these contending systems of authority ultimately proved wide of the mark, his structural analysis rang true. The FBI pulled out the stops. The night of Comey's firing, Peter Strzok—a lead FBI agent in both the Clinton email and Russia investigations—urged action: "We need to open the case we've been waiting on while Andy [McCabe] is acting [director]." That case was an investigation into Trump himself for evidence of his colluding with Russia and obstructing the investigation into Russian interference. The action that had precipitated Comey's firing—his refusal to say publicly that the president was not under investigation—occurred at a time when the bureau was contemplating that very move, and the president's hardball tactics appear to have tipped the scales. Expecting that the president might fire him too, McCabe agreed with Strzok. He opened the investigation so as to "put the Russia case on absolutely solid ground in an indelible fashion [so] that were I removed quickly or reassigned or fired that the case could not be closed or vanish in the night without a trace."[27]

The reaction against Trump was not limited to the bureau. Earlier, Jeff Sessions, the attorney general, had recused himself from oversight of the matter out of concern that revelations of his own Russian contacts might appear to compromise investigatory independence. Supervision passed to the deputy attorney general, Rod Rosenstein. For his part, Rosenstein was being squeezed between the White House's enlistment of his support in Comey's firing and the fierce reaction from colleagues and the wider media to it. One DOJ official charged: "Either [Rosenstein] knowingly helped the president fire the FBI director to try to rid himself of this investigation, or Rod was an unwitting tool who got used by the president." Hoping to contain the damage to reputations, Rosenstein himself raised the flag for investigatory independence. He appointed a special counsel for the probe, the onetime director of the FBI, Robert Mueller.[28]

Comey had played a part in this. Concerned about what Rosenstein might do with the case against Trump, he had tried to force the deputy's hand. Rather than simply turn over to the DOJ the contemporaneous memos he had written about his interactions with the president, the ousted director had an associate leak their existence to the press. The intent was to leave Rosenstein no option but to create an arms-length investigation.[29] Then, seizing upon an opportunity to testify to Congress about his dismissal, Comey presented himself to the nation as a model of integrity in public service. Implying presidential indifference to norms protective of the rule of law, he explained why the "statue of justice" was blindfolded: "You're not supposed to peek out to see whether your patron was pleased with what you're doing."[30]

"Witch Hunt": Only a few months in, Trump's efforts to assert control over the FBI and DOJ appeared to be in tatters. The president recognized the threat posed by Mueller's appointment, exclaiming, "Oh my God. This is terrible. This is the end of my presidency."[31]

But the two sides were only beginning to draw each other out. Just as officials at the FBI and DOJ were testing the limits of their authority to resist presidential control and to turn their investigatory powers back on the president himself, the administration was radicalizing its own claims to authority. Soon the White House found its bearings, and the administrators found earlier stumbles coming back to haunt them. Trump rejected the premise of the special counsel investigation, repudiating it as a politically inspired "Witch Hunt." Despite some initial cooperation by White House lawyers, the president himself would persistently challenge the legitimacy of the inquiry and repeatedly threaten to remove those in the DOJ who protected it.[32] All along the way, the Mueller probe provided a political foil against which the White House could expound the case for executive branch unity.

As the investigation progressed, the president's lawyers elaborated their theory, and by the time they were done, they had given constitutional sanction to presidential rule by personal instinct. In a letter rebuffing Mueller's request for a presidential interview, John Dowd and Jay Sekulow argued that "by virtue of [the president's] position as the chief law enforcement officer," his actions "could neither constitutionally nor legally constitute obstruction because that would amount to him obstructing himself." Moreover, Trump could take further actions to constrain the inquiry: "he could, if he wished, terminate the inquiry, or even exercise his power to pardon if he so desired." The president's reasons did not matter, they contended, because the powers Trump exercised were inherently his by the Constitution: "every action that the President took was taken with full constitutional authority pursuant to Article II of the United States Constitution. As such, these actions cannot constitute obstruction, whether viewed separately or even as a totality."[33] The strong assertion of unitary principles delighted the president. "I love that letter," Trump told Dowd.[34] Nor did Dowd shy away from making these claims to Mueller himself. In a meeting where Mueller stated that he wanted to find out if the president had exhibited "corrupt intent" when he fired Comey, Dowd insisted, "I'm not sure constitutionally you can question that."[35] This echoed the broader unitarian position that any attempt to decipher the chief executive's "real motive . . . represents a serious intrusion on the President's constitutional prerogatives."[36]

Despite his threats, the president never did shut down the Mueller investigation. Score that also to the abiding constraint of norms. The larger case for administrative insulation did not fare nearly as well. The president risked substantial political costs with his assault on norms, but he did not stop until he had shattered the distinction between public servants heroically defending the rule of law and self-serving bureaucrats illegitimately resisting constitutional authority. Pushing beyond the formalistic reasoning behind its defense of the unitary executive, the president's lawyers ripped into his tormentors' status as straight shooters dedicated to nothing but fair dealing and the truth. The response of Trump's attorney Marc Kasowitz to Comey's congressional testimony illustrated the link: "Of course, the Office of the President is entitled to expect loyalty from those serving in an administration . . . it is overwhelmingly clear that there have been and continue to be those in government who are actively attempting to undermine this administration with selective and illegal leaks of classified information and privileged communications."[37] Dowd and Sekulow continued that line of attack, decrying "the astounding public revelations about the corruption within the FBI and Department of Justice which appears to have led to the alleged Russia collusion investigation and the establishment of the Office of Special Counsel in the first place."[38] Dowd pressed this thesis to Mueller directly: "The entire inquiry appears to be the product of a conspiracy by the DNC, Fusion GPS . . . and senior FBI intelligence officials to undermine the Trump presidency."[39]

The charge that it was all a "Witch Hunt" initially seemed little more than Deep State hyperbole, but it did raise the stakes for all who were involved in the investigation. Any evidence indicating that FBI administrators might be pretenders, hypocritical purveyors of good government values, bureaucrats biased against the president and collaborating with the administration's political opponents, would serve to seal the president's case for a clampdown. Mueller's appointment had itself been calculated as firewall protection against such charges. Politicians on both sides of the aisle attested to his sterling reputation for independence. Yet Mueller's credentials aside, Trump's supporters did not have to dig too deeply to add substance to their charge and rip the administrators' reputations. Comey had compromised his defense of norms by admitting that he was one of the leakers and that he had used the release of his memos to prod a special counsel appointment. In a scathing review, the DOJ inspector general, Michael Horowitz, wrote that the memos had been government documents and that "Comey's own, personal conception of what was necessary was not an appropriate basis for ignoring the policies and agreements governing the use of FBI records."[40] (That judgment echoed Horowitz's earlier findings about Comey's public statements in the Clinton email investigation. The IG faulted Comey for having "engaged in ad hoc decisionmaking based on his personal views even if it meant rejecting longstanding Department policy or practice."[41])

Trump's allegation of a Deep State conspiracy advanced further on revealed text messages between Strzok and another bureau official involved in the FBI probe and Mueller's Russia investigation, Lisa Page. The personal relationship between Strzok and Page was itself a violation of FBI norms, and their communications were devastating to the bureau, undermining trust and confidence that had been hard won in the wake of the Hoover years. After the initial revelations in the summer of 2016 about potential Russian assistance to the Trump campaign, Page had texted Strzok, "[Trump is] not ever going to become president, right? Right?!" Strzok had responded, "No. No he's not. We'll stop it." After Trump's election, Page again texted Strzok, "I bought *All the President's Men*. Figure I needed to brush up on Watergate."[42]

Exchanges like these, where FBI officials revealed personal political hostility to Trump, all but confirmed a core precept of the Deep State charge, that an insulated class of administrators was using the resources of the executive branch to obstruct and undercut the chief executive. The damage to the reputational assets on which the administrators relied for a political defense of investigatory independence was severe. Mueller understood the Strzok-Page text messages as a direct threat to the credibility of his work, and Strzok was immediately removed from the Special Counsel's office.[43] But the stain was indelible. In one of a series of reports on the FBI's actions with regard to the 2016 elections, Inspector General Horowitz took the opportunity to excoriate Strzok and Page. For Horowitz, the "We'll stop it" text message was "not only indicative of a biased state of mind but, even more seriously, implie[d] a willingness to take official action" to that end. While he acknowledged that officials have a right to "their own political views," Horowitz suggested that sharing such sentiments on FBI communication devices likely broke agency rules. His summation was a sharp rebuke to the defenders of depth. The text messages had expressed sentiments "antithetical to the core values of the FBI and the Department of Justice," and the use of FBI devices "to send the identified messages demonstrated extremely poor judgment and a gross lack of professionalism."[44]

A later report by Inspector General Horowitz pointedly stopped short of toppling the foundation of the investigation itself, concluding that, despite it all, there had still been a sound basis for opening the Russian probe. He found no conclusive evidence of political bias as the motivation among key officials for that action. Horowitz again acknowledged the problematic Strzok-Page text messages, but he noted that they were only two of the many officials involved in the decision to investigate. The FBI, he stated, had "an authorized purpose when it opened Crossfire Hurricane to obtain information about, or protect against, a national security threat or federal crime." Nevertheless, his indictment of the bureau continued. He found the FBI guilty of procedural sloppiness in its pursuit of the case, a charge that all but voided the value of his rejection of the conspiracy allegations. Horowitz criticized the FBI for "significant inaccuracies and omissions" made in its applications to the FISA court for permission to surveil Trump campaign adviser Carter Page during the 2016 election. He faulted officials at all levels of the bureau for these errors, stating that they "demonstrated a failure on the part of the managers and supervisors in the Crossfire Hurricane chain of command, including FBI senior officials."[45] Following up, Horowitz looked into a random sample of twenty-nine FISA requests and found procedural problems in all of them.[46] The rout of the defenders of depth was near complete.

Precarious foundations: Every aspect of this episode is sobering commentary on the structure of the modern American state. The first and most obvious lesson is the fragility of its reliance on norms. The insulation that instills faith in the separation of the administration of justice from politics is perilously dependent on the behavior of those who rely on it most directly. The personnel of the FBI and DOJ may have a sincerely held faith in their own neutrality and competence, but when, as in this case, that *ésprit de corps* becomes a conceit, and the conceit a license, the results are self-defeating. Neutrality and independence are an offense to the unitary executive and susceptible on that ground alone to the Deep State charge. Those norms may have other good defenses, but when faced with a hostile president, there is no slack in the case for mistakes, sloppiness, or hints of bias. The former DOJ official and legal scholar Jack Goldsmith observes that "when the President and DOJ are in conflict, it is not always easy to tell whether DOJ is acting on the basis of the rule of law or some self-serving bureaucratic imperative."[47] Administrators who put their professional authority on the line are prone to self-indictment for any ambiguity between their personal motives and their claims of independence. When the self-styled straight shooters are hoisted on their own petard, the damage to the case for neutral competence reverberates throughout the administrative realm.

This points to a second lesson to be drawn from this episode. When it comes to stripping away depth, a unitary executive can be devastatingly effective. Trump did not rest content with pointing out evidence at the FBI that served his "Witch Hunt" narrative. He also fixed his personnel problem at the top of the DOJ to ensure a full-throated affirmation of his claims. By the time the Mueller report was released, Trump had appointed a committed unitarian, William Barr, as attorney general. As AG in the George H. W. Bush administration, Barr had been a skeptic of investigations into the Iran-Contra affair, and in a similar spirit, he had written to the Trump DOJ prior to his new appointment opining that the Mueller investigation was "fatally misconceived."[48] Now in charge again, he knew just what to do to take back control of what Trump had called the "Deep State Justice Department."[49] Offering a public summary of the Mueller report prior to its formal release, Barr made hash of the investigation's conclusions. His interpretation of the report's delicately worded findings appeared to absolve the president of all charges. Mueller attempted to correct the record, complaining that Barr had seized the opportunity to sow "public confusion" and distort his work before it could be publicly reviewed.[50] But the attorney general went even further, alleging at a press conference that Trump's actions were justified by suspicions of a Deep State conspiracy: "as the Special Counsel's report acknowledges, there is substantial evidence to show that the President was frustrated and angered by a sincere belief that the investigation was undermining his presidency, propelled by his political opponents, and fueled by illegal leaks."[51]

For those who cared to read it, the two-volume report departed significantly from Barr's summary. Beyond confirming Russian interference in the election and bringing multiple indictments against actors engaged in that sabotage, it detailed numerous contacts between the Trump campaign and Russia during the election, bolstering the original basis of the investigation. In fact, the report raised substantial concerns about the threat that a president wielding the powers of a unitary executive might pose to the rule of law. And it implicitly endorsed the resistance afforded by depth. "The President's efforts to influence the investigation were mostly unsuccessful," Mueller wrote, "but that is largely because the persons who surrounded the President declined to carry out orders or accede to his requests."[52]

What Mueller had not been able to do, however, was resolve the structural ambiguities surrounding his work. These had restricted the scope of his investigation, and they would significantly affect its conclusions. From the beginning, Mueller had been advised to avoid a drawn-out inquiry. In his first meeting with Mueller, Rosenstein warned against conducting "a fishing expedition," saying, "This is a criminal investigation. Do your job, and then shut it down." Wary of his ground, Mueller himself shied away from a potential constitutional confrontation over whether he could interview the president personally. Moreover, Rosenstein's charge to Mueller limited inquiry into the counterintelligence aspects of the case, and with Strzok's removal from the probe, any lingering hope of pursuing that angle was lost.[53] The most revealing indication of Mueller's ambiguous position, however, came in the report's conclusion. Reacting to investigations of wrongdoing in 1973 and 1998, the DOJ's Office of Legal Counsel had said that as a matter of law and policy a sitting president cannot be indicted. Mueller, technically not independent of the DOJ, evidently felt compelled to comply with those opinions. As one of his deputies told the Barr team, "We're going to follow the OLC opinion and conclude it wasn't appropriate for us to make a final determination as to whether or not there was a crime."[54]

The special counsel had been caught in a Catch-22. Appointed to ensure independence, Mueller was playing a game with rules already tilted in favor of the person he was investigating. His ringing declaration that no one "in this country is so high that he is above the law" was followed by tortured conclusions. He pointedly declined to say whether or not the president had obstructed justice: "while this report does not conclude the President committed a crime, it also does not exonerate him."[55] That muddy formulation was the best the investigation could muster against the head of the executive branch.

Since he had acceded to advice to let the investigation play itself out, Trump might have simply endorsed his AG's interpretation of its conclusions. He might even have declared that his "exoneration" vindicated the merits of independent processes. But once the damage contained in the report was neutralized, the president ramped up his efforts to root out the sources of the resistance. Every element of bias or sloppy decision making that had been discovered added credence to the case for hierarchy and subordination. "This was an illegal takedown that failed," Trump asserted.[56] Serious consequences had already befallen the instigators of the investigation. McCabe was fired hours before his scheduled retirement, Strzok was fired, and both Strzok and Page were made the public faces of the Deep State.[57] Barr then escalated the campaign to erase all vestiges of depth. "Republics have fallen because of a Praetorian Guard mentality," he warned. Echoing Trump's appeal to the will of the people, he cast those responsible for the investigation as a threat to democracy: "there is that tendency that they know better and that they're there to protect as guardians of the people. That can easily translate into essentially supervening the will of the majority and getting your own way as a government official."[58]

Going further, Barr opened inquiries of his own, suggesting not only that the IG investigation was insufficient, but that the DOJ itself needed to be investigated more directly on behalf of the president. The AG wanted to push against the widely accepted determination that Russia had interfered in 2016 to support Trump's candidacy, and ultimately beyond that, to bring into question the aims of the Obama administration in the whole affair. In one move, he appointed a respected US Attorney, John Durham, to probe the motives of FBI administrators and to scrutinize any sign of disagreement among officials in the wider Intelligence Community on the central question of Russian interference. In a later move stemming from Durham's inquiry, Barr appointed US Attorney John Bash to examine the actions of the Obama administration, focusing particularly on "unmasking," an intelligence practice in which senior government officials request access to the identity of a US resident whose communications were intercepted by government surveillance.[59]

Seeking to identify political enemies lurking within, the Durham inquiry effectively collapsed the distinction between administrators' motives and their private political views. It "asked witnesses pointed questions about any anti-Trump bias among former F.B.I. officials who are frequent targets of President Trump and about the earliest steps they took in the Russia inquiry."[60] It also sought to identify officials who had leaked information to the media and ramped up public pressure to pursue the story, such as the disclosures that had led to Flynn's ouster as national security adviser.[61] When IG Horowitz, in his own overlapping investigation, upheld the agency's rationale for opening the inquiry, both Barr and Durham publicly took issue with him. In a highly unusual demur, Durham said that "we advised the inspector general' that we do not agree with some of the report's conclusions as to predication and how the F.B.I. case was opened."[62] "We stand by our finding," Horowitz fired back. "Ongoing investigations . . . need to be protected from outside influence."[63]

The president's man at the top of DOJ was taking aim at the institution and turning it inside out. But with credible, independent authority in short supply, even the unitary executive appeared at wit's end. The AG and the president were as desperate as everyone else to find someone with enough credibility, enough independence, to speak with authority and to set the record straight. Barr had appointed Durham because of his impeccable credentials and his past experience investigating abuses at the FBI and CIA. But with Durham countering Horowitz's findings, with Horowitz standing firm, and with Barr clearly pressing the president's political case, no one's charges rang true. Was Durham's work the final vindication of the president's legitimacy against the Deep State conspiracy? Or was it just another "vehicle for President Trump's political revenge"?[64] By his own actions, Barr had made it nearly impossible to provide a convincing answer. As he did with the Mueller report, the attorney general moved to preempt Durham's findings, assuring the public that proof certain would soon be forthcoming of the FBI's intent to "to sabotage the presidency."[65]

Norms had collapsed on all sides, dissolved in the competing narratives. In August 2020, the Senate Intelligence Committee issued its fifth and final report on Russia's interference in the American elections. Again, it reached a strong bipartisan consensus on the seriousness of the threat. Going beyond the findings of Mueller's criminal investigation, the Intelligence Committee found that the Trump campaign had actively welcomed Russia's involvement on its behalf, and it suggested that Trump administration insiders had lied to Congress about their Russian contacts.[66] On the other side, allegations of bias at high levels of the FBI continued to undermine the bureau's reputation and to paint Trump as the victim. The Senate Judiciary Committee countered the Intelligence Committee with documents suggesting that the FBI had targeted Trump campaign officials, displaying bias against *them*, not the Clinton campaign. Meanwhile, the president awaited Durham's findings, expecting that inquiry to give him the last word. An initial case in mid-August was heralded by Barr as an indication of bigger things to come. It followed up on IG Horowitz's findings of malpractice in the process of obtaining FISA warrants and yielded a guilty plea from an FBI lawyer, Kevin Clinesmith, who had been assigned to the Russia investigation. Clinesmith too had a message trail expressing personal animus toward the president: "viva le resistance."[67]

You don't know what you got till it's gone: All this points to the most important lesson to be drawn from this episode. No one wins when expectations of neutrality and independence lose their grip. Each stage in this unfolding debacle offers vivid reminders of why those norms took hold in the first place and why collective buy-in is so important. Ultimately, however, this is not a story about the critical role of norms in making government work; it is, rather, the story of a president who made no pretense of respect for norms and who had no interest in restoring them. As Trump said of the efforts of Barr and Durham to investigate the FBI, "I hope they won't be politically correct."[68]

Earlier, Jeff Sessions, whom Trump had repeatedly and mercilessly berated for recusing himself from the Russia investigation, had felt compelled to make a public defense of independent investigations: "While I am Attorney General the actions of the Department of Justice will not be improperly influenced by political considerations."[69] Trump took the opposite view: "you were supposed to protect me."[70] Sessions never recovered from that offense and was ultimately dismissed.

Even Barr eventually tried to put some distance between his office and the president. The president's public commentary on ongoing cases, he admitted, "makes it impossible for me to do my job."[71] Other unitarians began talking about the importance of maintaining a line as well. When pressed on the DOJ imbroglio, John Yoo echoed the position of Carter's AG Griffin Bell: "while the President is in charge constitutionally, as a matter of good policy, presidents have kept law enforcement at arm's length. Neutrality in law enforcement is important if the government is to have the credibility and integrity to convince judges and juries, who are the ones who ultimately render the verdict."[72]

But the lines were hopelessly compromised. By the time Barr admitted his own need for distance, he had taken charge of criminal cases of direct interest to the president, including those of Michael Flynn and Trump intimate Roger Stone, that were referred from the Mueller investigation. After the president complained on Twitter that DOJ prosecutors in the Stone case were demanding too stiff a sentence, higher-ups at the DOJ overruled those prosecutors. The appearance that DOJ was acting in direct response to the president led the department to protest its independence, but after publicly asserting that there had been no communication with Trump about revising the recommendation, the president intruded again: "Congratulations to Attorney General Bill Barr for taking charge of a case that was totally out of control." It was left to the four prosecutors to mount the ultimate defense of norms. When their sentencing request was overruled, three of them withdrew from the case and the fourth resigned from the department altogether.[73] Soon the wider legal community stepped up behind them. In an open letter, more than 2,000 former DOJ officials accused Trump and Barr of having "flouted [the] fundamental principle" that "political interference in the conduct of a criminal prosecution is anathema to the Department's core mission and to its sacred obligation to ensure equal justice under the law."[74] One of the prosecutors who withdrew from the case later stated in congressional testimony what everyone suspected, that Roger Stone had been "treated differently because of politics."[75]

The sequence repeated itself in the Flynn case. With the president cheering on the effort publicly, Barr found political appointees to raise procedural questions that he deemed sufficient to drop the charges to which the defendant had already pled guilty twice. The career prosecutor in charge of the case withdrew. In fact, no career prosecutors signed on to the brief seeking the dismissal, and indeed, no one seemed to be able to come up with any precedent for such an action. Officials again spoke out in protest. One lamented, "It's deeply disheartening to see politics infect Justice."[76] Former acting assistant attorney general Mary McCord, whose views were cited more than twenty-five times in the motion to dismiss the case, wrote that it was "disingenuous for the department to twist my words" to support the action.[77] And again, more than

2,000 former DOJ officials denounced Barr's move, saying, "Our democracy depends on a Department of Justice that acts as an independent arbiter of equal justice, not as an arm of the president's political apparatus."[78]

Protest and resignation are the last refuge for norms. Trump shrugged off even Barr's belated attempt to draw a line, asserting that the president is allowed to be "totally involved" in DOJ investigations. Then, he appropriated a designation usually applied to the attorney general, and pressed his own constitutional authority as the "chief law enforcement officer of the country."[79] He subsequently affirmed that status by pushing past Barr's objections and commuting Roger Stone's sentence.[80] That move drew Mueller back into the fray, with the former special counsel asserting that his inquiry had acted "in accordance with the rule of law" and defending his officials as having "acted with the highest integrity."[81] But Trump was having none of it: "I won the Mueller Witch Hunt."[82]

At the root of Trump's dispute with DOJ independence lies a long-festering structural problem, one that the theory of the unitary executive makes plain and that depth in norms has manifestly failed to resolve. Fittingly, the value of the theory in shutting down concerns about the lack of credible, independent authority at DOJ was demonstrated by Neomi Rao, the Trump administration stalwart now sitting as a judge on the DC Circuit Court of Appeals. Writing for a three-judge panel, she defended "the Executive Branch's exclusive prosecutorial power" and dismissed a last, desperate effort by the lower court to get at the question of prosecutorial abuse in the DOJ's summary decision to reverse course and drop the charges against Flynn. Proceeding with a judicial inquiry into the Department's intent would, she reasoned, "likely require the Executive to reveal the internal deliberative process behind its exercise of prosecutorial discretion, interfering with the Article II charging authority." In other words, a judicial inquiry would be a "usurpation" and was foreclosed by the separation of powers: "the district court's . . . intent to scrutinize the reasoning and motives of the Department of Justice constitute irreparable harms that cannot be remedied on appeal."[83]

The full circuit court set Rao's outburst aside. Reviewing the matter again *en banc*, the court decided overwhelmingly to send the case back to the district court for a ruling on the Justice Department's extraordinary action. This intra-court dispute brought to the fore the dangers posed by an erosion of the norm of investigatory independence for the constitutional system at large. In the exercise of their judicial authority, courts rely on the assumption that actions taken by DOJ are credible. When that credibility is thrown into doubt, the legitimacy of the courts' own proceedings is placed in jeopardy. They can defer to the political judgments of others and risk "a formalism dangerous to the concept of legality itself." Or they can try to discern the motivations of the executive branch, placing themselves in the awkward position of using their own credibility to try to uphold the norms of another branch of government.[84] Either way, the constitutional system is thrown out of kilter.

7

Depth in Knowledge

The modern American state was built in significant part on the common ground of knowledge-based authority. Science and expertise operated as public goods to ease the separation of powers and to facilitate institutional cooperation in the expansion of national administrative capacities. The aspirations of the time for a partnership arrangement echo through a 1945 report commissioned by President Franklin Roosevelt and released as *Science: The Endless Frontier*. Government and science must work in concert with one another, the author opined, for science could "be effective in the national welfare only as a member of a team."[1]

Teamwork assumes a deep well of diverse resources. It seeks unity in collaboration. Dare we invoke the sports coach cliché? There is no "I" in "team."

The expectation that executive branch action will be based on the best available knowledge is not just a norm. It's a standard set more firmly in law and in rules. It is anchored by statutes regulating the appointment, tenure, dismissal, and behavior of civil servants. Civil service rules stipulate the recruitment of administrators based on job-specific qualifications and demonstrations of merit, and they protect the technical workforce of government from political manipulation or casual dismissal. The Administrative Procedure Act of 1946, with its long progeny of judicial opinions, underwrites the integrity of agency decision making. The statute proscribes regulations that are "arbitrary" or "capricious," "unsupported by substantial evidence," or "unwarranted by the facts."[2] Statutes and rules saddle agencies with scientific advisory boards, outside experts charged to review their research and methods.[3] As recently as 2012, a Republican House and a Democratic Senate provided a shield for administrators seeking to report concerns about scientific integrity. The Whistleblower Protection Enhancement Act declared, "It is essential that Congress and the public receive accurate data and findings from federal researchers and analysts to inform lawmaking and other public policy decisions."[4]

Through the middle decades of the twentieth century, the president and Congress found ways to tap the mutual benefits of depth in knowledge without sacrificing their other political and institutional interests. So, for example, presidents kept agency actions aligned with their priorities by clearing administrators' public statements and requests through the central budget office, and Congress kept its constituents apprised of administrative action through "notice and comment" requirements compelling agencies to publicize their proposals before enactment and to respond to the feedback. But since the 1970s, the notion that a happy balance can be struck among these competing values has been subject to increasingly severe strains. Knowledge-based authority is now another battleground in the confrontation between unity and depth.

"Procedural politicking"—agency administrators bending the rules to advance their own interests—has provided ample fodder for the Deep State charge. In one brazen scheme, officials in the Obama administration's Environmental Protection Agency (EPA) manipulated the notice-and-comment period on a proposed regulation that would have expanded the waters covered under EPA jurisdiction by the Clean Water Act. Anticipating Republican and industry opposition, the agency engineered an outpouring of public support for their proposal. Partnering with allies such as the Sierra Club, the EPA enlisted social media to produce a wave of positive comments.[5] In another recent ploy—this one to provide congressional testimony at odds with Trump administration policy—a climate scientist at the National Park Service (NPS) circumvented clearance procedures by appearing under the auspices of his other, auxiliary appointment as an adjunct professor at the University of California.[6]

It is hard to deny that knowledge-based authority has deep resources to draw on, that it can deploy those resources to resist the political pressures arrayed against it, and that it often has a political edge of its own. But as we saw with depth in staff and depth in norms, the most striking thing about depth in knowledge is how easily its abusers are quashed. Those phantoms of the Deep State at EPA and NPS were quickly dispelled. The Government Accountability Office ruled that the EPA's effort to use federal funds for grassroots lobbying violated the law.[7] President Trump went further and rescinded the water rule.[8] The White House made short work of the shield of academic appointment as well, ordering the NPS scientist to cease and desist.[9]

Much harder to regulate these days is the politicking occurring the other way around—*against* knowledge-based authority and for a more rigid hierarchy of political control over administrative action. Consider by way of introduction the complicated sequence that followed a political clampdown on the work of the EPA by the George W. Bush administration. Reaction to that manipulation was as swift as the reaction against the EPA's own manipulation of notice and comment. An activist group, the Union of Concerned Scientists, pushed back, charging that the administration was deliberately suppressing science-based policy.[10] The Court pushed back as well. Its decision in *Massachusetts v. Environment Protection Agency* (2007) admonished political overseers at the agency and urged the experts to show more backbone.[11] Even more impressive was the Obama administration's promise to reverse course and "restore science to its rightful place."[12]

For a moment, it appeared that a happy balance was being reestablished, and that the impositions of a unitary executive were giving way before a presidential pledge to partner with administrative expertise in policy making. Obama's "Memorandum on Scientific Integrity" aimed to deepen existing protections. The new president promised deference: "the scientific process must inform and guide decisions of my Administration." To that end, he included a stipulation that every agency "should have appropriate rules and procedures to ensure the integrity of the scientific process within the agency."[13] Most agencies of the executive branch followed up by promulgating new rules (described as "scientific integrity" policies) and listing them in the *Federal Register*.[14]

But conspicuous as Obama's initiatives were in support of knowledge-based teams, they did not foreclose an opt-out. How these rules, which apply to action "within the agency," would constrain those in charge of the agency was unclear. As one recent review notes, rules concerning scientific integrity "do not give rise to legally enforceable constraints."[15] Obama's own political appointees played fast and loose with the rules when the guidance they received ran counter to the administration's political interests. Political overseers sidelined EPA concerns that fracking would contaminate well water.[16] They ignored findings by Food and Drug Administration (FDA) scientists in order to keep over-the-counter contraceptives beyond the reach of minors.[17] Public statements by political officers at the National Oceanic and Atmospheric Administration (NOAA) significantly and deliberately downplayed estimates by agency scientists of the severity of the Deepwater Horizon oil spill.[18] During talks over the Paris Agreement on combatting climate change, higher-ups at the Energy Department delayed publication of a report questioning the feasibility of the US reaching its remediation goals under the administration's policies.[19]

The presidents of this beleaguered republic are fickle promoters of depth in knowledge, and although rules may provide firmer footings for depth than norms do, even rules strain under a chief executive bent on political control. The so-called war on science ramped up again in the Trump administration, and questions about whether and to what extent rules protect government research and expertise from the unitary executive have been pushed front and center.[20] Here we examine four cases in which knowledge-based authority was besieged.

Truth and power: When President Trump intruded upon the work of the National Weather Service, he quickly ran up against barriers to political interference, and, in the near-term at least, the barriers held. That may be because the president's assault was so absurd as to defy satire. We look to this dispute, over a hurricane forecast, because it would seem far removed from contentious issues of policy or the regulation of private interests. As a pure case of knowledge-based authority colliding with assertions of personal control, it expressed perfectly the intrinsic resistance of established institutional arrangements to hierarchical impositions. At issue here again is the government's dependence on its own credibility, the expectation that the information it provides the public is reliable.

When Hurricane Dorian approached the southeastern United States in the late summer of 2019, the NWS forecast that the storm would significantly impact states on the east coast from Florida to North Carolina. President Trump asserted otherwise, tweeting, "In addition to Florida—South Carolina, North Carolina, Georgia, and Alabama will most likely be hit (much) harder than anticipated."[21] Trump's inclusion of Alabama in the storm path was erroneous, as the system would remain too far east. Initially unaware of Trump's tweet, but suddenly deluged by worried phone calls, the NWS in Birmingham responded minutes later: "Alabama will NOT see any impacts from #Dorian."[22]

The president could have simply acknowledged his error. Instead, he clamped down. The point was to establish who was in charge and to solicit a show of deference. Trump not only asserted he had been correct about the forecast, but he tried to bend the forecasters to his line. Speaking from the Oval Office, he presented the public an obviously doctored forecast map in which the area of the storm's projected impact had been extended in black marker to encompass part of Alabama.[23] Trump also directed his acting chief of staff, Mick Mulvaney, to fix the contradiction in his favor. Mulvaney contacted Secretary of Commerce Wilbur Ross, under whose remit the weather service fell, to address the issue: "it appears as if the NWS intentionally contradicted the president. And we need to know why. . . . [Trump] wants either a correction or an explanation or both." Ross responded with a demand that the political staff rebut the forecasters' correction. As the NOAA's acting administrator, Neil Jacobs, saw the situation, the political appointees thought their jobs were on the line: "we could definitely lose our jobs over this if we don't do what, you know, we're told."[24] Soon NOAA issued an unsigned statement, spearheaded by top officials from the Commerce Department, including Jacobs and Ross's chief of staff, directly criticizing the Birmingham NWS and implying that their tweet had been inaccurate: "The Birmingham National Weather Service's Sunday morning tweet spoke in absolute terms that were inconsistent with probabilities from the best forecast products available at the time."[25] Raising the specter of a Deep State plot, an anonymous senior administration official suggested that "the [original] Twitter post by the Birmingham forecasters had been motivated by a desire to embarrass the president more than concern for the safety of people in Alabama."[26]

Pushback against the president's clampdown was fierce. It focused directly on the threat to the scientific integrity of governmental pronouncements. The Commerce Department's inspector general began to look into allegations of political interference, suggesting the incident could "call into question the NWS's processes, scientific independence, and ability to communicate accurate and timely weather warnings and data to the nation in times of national emergency."[27] Other scientists sounded the alarm as well. NOAA's acting chief scientist, Craig McLean, emailed fellow employees: "My understanding is that this intervention to contradict the fore-caster was not based on science but on external factors including reputation and appearance, or simply put, political." The director of the NWS, Louis Uccellini, told a gathering of meteorologists that "the integrity of the forecast process was maintained by the Birmingham office," and praised it for doing "what any office would do" in responding to a rumor.[28] Jacobs, NOAA's embattled acting administrator, gave a speech to the same weather conference. In full damage-control mode, Jacobs told his colleagues, "There is no pressure to change the way you communicate or forecast risk in the future," and he further pledged, "This administration is committed to the important mission of weather forecasting." Notwithstanding these assurances, Jacobs's remarks were an attempt to reconcile two irreconcilable positions.[29] His own emails revealed the real story. In a reply to a NOAA biologist who implored him to "not allow the science and support that we perform on behalf of the American public to be tossed into the trash heap by political expediencies," Jacobs wrote, "You have no idea how hard I'm fighting to keep politics out of science."[30]

The reaction at the NWS had explicit rule-based authority to draw on. As the NOAA scientific integrity policy stated, "In no circumstance may any NOAA official ask or direct Federal scientists or other NOAA employees to suppress or alter scientific findings."[31] On that basis, Representative Paul Tonko (D-NY), along with two NOAA employees, requested an independent investigation of the affair by the National Academy of Public Administration (NAPA), a non-profit learned society chartered by Congress. The final report, issued in June 2020, concluded that the anonymous reprimand of agency scientists did in fact violate NOAA's integrity policy, and it suggested strengthening the rules. Although it did not recommend action against those who had issued the reprimand, the report did implicate the acting administrator, Neil Jacobs, and it complicated his Senate confirmation to the full-time position.[32] The IG report followed up and also found fault with political officials in the

Commerce Department: "the Department and NOAA acted contrary to the apolitical mission of NWS."[33]

Still, more questions were left hanging by this episode than were resolved. Was NOAA's work really protected by its scientific integrity policy? No one was fired for violating it, and to the extent that the agency did find protection, other factors seem more decisive. First were the civil service rules insulating the meteorologists. That boundary was recognized implicitly by the Trump administration when it demanded redress from the *political* appointees at NOAA. The weather service was in fact among the first agencies to be brought under the civil service protections of the Pendleton Act of 1883.[34] It renders a service in which neutrality, competence, and expertise have long been prized as indispensable to public safety. And of course, there is a reason that NWS is lodged in the Commerce Department: business interests rely on it.

That said, the unitary executive chafes against restrictions on administrative appointment and removal. As we shall see, the Trump administration was active all along the way in efforts to strip away civil service protections for career officers. Initially, it sought to enlist Congress in this project, but, as one might expect, legislators proved more protective of depth.[35] At NOAA, the congressional backstop was critical. At the time of the hurricane controversy, consideration of Trump's original nominee to head the agency, Barry Myers, had long been held up by the Senate. As the CEO of AccuWeather, Myers had a history of hostility toward the NWS. His former advocacy for the privatization of weather forecasting raised concerns at his confirmation hearings that even the weather service might become a vehicle to advance special interests. Had he been confirmed, the assault on agency integrity would almost certainly have cut much deeper than it did. As it was, objections to Myers's conflicts of interest tied up his nomination. It languished for two years without ever receiving a floor vote. Two months after the hurricane forecast controversy, Myers withdrew from consideration, citing medical issues.[36]

And that raises the question of whether this was all just a matter of political calculation. While the contradiction in forecasting was not resolved in Trump's favor, neither did the administration ever acknowledge the inappropriate nature of its demand for deference. In fact, when the NAPA investigators sought to interview political appointees at the Commerce Department about their role in the anonymous reprimand of the agency's actions, they were told that those officials were not bound by NOAA's scientific integrity policy.[37] Perhaps the president perceived a misfire and simply altered his approach. Notwithstanding the policy on scientific integrity, it is the secretary of commerce who is charged by law with "the forecasting of weather," and soon Trump pushed Ross further. In the summer of 2020, the secretary moved again to bring NOAA to heel. New directives gagged career officials, shook up the staff, and restricted reporting on climate change.[38]

Political science: The work of the EPA is steeped in conflicts of policy and interest. Consequently, the agency has long been the leading example of the regulatory whipsaw produced by presidents each bent, one to the next, on creating administrations of their own. Pressure on rules-based protections for expertise in government policy making mount precipitously when the president's policy preferences run directly counter to the recommendations of scientists, as they often do at the EPA. It's a perfect setting for the phantom twins to draw each other out.

Trump's selection of Scott Pruitt to head the EPA made no pretense of teamwork or cooperation. As a former Oklahoma attorney general with close ties to the fossil fuel industry, Pruitt had sued the EPA frequently. He described himself in his official state biography as "a leading advocate against the EPA's activist agenda."[39] Hostility at the top bore down hard on those below. The release of information was suppressed systematically, most especially in the area of climate science. Career scientists reported the rise of a new culture of self-censorship.[40]

For stalwart resisters, the only hope was to extend the timeline of battle and to arm agency allies with resources to fight the inevitable rollbacks later on in court. By embedding data, statistics, and projections into draft analyses of proposed rule changes, EPA scientists sought to clarify the stakes of the impending alterations and to leave them open to legal challenges down the road. For example, in a draft analysis for a review of a regulation of industrial soot emissions, scientists showed that a 25 percent tightening of the existing standard for the pollutant could save up to 12,150 lives annually.[41] In another case, related to climate change, scientists showed the costs of replacing the Obama administration's Clean Power Plan rule for coal with the Trump administration's proposed Affordable Clean Energy rule. While the Obama administration rule was estimated to *prevent* between 1,500 and 3,600 premature deaths annually, the new Trump administration proposal was projected to lead to an *increase* of 1,400 annual premature deaths by 2030.[42]

Efforts like these reached out to the external supporters of knowledge-based authority—environmental lawyers and interest groups—who might appeal the rule changes in court.[43] The draft preliminary assessment of the change in soot policy explicitly stated that it was "intended to be a useful reference to all parties interested in the review," and that it was "written to be understandable to a broad audience."[44] The draft regulatory impact analysis of the coal rule also spoke to an audience beyond direct political superiors: "By analyzing against the existing [Clean Power Plan], the reader can understand the combined impact of a repeal and replacement."[45] But though a defiant spirit of service to a larger public ran deep at the agency, these were acts of desperation. Invested in policies they had developed, the scientists lashed out at unitary pretensions as a direct threat to evidence-based decision making: "what these guys have done is come in and repeal and replace [rules and regulations], without relying on data and facts." A former employee who worked on clean air policy put it this way: "You work hard on stuff that is good for the world, for a long time, for years, and then it's trashed, and you're told you have to participate in trashing it, and now you have to figure out what to do."[46]

Of course, for supporters of the Trump administration's policies, these were the subversive acts of a Deep State. As Steven Milloy, who worked on Trump's EPA transition team, complained, "It's been obvious since the beginning of the Trump administration that the career staff is sabotaging the rulemakings, deliberately seeding them with numbers that can help the enviros sue." Milloy's regret was that civil service protections provided by Congress to support careers in public administration prevented peremptory dismissals: "I was hoping Trump would be able to fire these people, but you can't legally. . . . You can't discipline them." What the administration could do, however, was ignore them. The final draft report on fine soot eliminated the reference to preventing deaths, only acknowledging that stricter soot standards would reduce "health risks." Trump's second EPA administrator, Andrew Wheeler, acknowledged the scientists' work but said he placed "little weight on quantitative estimates." The number of annual premature deaths was also deleted in the final rule proposal on coal.[47]

In the near term at least, the unitary executive prevailed. By the summer of 2020, work weakening 68 separate environmental rules had been completed. Another 32 rollbacks were still in progress.[48] The administration was thinking long term as well. Its broader strategy for dealing with depth in knowledge sought a more systemic change, albeit one that avoided a frontal assault on scientific findings. In fact, one of its initiatives would re-appropriate the motif of scientific integrity for its own purposes.

Specifically, the administration called for a change in the rules that would make data collection and usage more difficult. By imposing new restrictions on the kind of evidence that could be presented to justify administrative action, these changes would, by extension, also limit judicial scrutiny of presidential priorities. In this case, depth was to be stripped away indirectly, in the name of better science. The demand was that EPA scientists make their findings more transparent.

The proposed change was prompted by a study that had recommended a ban on the insecticide chlorpyrifos. Under the Obama administration, the EPA had begun to rely on epidemiological studies—which examine the factors that influence diseases in particular groups of people over time—as a basis for environmental decisions about public health, and in particular, for the regulation of pesticides like chlorpyrifos. A long-standing research project called "Chamacos," partly funded by the EPA and run by scientists from the University of California, had shown negative health impacts in the children of farmworkers, and it had linked them to pregnant mothers' exposure to the pesticides. The EPA proposed banning chlorpyrifos in late 2016.[49]

Companies such as Monsanto and Dow Chemical opposed the ban. In December 2016, just a month before Trump took office, CropLife America, a group representing agrochemical companies, petitioned the EPA to stop making regulatory decisions about pesticides based on epidemiological studies. The group complained that such studies "do not meet well-defined data quality standards" and that "the public has no means of knowing how EPA is determining the data quality of such studies."[50] Similarly, in September 2017, the California Specialty Crops Council, representing crop growers, complained to the EPA about the "inappropriate use" of such studies.[51]

Pruitt disregarded the recommendations of EPA scientists and rejected the proposed ban on chlorpyrifos.[52] But the deeper cut against administrative fact-finding was already in view. Borrowing from long-standing business interests and earlier Republican initiatives in Congress, the administration latched onto standards of transparency and replicability in research and set out in effect to "out-science" the EPA scientists.[53] As part of his overall deregulatory agenda, President Trump issued an executive order in February 2017 that called for officials to identify "regulations that rely in whole or in part on data, information, or methods that are not publicly available or that are insufficiently transparent to meet the standard for reproducibility."[54] The intended beneficiaries of the directive were clear from the audience of business leaders present in the Oval Office for the signing. Chief among them was Andrew Liveris, the CEO of Dow Chemical and the head of Trump's short-lived American Manufacturing Council.[55]

The presence of the Dow Chemical CEO at the signing indicated that this directive would be applied broadly, and in April 2018, Pruitt got the ball rolling. He proposed a rule that would require many public health studies to provide public data for replication before they could be used in making regulatory decisions. Invoking transparency, Pruitt declared, "The era of secret science at EPA is coming to an end. . . . The ability to test, authenticate, and reproduce scientific findings is vital for the integrity of [the] rulemaking process. Americans deserve to assess the legitimacy of the science underpinning EPA decisions that may impact their lives." In its press release, the EPA further claimed, "This proposed rule is in line with the scientific community's moves toward increased data sharing to address the 'replication crisis'—a growing recognition that a significant proportion of published research may not be reproducible."[56]

Stripping away the insulation that promotes data collection about public health is a political tactic, a way of thwarting governmental action and turning administration into an arm of the presidential party. Because these studies rely on patient data protected by privacy laws, the rule would stifle the research on which many regulatory decisions must be based. Indeed, the EPA subsequently emailed the Chamacos director, Brenda Eskenazi, to request "the original data" from the pesticide study, suggesting that there was "uncertainty around neurodevelopmental effects" and implying that withholding the relevant data would render the study unusable as a basis for regulatory decisions.[57] Under pressure from the courts to respond to a petition from environmental groups seeking to ban the pesticides, Pruitt's successor, Andrew Wheeler, upheld the decision to reject the ban.[58]

The use of transparency rules to strip away protections for government research is potentially far-reaching. Building on Pruitt's efforts, Wheeler—a former coal industry lobbyist—proposed an even more sweeping requirement.[59] Rather than apply the transparency rule only to certain types of studies, his proposal required access to all data, including medical data, used in any study involved in regulatory decision making. Moreover, the new rule would have been retroactively applicable, putting existing regulations based on public health studies at risk. For example, it might have been used to invalidate EPA regulations that relied on a 1993 Harvard study that had tracked more than 22,000 people for years for evidence of premature death from air pollution. That study too rested on confidentiality agreements on the use of health data.[60]

Although Wheeler claimed that his rule would "ensure that the science supporting agency decisions is transparent and available for evaluation by the public and stakeholders," scientists both within and outside the administration took a different view. The proposal raised concerns that "the politically appointed agency administrator would have wide-ranging discretion over which studies to accept or reject." Speaking for the Union of Concerned Scientists, Michael Halpern said, "It was hard to imagine that they could have made this worse, but they did. . . . This is a wholesale politicization of the process."[61] Even scientists appointed by the Trump administration to the EPA's Scientific Advisory Board, a body authorized to oversee and evaluate the scientific integrity of EPA regulations, criticized the administration's efforts. Their internal report argued that "privacy and confidentiality must be taken into consideration," and it warned that "the proposed rule could be viewed as a license to politicize the scientific evaluation required under the statute based on administratively determined criteria for what is practicable."[62]

The criticisms did have some effect. As the White House came closer to finalizing the proposal, it modified the rule to relax the total restriction on using studies without public data, and it omitted any mention of applying the new rule retroactively. Still, existing regulations based on studies with confidential data frequently come up for renewal, leaving open the possibility that research such as the seminal Harvard pollution study would eventually be precluded under the new framework. The crux of the proposal remained the same. Authority to determine which studies would be admissible in regulatory decision making would be lodged in the politically appointed EPA administrator. The Union of Concerned Scientists charged that such discretion would favor outside interests: "It makes it easier for industry in most cases to say, 'There's too much uncertainty; you shouldn't move forward.'"[63]

The transparency rule deploys scientific standards on behalf of unity against depth. It seeks a systemic shift in authority, a change in the game itself. The across-the-board character of the rule is what distinguishes it as a priority. Trump administration officials anticipated applying the rule broadly and putting "each of our major [environmental] statutes" under scrutiny.[64]

Procedures in place dictate that alterations of this kind are not adopted precipitously. Rule changes take time. Action on behalf of the transparency rule stretched over several years, bumping up against a significant deadline. The Congressional Review Act allows Congress to overturn a rule within sixty days of its final adoption, and with the outcome of the 2020 elections in doubt, the push to finalize the transparency rule in time to secure its long-term survival became a race against the clock. While time was ticking, however, the administration tested its arguments in a case about that controversial pesticide. It opined in court that Wheeler's approval of chlorpyrifos should be upheld because EPA decisions could not be based on inaccessible data.[65]

Ship 'em out: It bears notice that the Trump administration steered clear of any forthright renunciation of the use of science in government decision making. It advocated "transparency" as a principle of scientific integrity, merely changing the rules of best practice to achieve its political ends. At the EPA and elsewhere, it left the Obama-era scientific integrity rules in place.[66] As a spokesman for the Union of Concerned Scientists put it, rescinding the integrity rules would be tantamount to an announcement that "we think political manipulation of the sciences is a good thing."[67]

Candor on this point remains a step too far. The recognition that there are other kinds of authority at work in the executive branch may be implicit, but there is in that acknowledgment a limit to the assault on administrative depth. The administration had to work its will surreptitiously. Extending presidential control in this arena was a matter of crowding out the competition.

At the Department of Agriculture (USDA), the administration targeted depth in knowledge without either challenging the basis of research findings or changing the rules of scientific integrity.[68] The strategy employed there was different, but the crowding-out effect was the same. President Trump's USDA simply relocated scientific agencies, moving them geographically closer to the outside interests the administration sought to serve.

The potential use of harassment and reassignment to sideline individual civil servants whose jobs are otherwise insulated from political control had long been recognized. In 1974, one *National Review* writer recommended that a president at odds with a powerful bureaucrat over policy should just "have him posted to Nome, Alaska or some such place."[69] A more brazen approach was to marginalize entire agencies through the use of reorganization authority.

As it happened, the broad authority to reorganize the executive branch that Congress had extended to the president in 1939 was pared back in the 1970s. And after the Supreme Court ruling in *INS v. Chadha* (1983) deprived Congress of the protection of the legislative veto, presidential reorganization authority was ended altogether.[70] Nonetheless, pockets of such authority remained scattered throughout the executive branch, lodged in provisions that had been enacted in the interim. With *Chadha* clouding the validity of those *previous* reorganizations, Congress feared chaos and felt compelled to act affirmatively. In 1984, it passed a statute "ratifying all [preexisting] reorganization plans as a matter of law."[71] Thus, the authority granted to the secretary of agriculture by President Eisenhower's

Reorganization Plan No. 2 of 1953 "to adjust the organization of the Department" remained intact for use by the Trump administration.[72]

Secretary of Agriculture Sonny Perdue seized upon it. In June 2019, he announced a transfer of the department's National Institute of Food and Agriculture (NIFA) and its Economic Research Service (ERS) from Washington, DC, to Kansas City. Employees were forced to decide within months whether to uproot their lives or quit. The choice to move these particular agencies was conspicuous because they had clashed with the secretary on matters of political interest and policy.[73] The ERS had been a source of multiple agriculture studies with results the Trump administration disputed, including findings that farmers had been harmed by the president's imposition of tariffs and by the administration's tax reform. The secretary's office had previously issued an internal memo to direct the ERS to include disclaimers at the top of their studies declaring that their findings were "preliminary" and "should not be construed to represent any agency determination or policy."[74]

Unable to dismiss the agencies' experts and not content simply to cabin their work, Secretary Perdue decided to displace them to the hinterlands. Moving government researchers nearer to concerned stakeholders might appear to augment depth, not strip it away. This was, in fact, USDA's stated rationale. The move to the Kansas City region was heralded as a way to "increase efficiencies and effectiveness and bring important resources and manpower closer to all of our customers."[75] But stripping away is exactly what happened. Policy networks were broken up. As the Union of Concerned Scientists saw it, the effort was designed to "disconnect the perspective and expertise of USDA scientists from direct contact with policymaking on Capitol Hill."[76] A report summing up the views of ERS employees explained that "the specialties of those who are being asked to move corresponds closely to the areas where economic assessments often clash with the president's policies." One opined, "This was a clear politicization of the agency many of us loved for its non-partisan research and analysis."[77]

Each agency was decimated. Two-thirds of the workers affected decided to leave their positions rather than move. Hundreds of millions of dollars allocated to research projects were put on hold. The reaction of Acting Chief of Staff Mulvaney at a Republican Party event belied claims that the agency's scientific activities would go forward unimpeded. "It's nearly impossible to fire a federal worker," he gloated. "What a wonderful way to sort of streamline government and do what we haven't been able to do for a long time."[78] Surveying the damage, the House Appropriations Committee concluded that "ERS and NIFA are shells of their former selves, and the loss of institutional knowledge each agency has suffered will take years to overcome."[79] The administration applied a similar tactic to shift the Interior Department's Bureau of Land Management headquarters to Colorado.[80]

Mobilizing a team: The American Constitution does not contain a very robust conception of national political leadership, and the theory of the unitary executive, a proposition derived from the Constitution, is a poor substitute for one. The unitary executive relies on formal authority to command the respect of others and to get them to do the president's bidding. Political leadership, by contrast, is team play. It is a relationship of reciprocity, a mobilization of diverse assets, and a recognition of the indispensability of others.[81] An effective political leader gains control by signaling cooperation and building trust, and in a crisis, when a president has to call upon all the resources at his disposal to mount an effective response, it is trust and cooperation that count most.[82]

Little wonder, then, that President Trump's preference for mandate claims, unitary authority, and personal control left him flat-footed during the coronavirus pandemic of 2020. This episode stands out for attention since, at first glance, it might appear custom-made for a unitary executive. It should have been a moment of certain proof of the value of a strongman at the top. This was exactly the kind of circumstance that advocates of presidentialism imagine when they say that the nation has "no real choice but to hand the reins to the executive and hope for the best."[83] The public expects no less than presidentialism when it suspends its usual skepticism and opens itself up to the extraordinary demands of crisis management. It is what Congress itself anticipated when it provided for the suspension of rules and regulations during national emergencies.[84]

But it is precisely at these times—when presidents command center stage, when everyone expects them to take charge and to vindicate the full powers of their office—that their dependence on others is most acute. Crisis management is not a unilateral imposition, nor is it a matter of serving political interests.[85] Managing a group effort is something entirely different. As experts on crisis management tell us, "team response" is enhanced if "the preexisting interpersonal and inter-organizational relationships among the chief actors represented in the crisis group are marked by a reasonable degree of mutual trust."[86]

President Trump's suspicion of alternative and potentially competing sites of executive branch authority did little to cultivate trust in those he would need most to deal with the pandemic. His hostility to the independent voice of public health professionals was baked into his top-down conception of executive branch control. Those "preexisting interpersonal and inter-organizational relationships" were toxic.

Stripping away depth had been the administration's priority. It had tried (unsuccessfully) to cut funding for the National Institutes of Health and the National Science Foundation.[87] In 2018, it disbanded the National Security Council's pandemic response team, a group organized by the Obama administration in anticipation of just such emergencies,[88] and it ignored their playbook, outlining step-by-step responses to such threats.[89] The president snubbed a warning in January 2019 from the director of national intelligence "that the United States and the world will remain vulnerable to the next flu pandemic or large-scale outbreak of a contagious disease."[90] The Department of Health and Human Services

(HHS) got a similar response that year to a simulation of an influenza pandemic that showed significant problems in funding, supplies, preparedness, and government coordination.[91] In the months leading up to the coronavirus outbreak, the administration reduced the staff presence of the US Centers for Disease Control (CDC) in China, where the outbreak would originate, by two-thirds.[92] It eliminated provision for an American epidemiologist to be embedded in China's public health agency and provide early warning of disease outbreaks.[93] Most portentous of all, the administration ended the PREDICT initiative, another early-warning program with operations in the outbreak's epicenter of Wuhan, China.[94]

The marginalization of knowledge-based authority continued through the early days of the outbreak. The president downplayed the threat even as his advisers alerted him to its scope and significance. He dismissed the warnings of his HHS secretary, Alex Azar, as "alarmist."[95] Other than curtailing travel from China, he resisted attempts to plan for increasingly likely worst-case scenarios, and he shunned bad news.[96] Warnings about the spread of the coronavirus pandemic became a staple of the President's Daily Brief, but Trump still preferred to trust his gut instincts.[97] He spoke of his confidence in his own "natural ability" to deal with complex public health issues.[98]

To the extent that the president focused on the crisis, it was to control public perceptions and contain political fallout. Long after the warnings became urgent, he still seemed determined to dismiss the threat as just another hoax engineered by his political opponents.[99] In one case, the president seemed less concerned with the logistics of allowing infected passengers from a cruise ship to disembark than with how the infection count would be impacted: "I don't need to have the numbers double because of one ship that wasn't our fault."[100] Though former Trump administration officials had taken to the op-ed pages, calling upon the president to "Act Now,"[101] Trump relied on a charismatic trope: "One day, it's like a miracle, it will disappear." Repeatedly, he offered assurances that the coronavirus was "very well under control in our country," even predicting in late February that "the 15 [cases] within a couple of days is going to be down close to zero."[102] As the scope of the outbreak began to register, the president appeared nonplussed. Traveling to the CDC in Atlanta, he said, "Who would have thought we would even be having the subject?"[103]

It was not as if agency experts were doing a fine job responding all on their own. There was infighting at HHS. A costly delay in ramping up the nation's capacity to test for the virus meant that, at a critical moment in the infection's spread, there was no way to tell how many Americans had contracted it and where the "hotspots" lay. The immediate reason for the delay was a flaw in the test initially developed by the CDC. Bureaucratic rigidity and "institutional arrogance" hampered efforts to fix the problem. The CDC insisted on the use of its own test when others had proven effective, and its criteria for selecting Americans eligible for a test proved far too restrictive. At the same time, the FDA stuck to a slow approval process for the new tests developed by private manufacturers, academic researchers, hospitals, and other health organizations. Obfuscation at the top and floundering in the agencies below cost the government a vital month in understanding the pace of the outbreak.[104] Under questioning by Congress, the National Institute for Allergies and Infectious Diseases (NIAID) director Anthony Fauci—testifying alongside the CDC director Robert Redfield—conceded the problem of testing in blunt terms: "It is failing. Let's admit it."[105]

All of this calls into question the practical value of a unitary executive. Short of political leadership—mobilizing a team and recognizing what others have to bring to the table, promulgating a national plan and coordinating a collective response, communicating useful information to the public and steeling national resolve—it is not clear what presidents have to offer in such circumstances. Trump's performance exposed the false equation of personal control with the effective mobilization of national resources. An even more devastating indictment of the unitary idea was the president's attempt to shift blame for shortcomings in the response to others. Asked about his role in the testing failure, the president's response—"I don't take responsibility at all"—knocked the bottom out of a theory that legitimates concentrated power in the name of accountability.[106]

The disconnect between the agencies and the White House proved unsustainable, but once a group was assembled to manage the crisis, the leadership problems became even more glaring. Forced to defer to the authority of others, the president had a hard time settling into a power-sharing arrangement. By late February, scientists and political appointees meeting under the auspices of the HHS secretary realized that drastic action would be needed. Widespread lockdowns, social distancing, and a suspension of economic activity were on the table, and someone would have to explain to the public why this was all necessary.[107] As officials prepared to detail the situation to the president, Nancy Messonnier, an official at the CDC, went public to force the issue: "It's not a question of if but rather a question of when and how many people in this country will have severe illness."[108] With markets falling sharply on that warning, the president grew angry. But with public concern mounting, he raised the profile of the HHS group and put Vice President Mike Pence in charge of the effort.[109]

Pence's appointment suggested a national priority, but it also hinted at a problem that would plague the team's response. The bypass of medical professionals who might have led the task force suggested lingering White House suspicions about the authority of the experts and an abiding determination to retain a tight grip on the operation. The new approach was as much a clampdown as an opening to others. Indeed, when the White House took over public communications, the CDC's reliance on long-standing Epidemic Intelligence Service communications protocols fell away, and its employees were silenced: "They can't speak to the media. These are people who have trained their entire lives for epidemics—the finest public-health army in history—and they've been told to shut up!"[110]

With the president content for the moment to stay in the background, the vice president reassured the nation with elaborate displays of the administration's newfound deference to knowledge-based authorities: "The president is very clear. We're going to follow the facts and listen to the experts every step of the way."[111] Each of Pence's televised briefings on the task force's work put a gaggle of experts on public view. Repeatedly stepping aside to give the professionals the microphone, he nodded to their invocation of "models" and "data" and then endorsed their "guidance." Praise for the president's "whole-of-government-approach" mixed freely with assurances that the scientists had come to the nation's rescue.[112] NIAID director Fauci was widely perceived as "the one person everyone in Washington trusts right now," and Republican senators urged the president to make him "the face" of the government's response.[113] Deborah Birx, whom President Obama had named as the government's coordinator in charge of addressing the global AIDS epidemic in 2014, became the White House coronavirus response coordinator, with Pence describing her as "my right arm."[114]

The inversion of authority was striking. It was also unsteady, and it proved short-lived. In the first place, the task force fell short of its promise as a central coordinating mechanism. It had to compete with other centers of power in the White House. Jared Kushner ran the procurement operation, and he was part of another group run by Chief of Staff Mark Meadows that sought to reconcile the data with the president's political interests in a quick resolution.[115] The task force members put a public face of unity on an effort that they never entirely controlled.[116] The two groups epitomized the different systems of authority in play.

The president himself seemed torn. He would repeatedly concede authority to the public health professionals, then renege, and then concede it again. Uneasy with sharing, Trump soon shoved the vice president aside and took over the daily task force briefings himself. The result was a team that appeared increasingly at odds with itself. The back and forth between the experts and the president became a communications nightmare. Trump followed the public health experts' recommendations by announcing in mid-March a set of stay-at-home guidelines to help the country "flatten the curve."[117] But when a record number of unemployment claims were filed, the president got out ahead of the team to announce the possibility of ending the guidelines as early as Easter: "WE CANNOT LET THE CURE BE WORSE THAN THE PROBLEM ITSELF."[118] The experts pushed back, with Fauci saying that they had "made it very clear to [the president] that if we pull back on what we were doing and didn't extend [the recommendations], there would be more avoidable suffering and avoidable death." Trump relented: "I guess we got to do it." He tried to make the best of it: "I listened to experts . . . I'm going to rely on them."[119]

The task force briefings were meant to demonstrate presidential leadership and present a united front, but they backfired repeatedly. Each day's press conference became an opportunity for the president to put his personal stamp on the response and to spin the meaning of the collective effort. He turned the events into surrogate campaign rallies. He bragged about his high "ratings" and played a video clip praising his "DECISIVE ACTION."[120] Sharing the stage with his medical experts, he repeatedly stepped on their message. When the CDC recommended that Americans wear face masks outside their homes, Trump undercut the advice: "You can do it. You don't have to do it. I am choosing not to do it."[121] While the president mused that it was "possible [the virus] doesn't come back at all," Fauci pushed back: "There will be coronavirus in the fall."[122] After an interview in which Fauci had emphasized the need to "significantly ramp up" testing to reopen the country, Trump undercut him directly: "I don't agree with him on that, no. I think we're doing a great job on testing."[123] On the question of who would control the reopening, Trump proclaimed, "When somebody's the president of the United States, the authority is total." But the next day, he reversed himself and shifted the burden to others: "The governors are responsible. They have to take charge."[124] When states did begin reopening for business, the administration briefed that it was ready to wind down the task force, but the next day, the president said it would run indefinitely.[125] After Fauci testified to the Senate expressing caution about opening schools in the fall, the president countered, "To me it's not an acceptable answer, especially when it comes to schools."[126]

The back and forth, the mutual undercutting, took its toll. The public messaging was muddled, and presidential skepticism politicized expert advice. Fauci admitted his predicament: "I can't just jump in front of a microphone and push him down. OK, he said it. Let's try and get it corrected for the next time."[127] For his part, the president was increasingly uneasy with his most trusted science adviser, saying privately, "I made Fauci a star. The least he could do is give me a little credit."[128]

It was not just about upstaging. At times, the president would offer his own prescriptions, speculating on the fly about miracle cures and brushing past the caution expressed by his advisers about untested treatments. Touting a combination of drugs—hydroxychloroquine and azithromycin—as one possibility, Trump said it had a "real chance to be one of the biggest game changers in the history of medicine." Urging its use, he asked, "What do you have to lose?"[129] FDA commissioner Stephen Hahn acknowledged the president's interest—"that's a drug that the president has directed us to take a closer look at"—and a few days later, the agency granted emergency authorization to use the drugs to treat patients hospitalized with the virus.[130] The president's enthusiastic endorsement caused hoarding of the drugs across the country.[131] Within weeks, however, a panel of experts at Fauci's NIAID recommended against using that drug combination for treating patients, and the FDA revoked its temporary authorization, citing the drugs' risks and lack of effectiveness.[132] The casual discussion of treatment ideas took its most absurd turn when Trump mused publicly about transparently dangerous remedies, including the use of toxic disinfectants: "I see the disinfectant, where it knocks [the virus] out in a minute. One minute. And is there a way we can do something like that, by injection inside or almost a cleaning?" The reaction was fierce. Disinfectant manufacturers issued warnings that people should not ingest their products.[133]

The alarming spectacle exposed an uncomfortable truth. The president had finally gotten a chance to suspend rules and regulations en masse, but cutting through red tape was not in this instance meant to give him more say-so; it was meant to give the experts a freer hand. The pandemic did more to enhance the credibility of those around the president than the credibility of the president himself. Authority flowed naturally to others, and presidentialism lost its purchase. Rather than redound to his benefit, the crisis rendered what Trump had to offer confusing and counterproductive. Representative Greg Walden (R-OR) put it gently: "Any of us can be onstage too much."[134] Senate Majority Leader Mitch McConnell (R-KY) was more direct: "certainly what the American people are most interested in is the advice from health professionals. . . . To the extent that the White House decides to re-craft those briefings to reflect that goal—[it] would probably be a good idea."[135] The yearning for a concerted, competent, collaborative effort cut hard against the pretensions of a unitary executive. Ron Klain, who had coordinated the Obama administration's response to the Ebola virus, pressed the point: "You're going to have to beat this with the 'deep state.'"[136] *Politico* too recommended "leaning into the 'deep state.'"[137] Joe Biden, Trump's 2020 opponent, piled on, admonishing the president to "lead with the science" and "listen to the experts."[138]

With his credibility in tatters and the election season looming, Trump became increasingly desperate to move on. As the death toll from the pandemic surged past 100,000, his focus shifted to reopening the economy. One adviser conceded that Trump had "been over coronavirus for a long time."[139] Growing tired of Fauci and his penchant for contradicting the president, the White House marginalized him and cast aspersions on his credibility.[140] When task force coordinator Deborah Birx warned that the outbreak was "extraordinarily widespread," Trump dismissed her statement as "pathetic."[141] The clampdown on the CDC tightened as well. The administration concluded that CDC guidelines for reopening schools were too tough and directed the agency to relax them. As one official explained, "There is a view [that] the CDC is staffed with 'deep state' Democrats that are trying to tweak the administration."[142] Kayleigh McEnany, the president's press secretary, put it plainly: "the science should not stand in the way."[143]

The springtime promise of teamwork and coordination in the work of the task force could not be sustained. It could not even make it through the summer. Between the president's urge to re-open quickly and the surge of cases in states that had followed his lead, the crisis spun out of control. The response became a national disgrace and an international embarrassment. When the president, under pressure from the growing death toll, resumed regular briefings, he stood alone. Behind the scenes, there was a new adviser. Dr. Scott Atlas, a neuroradiologist with no experience in the field of public health, joined the team to counter the strategy promoted by Fauci and Birx and to propagate the view that comprehensive mitigation was unnecessary and misguided. At about the same time, the credibility of public health professionals at both the CDC and FDA came under fire for once again relaxing guidelines and accelerating treatment approvals. Agency officials strained to deny the charge that they were bending under political pressure, but their authority had become hopelessly muddled.[144]

The political pressure Trump exerted on the CDC and FDA did little to enhance his own credibility. Indeed, his strong-arm tactics mixed uneasily with his determination to speed the development of a vaccine to combat the virus. By his own actions, Trump deepened public skepticism about the safety and efficacy of the remedies upon which he pegged his ultimate vindication. That self-defeating dynamic speaks to the risks he ran in subordinating knowledge-based authority at other sites. Determined as he was to crowd out the experts that stood in his way, the president was hard-pressed to lose the imprimatur of knowledge-based authority entirely.

There was something similar at work in Trump's attempt to substitute the voice of Dr. Atlas for the voice of Dr. Fauci. He sought out a physician from a prestigious hospital to counter the government's experts and promote his preferred line, but the careerists with real public health credentials were never entirely silenced. Even after the administration sidelined them, they continued to dog the president. Their messages were eagerly awaited by the news media, the public, and even many Republican officials.

The president's difficulties speak to a stubborn cultural boundary on unitary claims. They suggest the residual appeal of seemingly disinterested voices, a demand within the wider polity for political deference to those in the know. Disastrous as it was, the pandemic response confirmed that depth in knowledge is an indispensable resource, something the state can ill-afford to manipulate and squander. Unfortunately, respect for the authority of others is not an integral part of the toolkit of the unitary executive. The conceit that the president has "all the executive power" is indifferent, if not hostile, to the authority of experts. Effective political leaders will have no need for the theory of the unitary executive, and the theory will not compensate for what leadership alone can provide.

8

Depth in Appointment

The power of appointment sits at the center of the tension between unity and depth in American administration. The two values were tied together in the formulation of that power, and they have been vying with one another ever since. The framers of the Constitution wanted to shift appointment powers out of Congress and into more responsible hands. Nonetheless, they qualified that power in ways that just as pointedly conditioned presidential control. Presidents would nominate the principal officers, but the appointment would be subject to the advice and consent of the Senate, and inferior officers would be selected as Congress might prescribe. Almost immediately, the resulting ambiguities raised questions about the relationship between the power to appoint and the power to remove. So profound was the confusion of competing priorities on the removal question that Alexander Hamilton, the reputed champion of executive branch unity, argued for consistency through joint action and shared responsibility, while James Madison, the reputed champion of checks and balances, argued for consistency through hierarchy and unity.[1]

At times—as in the Four Year's Law of 1820 and the *Myers* decision of 1926—Congress and the Court have endorsed a stronger hand to presidents in creating administrations of their own. At other times—as in the Tenure of Office Act of 1867 and the *Humphrey's* decision of 1935—they have imposed restraints. The constitutional design is such that these issues are never really resolved, only more or less contingently settled. But striking the right balance has become a more difficult proposition as the executive branch has gotten larger and more powerful, and the risks of entrusting the government to the president's administration have grown as incumbents have become more independent in political action. The Trump presidency brought these new realities into sharp relief.

Trump's administration became notorious for short tenures and serial turnover in high-level management.[2] But if instability in management is one obvious consequence of stripping away depth, it is not the most telling one. What this administration brought to the fore are the suspicions harbored by a unitary executive toward qualifications per se and in the broadest sense of the term. Consider again the initial setup. Senate confirmation was meant to serve as a check on fitness for office. It "qualified" the president's appointment power out of concern for the selection of officers "qualified" to do their jobs. Both conditions acknowledged collective interests in the selection of administrative personnel. Even where appointments are entrusted to the president alone, a collective interest in qualifications remains a matter of faith. Ability, sound judgment, commitment to assigned duties—these are presumptive conditions on presidential control, implicit limits on political subordination, anticipated brakes on personal will. They are the essence of depth.

The received wisdom on this point comes from the Nixon era. Nixon's domestic policy adviser John Ehrlichman once described good management as "get-the-Secretary-to-do-what-the-President-needs-and-wants-him-to-do-whether-he-likes-it-or-not."[3] Nixon's insight was that a president cannot gain control over administrative programs unless he has control over administrative personnel.[4] Political science has been building on that insight ever since. It has recast the presidential interest in administrative competence to identify a more specific concern for "responsive competence."[5]

But something else was at work in the Trump administration. It threw into question the value of competence itself. Call these the Trump corollaries to the unitary executive theory: when the president's interest in responsiveness becomes absolute, it drives down the value of all other qualifications; when unity is the priority, loyalty becomes the ultimate credential.

The priority of loyalty popped up in Trump's initial meetings with FBI director James Comey. It subsequently took on near-comical proportions. When Trump selected his former body man, Johnny McEntee, to be head of the Office of Presidential Personnel, a White House official quipped that McEntee "does not have the relevant experience to do this job, unless the job is to purge Never Trumpers and reward loyalists."[6] That was exactly the job description Trump had in mind, and soon McEntee gained a reputation as the president's "loyalty cop."[7]

Here we offer snapshots of the drive to dissolve administrative qualifications into loyalty to the president. The point gains weight at steps further removed from presidential command and control. Accordingly, we sample sites at four different degrees of separation.

From holism to egoism: The National Security Council (NSC), created at the dawn of the Cold War, was intended to provide the president a holistic view of national security policy. Established in the National Security Act of 1947 and the 1949 amendments to that act, the innovation had all the hallmarks of the post–New Deal settlement on presidential power. Recognizing the altered scale and critical character of the challenges that had come to revolve around the commander in chief, Congress acted to institutionalize the exercise of the executive power.

The idea was to create a cohort of responsible officials to deliberate, assimilate, coordinate, and inform. The Council brought the collective wisdom of the foreign policy establishment together in one place and put it at the president's disposal. Alongside the president, the 1949 amendments made the vice president, secretary of state, secretary of defense, and the chair of the short-lived National Security Resources Board statutory members. Others were added later. The chairman of the new Joint Chiefs of Staff and director of the new Central Intelligence Agency were the Council's statutory military and intelligence advisers and attended meetings.[8] These

Senate-confirmed officers were to "advise the President with respect to the integration of domestic, foreign, and military policies, relating to the national security."[9]

President Truman was wary of the group approach, alert to suspicions about his own qualifications to exercise his most formidable powers. At first, he rarely deigned to meet with the Council.[10] Congress had been willing to empower the president for the new tasks at hand, but not as a separate and solitary figure. Legislators had an institutional interest in surrounding the president with advisers in whom they had confidence and in bringing collective judgments to bear on the president's constitutional authority. From their perspective, the business of the chief executive had become too pressing and important to rely solely on the next election to remediate personal conceits and shortcomings. To make presidential power safe as well as effective, Congress sought to integrate it more fully into the rest of the government, its preferences mediated through information sharing and broadened with far-flung contacts.

Congress's effort to fuse unity to depth was further elaborated in the statutory provision of a staff for the Council. The staff was made up of both permanent and appointed officials, many of them detailed from the departments. By dint of its congressional mandate, the staff of the Council was a bit different from the White House staff, but though further removed, it would in time evolve into a resource for presidents more important than the Council itself.[11] Describing this resource later in his memoirs, Truman used progressive boilerplate: "a small but highly competent permanent staff which was selected for its objectivity and lack of political ties."[12] Envisioning the staff as a source of expertise and institutional memory, Congress also provided for an unassuming "executive secretary" appointed by the president to oversee it. Truman's executive secretary described himself as "an anonymous servant of the Council" who "operates only as a broker of ideas in criss-crossing proposals among a team of responsible officials."[13]

Though institutional arrangements insinuated congressional interests in a more informed and collaborative mode of operations, legislators had limited control over the follow-through. They could provide the depth, but they could not mandate its use. Moreover, they had to avoid any direct challenge to the president's constitutional position.[14] The authorizing statute implicitly "recognized and reaffirmed presidential prerogatives in foreign affairs."[15] Again, the reconciliation of two quite different conceptions of good order was left to whatever shared understandings might evolve.

By 1949, Truman had grown comfortable enough with the idea to move the Council and its staff into the Executive Office of the President.[16] Even more significant for the balance of principles was Eisenhower's appointment of a special assistant for national security affairs (now the assistant to the president for national security affairs [APNSA]). National security advisers quickly superseded the executive secretaries in control over the NSC staff, and they took over the regular meetings of the Council. Akin to members of the president's personal entourage, they are not explicitly provided for in statute nor are they subject to Senate confirmation. The whole arrangement, then, is an institutional hybrid, an improvisation testing the potential for a fruitful balance of congressional interests in depth and presidential interests in command. The Council and the staff were created by Congress to broaden the president's horizons, but they are run by an officer with no congressional connections and responsible to the president alone.[17] As Robert Cutler, Eisenhower's first pick for the position, explained, "Congress provided the vehicle, but it is in the President's discretion to do with it what he wishes."[18]

In his role as Eisenhower's agent, Cutler continued to emphasize the institutional bridges Congress had constructed to the rest of the executive branch. The Council would "integrate" all aspects of national security policy, while the "scrupulously non-political" NSC staff would be "the backbone of continuity, the reservoir of past knowledge."[19] But the tilt toward responsiveness was unmistakable, and by the 1970s, the team concept was clearly under stress. During the Nixon and Carter administrations, the secretary of state, the traditional voice of American foreign policy, competed unsuccessfully with the national security adviser for influence and presidential favor. What remained of the original idea was the priority of competence. As a rule, and with the notable exception of the Reagan era, presidents reserved the position of APNSA for a reputed star. The choice was intended to impress, to leave the president basking in the intellectual firepower of his foreign policy adviser and to instill broad confidence in their shared grasp of grand strategy.

President Trump was a foreign policy novice and an admirer of military might. The received regimen promised both competence and responsiveness, and he was willing to give it a try. His first pick for APNSA was a loyalist from his campaign but also a man of experience, retired Army General Michael Flynn. Within weeks, however, Flynn was forced to resign for lying about his pre-inauguration contacts with the Russian ambassador.[20]

Still finding his legs, the president stuck to the regimen. Recognizing that he was "getting killed with bad stories on this Flynn thing," his next pick was Lieutenant General H. R. McMaster, an active-duty military officer with a sterling reputation in the field. "The media loves McMaster," noted the president's son-in-law, Jared Kushner.[21] Trump himself unveiled his selection with a celebration of competence: "He's a man of tremendous talent and tremendous experience. . . . He is highly respected by everyone in the military."[22]

But the president did not appreciate what McMaster's competence implied. His PhD dissertation in history, published as *Dereliction of Duty*, had been an argument for depth. Its thesis was that the Joint Chiefs of Staff should have stood up to President Lyndon Johnson more firmly during the Vietnam War. McMaster was primed by his sense of history to hold his ground and assert his expertise. Trump grew weary of his briefings. As in his tense interactions with his economic policy staff over trade, the president complained about being instructed. McMaster, he said, was always trying to "teach me something."[23] The president clashed with the APNSA over the Iran nuclear deal and the Afghanistan war: "I've been hearing about this nonsense about Afghanistan for 17 years with no success. . . . I don't know what the hell we're doing."[24] Periodically, Trump would undercut his adviser publicly. When McMaster acknowledged the "incontrovertible" evidence of Russian interference in the 2016 election, Trump tweeted, "General McMaster forgot to say that the results of the 2016 election were not impacted or changed by the Russians and that the only Collusion was between Russia and Crooked H, the DNC and the Dems." Before a phone call between Trump and the Russian president Vladimir Putin in March 2018, McMaster warned Trump that American officials did not view the recent Russian election as legitimate. Trump nevertheless congratulated Putin on his victory.[25]

There were problems on both sides. While Trump did not seem to know what to do with experience and expert advice, McMaster appeared to be in denial about the administration's thinking. In his first meeting with the NSC staff, the general explained that he disliked the term "radical Islamic terrorism"—a phrase frequently used by the president—and said that the United States should be tougher in response to Russian aggression. One incredulous staffer later reported the reaction: "We got back to the office and said, 'Does he know where he's working?'" Indeed, McMaster's determination to play it straight seemed out of place, the role itself at odds with the president's wariness toward advice. And the general seemed to treat his role as a source of leverage. "What we owe the President is options," he would say, but more often than not, his presentation of "advantages and disadvantages" cut against the president's well-known preferences. When McMaster persuaded Trump to send more US troops to Afghanistan, some inside and outside the administration believed he was singularly focused on his own view of the world. And though the administration's official "National Security Strategy," unveiled by McMaster in December

2017, emphasized great-power competition akin to Trump's foreign policy themes, it also praised the North Atlantic Treaty Organization and criticized the Russian government.[26]

By dint of his single-minded insistence on the integrity of the process, McMaster's NSC "had the veneer of something that Stephen Hadley, or Condi Rice, or Susan Rice would recognize." But it didn't work. "There are two parallel tracks," one insider commented: "there's the interagency process, and then Trump makes a decision. But there's often no suggestion that he is making decisions with *reference* to that process. It's two ships in the night."[27]

McMaster's departure provided Trump an opportunity to reset. But his next APNSA only magnified the mismatch between assigned roles and presidential preferences. John Bolton was an astonishing selection. Perhaps the aim was again to instill confidence and calm in the Republican ranks, but it was hard to fathom how this pick could have been thought to facilitate unity. Bolton represented the George W. Bush style of foreign policy that Trump had roundly repudiated in his presidential campaign. Moreover, far more than McMaster, Bolton was a national celebrity in his own right. A darling of the neoconservatives, his intellectual positions and hawkish policy views were not only at odds with Trump's rhetoric but widely understood. Even those who disagreed with Bolton knew that his worldview was inextricably bound up with his identity and sense of mission. Nonetheless, Bolton jumped at the chance to serve. Somehow, he thought he could make it work. Bolton pledged he would "absolutely go along with Trump."[28] As for the president, Trump saw Bolton's celebrity as an asset: "I want someone with gravitas, not some unknown."[29] And he seemed to relish the opportunity to display his willingness to entertain different perspectives: "He has strong views on things but that's okay. I actually temper John. . . . I have different sides. I have John Bolton and other people that are a little more dovish than him."[30]

But the arrangement soured quickly. Bolton's views clashed with Trump's on national security issues involving Russia (including the subject of election interference), on Ukraine (on releasing aid to combat Russian aggression), on Venezuela (on how hard to push for regime change), on Iran (with Trump rejecting Bolton's plan to retaliate after Iran shot down an American surveillance drone), on North Korea (with Bolton skeptical of Trump's negotiations with Kim Jong-un), and on Afghanistan (over Trump's plans to meet with the Taliban).[31] The final straw, in fact, was Bolton's thinly veiled outrage at Trump's plan to invite the Taliban to Camp David to finalize American withdrawal from Afghanistan.[32] In the end the contempt was mutual: "If it was up to John," Trump quipped, "we'd be in four wars now."[33]

By this point, Trump was in no mood to defer to received standards of appointment. His fourth pick was conspicuously off the charts. Robert O'Brien was a Los Angeles attorney with close ties to the Republican Party. While he was a year into his job as the State Department's hostage negotiator and had some foreign policy experience, O'Brien was a largely unknown commodity. A senior Bush administration official worried that "he's not qualified to be national security adviser . . . he has no experience on Russia, or arms control or intelligence or covert action or Latin America. Now he's got the whole world."[34] As Trump now saw things, however, that was the attraction. Being "unknown" was now an asset. In an implicit comparison to McMaster and Bolton, one official noted that O'Brien had "no outside agenda."[35] Independent standing had become a liability; credentials had lost purchase; competence was expendable. The president said as much shortly before announcing O'Brien's appointment: "It's very easy, actually, to work with me. You know why it's easy? Because I make all the decisions. They don't have to work."[36]

O'Brien was sensitive to the point. He attempted to preempt the media charge that he was just "a loyalist who enables [Trump's] ideas instead of challenging them."[37] In a *Washington Post* column, he reached back to the traditional " 'honest broker' model of the national security adviser." Invoking the textbook description of the position, he wrote, "My job as national security adviser is to distill and present to the president the views and options that come from the various departments and agencies. The NSC then ensures that those agencies actually execute the president's decisions."[38]

Yet O'Brien did not play the part of a respectful operative with a "passion for anonymity."[39] Instead, he advanced the role of APNSA as a political mouthpiece for the president. His posturing and obfuscation on deadly serious issues did little to enhance his credibility. Asked about the underlying intelligence of an imminent Iranian attack on US embassies (intelligence invoked to justify an air strike that killed a senior Iranian leader), O'Brien led with a political point: "Well, I think the American people are behind this president."[40] Weeks later, O'Brien cast doubt on US intelligence assessments that Russia would interfere in the 2020 elections and do so with a preference for Trump. His skepticism was rhetorical: "Why would Russia want the president who has rebuilt the American military, who has given the Ukrainians lethal arms, javelin missiles and has sanctioned the Russians far more than any president in recent history, why would they want him reelected? I mean, that just doesn't make common sense."[41]

Trump's success in finding a loyalist also altered the NSC process itself. This was apparent in the way O'Brien ran meetings. While McMaster had said, "My job is not to worry about Twitter," O'Brien took the opposite approach, "sometimes open[ing] by distributing printouts of Mr. Trump's latest messaging on the subject at hand."[42] Although the NSC was originally envisioned as team play, providing the president with policy options based on the best knowledge in the executive branch, O'Brien completed its transformation into an unmediated extension of the president's ego. His approach was to convey the president's thinking and plan for its implementation. One former Trump administration official explained the contrast between Bolton and O'Brien: "Bolton was viewed as very independent and having his own agenda not necessarily aligned with POTUS. . . . O'Brien was told he was going to be the opposite.

He would carry out the instructions of POTUS and coordinate the interagency and not be a separate policymaking organization."[43] Strikingly, early on in his tenure, O'Brien simply went along with the president's decision to announce an abrupt pullout of troops from Syria. There was no NSC review at all, no detailed evaluation of the likely consequences of that course of action.[44] Destabilizing a volatile region interlaced by complicated relationships among Syria, Turkey, Russia, the Kurds, and the Islamic State, Trump's abrupt action resulted in what one senior administration official called "total chaos."[45] Similarly, O'Brien tiptoed around the president's sensitivities regarding Russia, downplaying intelligence reports that Russia was offering bounties to Taliban-affiliated fighters for killing American troops in Afghanistan.[46]

There was a concomitant change in the way O'Brien approached the NSC staff, traditionally considered an invaluable resource for presidents. As one former Trump political appointee at the NSC admitted, the president had "a high degree of paranoia that he has a bloated National Security Council full of deep-state minders who are there to undermine him, not to fulfill his national security policy."[47] Fulfilling a promise to Trump, O'Brien reduced the NSC staff by a third. Truman had admired a "small" staff, and there was agreement in some quarters that the NSC staff had grown too large. But Truman had praised the staff for its professionalism and political neutrality. By contrast, the effect of O'Brien's housecleaning was to empower the politically appointed staff, largely by transferring back career officials loaned from other departments and agencies, including the CIA, Pentagon, and State Department. The NSC was left "gutted."[48] By stripping away depth and substituting loyalty, Trump eliminated the internal pushback that he found so irritating and became freer to act on his own instincts.

"I sort of like acting": A puzzle for many observers of Trump's presidency was the record number of vacancies in executive positions and the extensive use of "acting" officials to fill political appointments.[49] Even some of the president's congressional allies

expressed frustration. "It's a lot. It's way too many," said Senator James Lankford (R-OK). "You want to have confirmed individuals there because they have a lot more authority to be able to make decisions and implement policy when you have a confirmed person in that spot."[50]

Senator Lankford said a mouthful, much of it bearing directly on the relationship between administrative appointment and a unitary executive. Consider each point in turn. First, he says that confirmed officials have "a lot more authority." But for a unitary executive, the authority of other executive officers is problematic, and perhaps especially so when their experience, their competence, and their expertise are confirmed by others. Second, Lankford suggests that confirmed officials will "make decisions." This too is a potential problem, as even political appointees may recognize that their own authority and reputation provide some wiggle room in dealing with presidential preferences and requests. Finally, Lankford suggests that confirmed officials are better able to "implement policy." In some policy areas, however, the chief executive may not share the officer's sense of responsibility for the policies under his care.

Trump is not the first president to rely on acting officials or to leave positions vacant, and to be sure, the existence of vacancies and use of interim appointments may owe more to happenstance and expediency than anything else.[51] With so many positions to fill at the beginning of an administration, it is nearly impossible for a newly elected president to begin with a complete slate of qualified officials.[52] The problem was particularly acute for Trump, because no one expected him to win the election and his preparations for taking power were unusually rudimentary.[53] Moreover, presidents will vary in the priority they assign to management and in their tolerance for loose ends. Trump may just not have cared very much.[54] And it is also possible that Trump found it more difficult than other presidents to recruit qualified people, that the Deep State is wary of serving an administration hostile to its interests.[55] But the use of vacancies and interim appointments can be matters of strategy and choice. As political scientist Christina Kinane has found, presidents who seek retrenchment in a particular policy area often purposefully leave the pertinent positions unfilled, and in areas where presidents have particular ambitions of their own to pursue, they often prefer to use an interim appointee.[56] That is to say, vacancies and interim appointments can be instruments of presidential control.

Rules regarding acting appointments were laid out in the Federal Vacancies Reform Act of 1998. If a vacancy occurs, "the first assistant to the office"—an ambiguous term not defined in the statute—becomes the acting appointee. But presidents also have discretion. They can choose to name either a senior civil servant at the agency or another senior official who had previously been subject to Senate confirmation. More important, these acting officials can serve long enough to have an impact on their departments and agencies. They can stay in an "acting" status for up to 210 days from the date the position becomes vacant. They can serve longer if the president has a nomination for the position pending before the Senate, and they get an additional 210 days if that nomination is rejected. Moreover, acting officers can continue serving while a second nomination is pending, and if that nomination is rejected, they can serve a final 210 days. All told, an acting official can be left in place for many months—and potentially years—before the position must be filled via Senate confirmation or left vacant.[57]

Congress may have thought that this housekeeping arrangement would prove mutually beneficial, that the government could remain in operation while the appointing branches gained the luxury of time to find the right people for the jobs. But Senate bypass reduces depth, allowing presidents to subordinate qualifications to their political interests. There was nothing subtle about this in the Trump administration. The president was candid about his preference for the device: "I sort of like 'acting.' It gives me more flexibility. Do you understand that? I like 'acting.'" The administration's in-house critic, "Anonymous," bemoaned the use of acting officials as contributing to a "purge of the Steady State" because interim appointees were "less inclined to ask questions and more inclined to do what they are told."[58] Here, we consider the different ways in which Trump used the device, looking at three different sites: the Office of the Director of National Intelligence, the Department of Homeland Security, and the Consumer Financial Protection Bureau.

The position of director of national intelligence (DNI) was created a few years after the 9/11 attacks. It was designed to coordinate national security policy across multiple intelligence agencies. Not unlike the APNSA, the DNI was meant to bring together the resources of the executive branch and keep the president informed. But unlike the APNSA, the DNI was made subject to Senate confirmation. And though by convention national security advisers have been officers of independent stature in their field, Congress made its preference for the appointment of a qualified DNI explicit in statute. Indeed, it made competence a directive to the president: "Any individual *nominated* for appointment as Director of National Intelligence shall have extensive national security expertise."[59]

Initially, Trump stuck with the program. His first DNI, a former long-serving senator, Dan Coats, had extensive experience on the Senate Select Committee on Intelligence. His appointment was confirmed overwhelmingly.[60] By the same token, it was hard for the president to push around a man of Coats's experience, reputation, and connection to the party establishment. On numerous occasions, Coats presented and defended assessments by the Intelligence Community at odds with the president's statements and theories. For example, tensions flared in July 2018 after Trump, standing next to Russian president Vladimir Putin at a joint news conference, undercut the Intelligence Community's unanimous assessment that Russia had intervened in the 2016 election to help elect him. "I have great confidence in my intelligence people, but I will tell you that President Putin was extremely strong and powerful in his denial [of interference] today," Trump stated. Later that same day, Coats put out a starkly contrary statement: "We have been clear in our assessments of Russian meddling in the 2016 election and their ongoing, pervasive efforts to undermine our democracy, and we will continue to provide unvarnished and objective intelligence in support of our national security."[61] With the friction between the DNI and the president growing, Coats and Trump agreed on a scheduled resignation to take effect at the end of September 2019. But in the interim, Coats objected to altering a National Intelligence Estimate (NIE) assessment that Russia sought also to influence the 2020 election in favor of Trump. Soon after, the president blindsided Coats by publicly announcing a mid-August departure date for the DNI.[62]

Seeking a course correction, Trump nominated Representative John Ratcliffe (R-TX), an ally who had impressed him with sharp and critical questioning of Special Counsel Robert Mueller in congressional hearings on the Russia investigation.[63] But even Senate Republicans had "a distinct lack of enthusiasm" for Ratcliffe's selection, and their objections, along with allegations that Ratcliffe had inflated his resume, led Trump to withdraw the nomination.[64] He then turned back to a more experienced hand, selecting the director of the National Counterterrorism Center and retired naval admiral Joseph Maguire. Notably, however, Trump bypassed the Deputy DNI Sue Gordon, a career CIA official who was the preferred nominee of many in Congress, and he appointed Maguire in an acting capacity, signaling an uncertain commitment to his choice.[65]

With Coats's early departure, the NIE assessment about Russia's aims for the 2020 election was softened to eliminate any explicit reference to Russia acting in favor of Trump. According to a senior intelligence official, this was "a way to make sure Maguire doesn't get fired."[66] Nonetheless, events soon cut short any prospect that the acting DNI would be nominated to assume the job in full. Early in 2020, Shelby Pierson, the DNI's top adviser on election security issues, echoed the original NIE assessment to the House Intelligence Committee, explaining that Russia had again "developed a preference" for Trump and was planning interference to promote his reelection. Irate at what he took to be these unending slanders on his electoral legitimacy, Trump gave Maguire "a dressing-down" in the Oval Office. He accused the DNI's staff of disloyalty and of getting "played." The acting DNI left "despondent."[67] After only six months on the job, he was out.

Trump then selected another acting official, this one having no chance of being confirmed by the Senate. An affront to the nomination standard set by statute, Ambassador to Germany Richard Grenell had "little experience in intelligence or in running a large bureaucracy." He was, however, a presidential loyalist.[68] Trump did not plan to have Grenell in that spot for the long haul (he remained ambassador as well as DNI), but an interim seemed just the thing for the job the president now wanted done. Grenell ousted his experienced deputy, Andrew Hallman, whom Senate Intelligence Committee chairman Richard Burr (R-NC) had praised for "his extensive knowledge of intelligence matters." He hired Kashyap Patel, point man for the theory of Obama administration culpability in the Russia investigation, to help "clean house," and he requested the underlying intelligence behind Pierson's briefing on Russian interference that had offended the president.[69] Grenell was put in place, it seemed, to invert the Russia narrative in time for Trump's reelection campaign.

But that was not all. With Grenell disrupting the office, Trump renominated his original preference for DNI, the loyalist Representative Ratcliffe, for Senate confirmation.[70] Because Grenell was "seen as such a provocative figure," the White House believed that "senators may be more amenable to Ratcliffe in the role now."[71] Senators recognized that the president had backed them into a corner. His dismissal of Maguire raised concerns that any future DNI might be reluctant to speak candidly to Congress. Moreover, Republicans were so apprehensive about Grenell that they were willing to contemplate any replacement. Senator Angus King (I-ME) captured the dilemma: "If we vote down [Ratcliffe], we are still left with a partisan in the position. In effect, we are choosing between Grenell and Ratcliffe."[72] At Ratcliffe's confirmation hearing, the Intelligence Committee's ranking member, Mark Warner (D-VA), put the point equally bluntly: "Some have suggested that your main qualification for confirmation to this post is that you are not Ambassador Grenell. . . . But frankly, that is not enough."[73]

Yet it quickly became clear that this *was* enough, and that the president had forced the Senate's hand. Revealingly, while Republicans now steered Ratcliffe to confirmation on a party-line vote, Senate Democrats were so eager to get Grenell out of the DNI office that they agreed to accelerate the confirmation process.[74] It was not hard to see why. Trump himself was pleased with Grenell's efforts to discredit the Russia investigation, saying on his departure, "I think you'll go down as the all-time great acting ever."[75] With the election year upon him and new Russia stories brewing, Trump had dispensed with congressional concerns about qualifications to get what he really wanted in a DNI.

Trump's use of an acting appointment to achieve loyalty from the DNI was meant to countermand expert judgments that undercut his preferred line. At the Department of Homeland Security (DHS), he used the same appointment technique to push for loyalty of a different kind.

The president's expectation at DHS was that acting appointees would more aggressively advance his programmatic interests and public messaging. The DHS and its component agencies were critical to the implementation of Trump's immigration agenda, yet the president seemed perpetually dissatisfied with their performance. There may have been officials at DHS who objected to the thrust of the White House's policies, but the more telling resistance at this site was practical. Agency officials who agreed with the president's priorities urged caution on grounds of feasibility, liability, and legality.[76] Secretary of Homeland Security Kirstjen Nielsen and others invoked such concerns time and again, pushing back on a White House proposal to release migrants apprehended at the border into "sanctuary cities" and resisting a "hastily put together" and "less than half-baked" plan for a ten-city "blitz operation" to round up undocumented immigrants. Eventually, Trump and his hard-line immigration adviser, Stephen Miller, tired of these objections and delays. Trump removed Nielsen and the leaders of the major DHS agencies as part of a pledge to go in a "tougher direction." Tellingly, his replacements were interim appointees.[77]

The most illustrative of these moves was Trump's replacement of L. Francis Cissna, the Senate-confirmed director of US Customs and Immigration Services (USCIS), with Ken Cuccinelli in an acting role. Cissna had not resisted Trump on policy grounds. He was not at all opposed to Trump's restrictive immigration agenda. On the contrary, he was the model administrator, a committed, if low-profile, subordinate. He played a key role in the administration's controversial "zero-tolerance policy," separating migrant children from their families: "If you want unlawful crossings to diminish or end, then there need to be consequences." He established an expansive "denaturalization task force" to investigate immigration fraud, and he advocated a move away from "chain migration." He sought to increase restrictions on refugee settlement in the United States, and he proposed a "public charge" rule that would restrict green card access for immigrants likely to use welfare benefits.[78] Cissna even changed the agency's mission statement, removing the line, "USCIS secures America's promise as a nation of immigrants."[79]

It is hard to imagine what more the White House could have wanted from an administrator. The problem with Cissna, however, was that he cared about the agency he ran. His expertise on immigration law and regulations and his respect for the agents in his charge contributed mightily to his effectiveness in implementing Trump's preferred policies, but this was also what proved his undoing. Cissna's experience gave him a fine-honed sense of what was feasible and of what could and could not be done unilaterally without damage to the agency. That made him enough of an annoyance to grate on White House aide Stephen Miller. In the critical test, Miller urged a surge of USCIS employees to the border in response to an increase in the number of migrants seeking asylum. In addition to dispatching asylum claims more quickly, Miller hoped that redeploying USCIS staff to the border would delay the processing of green card requests and naturalizations, and that, indirectly, Democrats supportive of more extensive provisions for legal immigration would also "feel the pain." But there was only so much that Cissna thought he could do practically and legally with redeployments. Growing more frustrated, Miller called for a "culture change" at USCIS, believing that the agency's asylum officers were being too generous in approving credible-fear asylum requests. Again, Cissna resisted, defending his agents' faithful application of the legal standards. That sealed his fate. Cissna became part of the purge at DHS. He was replaced with Cuccinelli in an acting capacity.[80]

The purpose of Cuccinelli's interim appointment was to create a frictionless conduit for the president's preferences. Had it been possible, Trump would have put him in the top position at DHS. As it was, Cuccinelli's appointment at USCIS was suspect, a brazen attempt to get around the already loose stipulations of the Federal Vacancies Reform Act. He was neither a careerist nor an officer confirmed for some other post. Moreover, he stood no chance of confirmation in the Republican-controlled Senate, for he had previously supported primary challenges to incumbent Republican senators and had drawn the ire of Majority Leader Mitch McConnell (R-KY).[81] To appoint Cuccinelli, the administration had invented a position—principal deputy director for USCIS. Doing so made him appear to be the "first assistant" and thus eligible to serve as director in an acting capacity.[82]

Soon Cuccinelli was everywhere, at the department and in the media. No mere bureaucrat, he knew that his power as an acting director derived from service as the president's direct agent, in effect as Trump's immigration spokesman: "I am an aggressive communicator of the President's immigration policies—doing that is part of why he asked me to come on board." And he had the president's ear: "I do speak to him, what I would call regularly." Unlike Cissna, Cuccinelli was willing to push the envelope to achieve Trump's desired ends. Where Cissna protected his subordinates from White House pressures, Cuccinelli directed USCIS asylum officers to be more skeptical of migrants' "frivolous" claims, and he issued a range of new rules aimed at dispensing with asylum requests more quickly.[83] As an outside ally from an interest group advocating more restrictive immigration policies put it, "Cuccinelli doesn't know the guts of what USCIS does in a granular way, but his approach to moving the bureaucracy is as a kind of a bully pulpit. I don't know if that's more effective [than Cissna] or not, but it seems to be working."[84]

And it continued to work even as Cuccinelli's status at DHS grew murkier. His appointment at USCIS was ruled unlawful by DC District Court Judge Randolph Moss, who criticized the administration for having "created a position that is second in command in name only."[85] The Government Accountability Office declared his appointment as second-in-command at DHS invalid.[86] But the episode made crystal clear the attraction of acting officers for a unitary executive. Cuccinelli used "every tool in the toolbox" in pursuit of the president's priorities.[87] He accomplished much of the president's agenda while questions about the legality of his appointment were pending.

The weaponization of acting appointments at the Consumer Financial Protection Bureau (CFPB) reflected a third strategy. This was not, as with the DNI, a case of a president looking to make the agency more pliable, nor was it, as at DHS, an attempt to accelerate work on a priority program. The intent at CFPB was not to take over the agency; it was to take it down.

Established in the Dodd-Frank Wall Street Reform and Consumer Protection Act of 2010, the CFPB was the inspiration of Harvard Law professor (and later Democratic senator) Elizabeth Warren of Massachusetts. The agency had never been through a presidential transition, and from the start of the Trump administration, both sides knew what was coming. The CFPB was a flagship of progressive reform and a priority target on the Republican hit list. Claiming that "Financial Institutions have been devastated" by the bureau, Trump had renounced it as a "total disaster."[88]

But the CFPB had been designed for just such a battle. Its programmatic mission was to protect consumers from abuse by those selling financial products, but for its sponsors, the first order of business had been to fortify the agency to protect itself. To that end, Democrats in Congress created an institutional hybrid. Their improvisations prioritized depth without sacrificing muscular direction. The agency was given a single director, but that officer was set up to operate independently. Adapting a device usually reserved for commissions and boards, the director was to serve a fixed five-year term, removable only for cause. Another limit on the agency's political exposure was its unique funding structure. Circumventing Congress's annual appropriations process, the budget of the CFPB came directly from the Federal Reserve Board. Equally remarkable was the fact that the director was the sole political appointee of the agency. It was careerists all the way down.[89] In virtually every respect, this agency was an affront to executive branch unity. Insulation was the watchword of the whole arrangement.

When Trump took office, Richard Cordray, the Obama-appointed director of CFPB, still had more than a year left to serve on his five-year term. Cordray was no stranger to controversy. Initially one of Obama's recess appointments, he had fallen victim to a legal challenge successfully restricting the president's use of a Senate recess to bypass the confirmation process.[90] His confirmation slipped through later as part of a compromise over the use of filibusters to block presidential appointments.[91] The Trump administration was planning a court challenge of its own, this one targeting the anomaly of a bureau with a single director who was insulated from removal by the president.[92] But events prompted a more direct and immediate intervention.

In November 2017, Cordray decided to resign in order to run for governor of Ohio, and in preparing for his departure, he plotted with his leadership team to preempt a presidential interim appointment to replace him. If Cordray saw the handwriting on the wall at CFPB, he had no intention of leaving his agency defenseless.[93] Seizing upon statutory language that the deputy director shall "serve as Director in the absence or unavailability of the Director," he shifted his chief of staff, Leandra English, into the deputy director slot, and upon resigning, he declared that English would serve as acting director.[94]

Cordray's impertinence evoked a stiff response. On the very night that the director announced English's elevation, Trump announced that Mick Mulvaney—already serving as the Senate-confirmed director of the Office of Management and Budget (OMB)—would take on the additional post of acting director of CFPB.[95] That drew the battle lines politically and structurally. A former member of the House Financial Services Committee, Mulvaney had made his thinking clear. He was on the record saying that he "would like to get rid of" the CFPB, and he had cosponsored legislation to that end.[96] Trump's appointment was authorization to do the deed administratively. To sweep away any legal obstacles, the president backed up his move with an opinion from the Office of Legal Counsel stating that the president's appointment authority superseded the procedures outline in the CFPB statute: "The fact that the Deputy Director may serve as Acting Director by operation of the statute . . . does not displace the President's authority under the Vacancies Reform Act."[97] English, however, refused to stand down. She filed a suit seeking a temporary injunction to block Mulvaney's appointment: "The President's attempt to appoint a still-serving White House staffer to displace the acting head of an independent agency is contrary to the overall statutory design and independence of the bureau."[98]

For the CFPB, the contest was about the survival of the mission. For many in service at the agency, loyalty was to the program, and that test of wills inevitably pitted the Deep State conspiracy against the unitary executive. The two acting directors, English and Mulvaney, personified the phantom twins. The next day both of them showed up for work, ready to assume the duties of director. Anticipating an attempt by Mulvaney to take control, English staked her ground in an email that directed the senior staff to maintain their existing authority: "I am, in my capacity as acting Director, hereby ratifying all existing delegations of authority to the Bureau's senior leadership team."[99] Mulvaney soon countered, instructing all agency personnel to "disregard any instructions you receive from Ms. English in her presumed capacity as acting director." Sensing her vulnerability, English spent the rest of the day cultivating her congressional allies, but strategizing with Elizabeth Warren and other Democratic leaders on Capitol Hill did little to bridge the perception gap.[100]

Whatever cover English might have provided for the agency was quickly stripped away. The CFPB's own counsel, Mary McLeod, agreed with the OLC's opinion that Mulvaney's appointment was valid. Noting that this had been the "oral advice" she had already given "to the Senior Leadership Team," McLeod "advised all Bureau personnel to act consistently with the understanding that Director Mulvaney is the Acting Director of the CFPB."[101] Shortly thereafter, English's effort to obtain an emergency injunction was denied by the DC District Court.[102] Mulvaney now had a free hand to clamp down on the resistance brewing below.

Around the time of his departure, Cordray had mused that "this part of the agency's history is as important as the rocky beginnings. We have to be able to survive changes in administration." But continuity across administrations assumes some common ground, some basis of cooperation around a shared objective, and in this instance, that was notable for its absence. Employees were dumbfounded by Mulvaney's effort to put a business-friendly face on the mission of consumer protection. The acting director said that the CFPB should be for "everyone: those who use credit cards, and those who provide those cards; those who take loans, and those who make them; those who buy cars, and those who sell them." The reaction within was one of outrage: "It's a hell of a document . . . it pushes the envelope of 'Corporations are people, too.' "[103] One group of agency officials consciously acknowledged their surreptitious purposes by adopting the moniker "Dumbledore's Army," the name of the Hogwarts student resistance group in *Harry Potter and the Order of the Phoenix*. Using encrypted messaging apps to communicate with each other, career officials leaked internal bureau disputes to the media.[104] Mulvaney was having none of it. In an agency-wide email, he called out employees who "might be interested in undermining [his] leadership," and he threatened to have the inspector general investigate the media leaks.[105] He cited the president's election as the basis of his authority to revamp the agency: "Anybody who thinks that a Trump administration CFPB would be the same as an Obama administration CFPB is simply being naïve. Elections have consequences at every agency."[106]

As an acting director holding another, more important port-folio, Mulvaney was not in it for the long haul. He was not looking to adapt the agency to the new administration's priorities. He was there to strip it of the wherewithal to act and to reduce it to an ir-relevance. And he did not disappoint. Mulvaney requested $0 from the Fed for the CFPB's first quarter budget in 2018, and he urged the American Bankers Association to lobby Congress to change the CFPB funding structure.[107] He altered the agency's mission state-ment to provide for the removal of "burdensome regulations."[108] He fired all twenty-five members of the agency's Consumer Advisory Board after some of its members questioned his decision to cancel their legally required meetings.[109] He even appointed a "Name Correction Group" in an effort to rob the agency of its identifying acronym.[110]

Other actions were more consequential. Mulvaney pulled back on the agency's rulemaking, halting efforts to tighten rules regarding student loans and payday lending.[111] He stripped the CFPB's Office of Fair Lending and Equal Opportunity, which investigated discriminatory practices, of its enforcement powers.[112] No new cases about financial discrimination were opened.[113] Those cases that did go forward were settled at what career employees referred to as "The Mulvaney Discount."[114]

The key element of Mulvaney's takedown was the deployment of new political appointees. Career employees fumed at this violation of legislative intent, but Mulvaney was unperturbed, believing the careerists were every bit as political as he was: "Maybe they didn't think they needed to have any political people here because a lot of the people here were political anyway."[115] Mulvaney's method of Deep State control was to pair each senior career officer in charge of a bureau division—the "associate directors"—with a new political appointee that he selected—"policy associate directors." These new positions included a number of hires who had worked for Representative Jeb Hensarling (R-TX), a critic of CFPB and the chair of the House Financial Services Committee. Mulvaney then directed the new political appointee overseeing enforcement, Eric Blankenstein, to require lengthy memos to justify the continuation of any ongoing enforcement actions. Cases languished while awaiting a response to the memos.[116] At the same time, Mulvaney decided that civil investigative demands—a process by which the CFPB could ask for information from lenders—could only be approved by Blankenstein, further slowing the pace of investigations.[117] As one bureau attorney complained, "It has all ground to a halt. . . . It's sort of 'Hurry up and wait.' And it's very much by design. They want everyone to leave."[118]

Mulvaney's one-year stint as acting director of CFPB was a near-complete rout. Even as consumer complaints rose, the CFPB's enforcement actions declined by 75 percent. Only one case was opened against debt collectors, even though debt collection was the subject of most consumer complaints. Morale among employees plunged, and as a temporary hiring freeze at the agency was extended indefinitely, the agency workforce dropped precipitously.[119] Mulvaney was rewarded for his services with a promotion, becoming Trump's acting chief of staff in late 2018. By the time the Supreme Court ruled on the Trump administration's constitutional challenge to the statutory insulation of the position of CFPB director from presidential removal in June 2020, the decision was something of an anticlimax. As English put it, "much of the CFPB's core mission has been abandoned and its protections for consumers dismantled."[120]

What *Seila Law v. CFPB* added was a ringing endorsement of the unitary executive theory. The five-to-four decision written by Chief Justice John Roberts held that the statutory leadership structure of the agency "violate[d] the separation of powers." Writing for the four other conservatives on the Court, Roberts bought the whole package, not only that the "entire 'executive Power' belongs to the President alone" but also that "the Framers made the President the most democratic and politically accountable official in Government."[121]

Breaching the merit line: As a rule, political appointees promote executive branch unity. If Trump's approach to their deployment has been shocking, it is because it has stripped bare all qualifications on that objective and exposed the full effect of unmediated presidential direction. But political appointees can go only so far in reducing depth. Below them lies the ballast of the executive branch, the merit-based appointees. Civil service qualifications on appointment and removal present a formidable statutory impediment to unitary control. Nixon had complained about it. The Carter reforms had softened it up. The Trump administration utilized its working theory to plunge ahead.

In 2017, James Sherk, then an adviser on Trump's Domestic Policy Council, wrote a memo on the reform of personnel policy suggesting exploration of the "Constitutional Option." Echoing the unitary theory, he argued "that Article II executive power gives the president inherent authority to dismiss any federal employee.

This implies civil service legislation and union contracts impeding that authority are unconstitutional."[122] In the spring of 2018, the president followed up with a set of executive orders stripping away union protections for federal workers and giving political appointees a freer hand in disciplinary and removal proceedings against them.[123] According to public administration scholar Paul Light, changes along these lines launched "the biggest assault on the nation's civil service system since the 1883 Pendleton Act ended the spoils system."[124] Though the orders were tied up for a time in the courts, the assault was open-ended and anticipated more sweeping action to come. Other administration initiatives were more targeted and more immediate in effect. For example, the Trump administration exempted the appointment of US marshals from the competitive exam system, and it empowered a political appointee to overturn decisions by immigration judges. Ashley Tabaddor, the president of the National Association of Immigration Judges, denounced the latter move for "collapsing the policymaking role with the adjudication role into a single individual."[125]

Here we focus on another targeted change: the method of appointment for administrative law judges (ALJs). Next to the other cases we have reviewed thus far in this chapter, the changes set in motion with regard to the appointment of ALJs are comparatively technical, and the questions raised are more subtle. They do not split observers sharply along the predictable political lines, and the administration's follow-up had little of the bombast and bravado of the appointment battles that have played out in public view. But taken in conjunction with initiatives on other fronts, the thrust of these changes is unmistakable and their implications are profound. They upended some old progressive nostrums, and they significantly advanced the conception of executive branch unity that the conservative legal movement had been elaborating for decades.[126]

Described as both the "hidden judiciary" and "the workhorses of the administrative state," the ALJs serve within the agencies, outside the Article III judicial system. They "preside over thousands of hearings annually in areas such as disability benefits, international trade, taxation, environmental law, occupational safety, and communications law."[127] Congress anchored the position in the Administrative Procedure Act (APA) of 1946, the cornerstone of the modern administrative establishment. Originally referring to ALJs as "hearing examiners," the APA put some distance between their adjudicatory functions and the policy-making apparatus of the agencies. The idea was to re-create, so far as possible, a separation of powers within the administrative realm and "to keep examiners free of agency pressure."[128] The position was insulated by civil service protections on appointment and removal. Federal agencies had to select examiners from a shortlist of applicants deemed qualified by the Civil Service Commission, and the examiners could not be removed without cause.[129]

The APA was a progressive settlement of the question of how to reconcile administrative depth with the American Constitution. Just as it provided for public participation through notice-and-comment rulemaking on the policy side of agency work, it provided protections for independent proceedings and the rule of law on the judicial side. An elegant articulation of the administrative realm, the APA assumed broad support for forms of executive branch authority that were only loosely bound by formal constitutional controls. But as depth in all of its manifestations has become a more contested proposition for executive branch organization, so too have the APA's guiding principles. Questions that once seemed happily resolved now appear fraught. It was this newfound sense of vulnerability that prompted proponents of the unitary theory of the executive to take aim at the ALJs. *Bloomberg Businessweek* called it "Trump's War on 'Deep State' Judges."[130] In this instance, the administration was able to seize upon an opportunity it had helped to create through the appointment of Article III judges favorably disposed to its unitary precepts. It took its case to the Court.

The administration joined in an appeal of a case involving questions about how ALJs at the Securities and Exchange

Commission (SEC) were selected. The specifics involved a former radio host, Raymond Lucia. In 2013, Cameron Eliot, an ALJ at the SEC, found Lucia guilty of significantly misleading investors. He was fined $300,000 and barred from being a registered financial consultant. The Trump administration joined Lucia's appeal in November 2017, urging the Supreme Court to consider the question of whether ALJs were merely government employees or "inferior officers" of the United States.[131]

Pressing this distinction was of considerable interest to the business community. The US Chamber of Commerce thought that the method of appointing ALJs at the SEC "materially and adversely affects the rights and interests of business." But the case opened onto much larger questions about the separation of adjudication from politics in the operations of the executive branch. Believing its ALJs to be government employees, the SEC had allowed its career staff to select them from the civil service certified list of qualified applicants. But if, as the Trump administration argued, the ALJs were "inferior officers," they could, under constitutional provision, only be chosen by the president, courts, or heads of departments. In an immediate reaction to the Trump administration's decision to support the appeal, the SEC commissioners—equivalent to the head of department—altered their procedures and began to appoint the ALJs themselves. Sensing that a wide range of administrative cases could be called into question and overturned on appeal, the commissioners also formally ratified all the ALJ appointments that had previously been made by the staff.[132]

The administration's brief to the Court sizzled with unitary precepts. Solicitor General Noel Francisco outlined the connection between the vesting clause and the appointments clause of Article II. "The Constitution vests '[t]he executive Power' of the United States in the President," argued Francisco, but "the President would need to rely on the assistance of subordinate officials." Therefore, he continued, the Constitution allowed the establishment of additional "Officers of the United States." While principal officers would be appointed by the president with Senate consent, Article II states that "inferior Officers" could be specified in law as being appointed by "the President alone, in the Courts of Law, or in the Heads of Departments." The ALJs, Francisco then posited, should be classified as " 'inferior officers' rather than 'mere employees.'" They exercised "governmental authority" on behalf of the SEC in holding administrative law hearings, and despite possible appeals to the SEC and the courts, in practice, an ALJ's "initial decision" often stood as final. For Francisco, this circumstance of significant and often final authority meant that the ALJs had to be considered "inferior officers." Going further, Francisco revealed the administration's full intent. He urged the Court to consider the possibility that if the ALJs were "inferior officers," any restrictions on their removal should also be overturned. As Francisco suggested, "the question [of] whether the Commission's ALJs are impermissibly insulated from presidential oversight is informed by the conclusion that such ALJs are constitutional officers who exercise significant authority."[133]

In its June 2018 decision, the Supreme Court ruled that ALJs at the SEC are "Officers of the United States," constituting "a class of government officials distinct from mere employees," and therefore subject to the appointments clause.[134] The majority opinion was written by a supporter of "presidential administration" and an Obama appointee, Elena Kagan. Kagan was joined by all the justices on the conservative side: John Roberts, Anthony Kennedy, Clarence Thomas, Samuel Alito, and Neil Gorsuch. While garnering broad support from the conservatives for her opinion that ALJs were inferior officers, Kagan tried to craft the decision narrowly.[135] She held that Lucia was due a new hearing by an ALJ appointed by the SEC commissioners themselves, but she did not address broader questions about qualifications and she declined to take the bait on removal authority.[136] In her opinion, the issue could be resolved by a technical correction.

Others took a wider view. Thomas and Gorsuch, the concurring justices, used the occasion to lay some groundwork for broader changes. They tiptoed toward a stronger endorsement of the unitary precepts articulated in James Sherk's 2017 memo on personnel policy. While their concurrence did not assert a presidential claim to direct control over ALJs, it did suggest that the framers of the Constitution would have considered *any* official in the executive branch to be subject to the appointments clause: "The Founders likely understood the term 'Officers of the United States' to encompass all federal civil officials who perform an ongoing, statutory duty—no matter how important or significant the duty." Moreover, they described the purported benefits of the appointments clause in terms familiar to unitarians, saying "the Appointments Clause maintains clear lines of accountability—encouraging good appointments and giving the public someone to blame for bad ones."[137] For an administration looking for a signal regarding its larger ambitions in rolling back civil service protections, this language flashed unmistakably green.

The other opinions in the case also recognized the stakes at issue and indicated concern about their broader implications. In a separate opinion, Justice Stephen Breyer, a longtime defender of progressive administration, sought to avoid ruling the appointment illegal on constitutional grounds. He thought the correction would rest more safely on statutory reasoning. He implored the Court to "decide no more" than was necessary. Breyer was clear-eyed about the potential risk that ALJs, as "inferior officers," would become subject to at-will removal: "to hold that the administrative law judges are 'Officers of the United States' is, *perhaps*, to hold that their removal protections are unconstitutional. This would risk transforming administrative law judges from independent adjudicators into *dependent* decisionmakers, serving at the pleasure of the Commission." Speculating further, Breyer worried that applying such a potential rule "to high-level civil servants threatens to change the nature of our merit-based civil service as it has existed from the time of President Chester Alan Arthur."[138] If, as the Court's unitarians were implying, every employee in the executive branch was an officer of one sort or another, Breyer reasoned, the strong qualifications on politicized administration reflected in the APA and the civil service rules would lie fully exposed.

The dissenters in the case, Justices Sonia Sotomayor and Ruth Bader Ginsburg, likewise worried about the implications of Thomas's concurrence and tried to suggest an alternative. Sotomayor noted that the question of whether the ALJs were in fact the final authority was clouded by the potential for an appeal of ALJ decisions to the SEC commissioners. She insisted that the Court had "yet to articulate the types of powers that will be deemed significant enough to constitute 'significant authority.'" Feeling the foundations shift and sensing that they might give way, Sotomayor called upon the Court to draw some firmer distinctions and to rearticulate boundaries: "Confirming that final decision making authority is a prerequisite to officer status would go a long way to aiding Congress and the Executive Branch in sorting out who is an officer and who is a mere employee."[139]

The Trump administration did not wait for further clarification. Nor did it rest content with Kagan's narrowly focused reasoning about the appointment of ALJs at the SEC. Instead, it seized upon the spirit of Thomas's concurrence to expand the reach of the *Lucia* ruling. Within a month of the Court's decision, Trump issued an executive order. In it, he interpreted the *Lucia* decision to mean that "at least some—and perhaps all—ALJs are 'Officers of the United States' and thus subject to the Constitution's Appointments Clause." He then took aim at the merit-based appointment procedures prescribed by the APA. He exempted ALJs from the competitive examinations administered by the Office of Personnel Management (OPM, the successor to the Civil Service Commission). Political appointees were to gain greater control and discretion. The shift was meant to "provide agency heads with additional flexibility to assess prospective appointees without the limitations imposed by competitive examination and competitive service selection procedures."[140]

In conjunction with that order, the solicitor general issued a memo concluding that the ruling should not be bound to the SEC but should be taken to apply more widely: "The Department of Justice understands the Court's reasoning, however, to encompass all ALJs in traditional and independent agencies who preside over adversarial administrative proceedings and possess the adjudicative powers highlighted by the *Lucia* majority." Francisco explained that DOJ would no longer defend the position that any ALJs were "employees rather than inferior officers." Moreover, Francisco went further in considering the removal power question the Court had declined to address. Although he suggested DOJ could defend some degree of insulation for ALJs from presidential removal, his memo stipulated that the department would take that position in a case only if the Merit Systems Protection Board's review was "suitably deferential to the determination of the Department Head" on a rationale for removal. Only such deference would give "the President a constitutionally adequate degree of control over ALJs."[141]

Reactions to the Court's ruling and the president's order were mixed.[142] Criticisms of the ALJ selection process had been brewing for some time, and the "reforms effectuated by the executive order were welcomed by many agencies that for decades felt hamstrung by the OPM hiring process."[143] Scholars had previously raised the possibility of designating ALJs "inferior officers."[144] They did not, however, all follow the implications of that designation to the same conclusion. One proposal was to take the appointment of ALJs out of the executive branch and to give the power to the DC Circuit Court. The appointments clause allows for appointment by the courts of law, and that method promises to alleviate the obvious concern that the demise of merit appointment will politicize these positions.[145]

Opinion at the Federalist Society, the intellectual seedbed of the unitary theory, was understated. "President Trump's ALJ EO hardly deconstructs the administrative state. To that end, 'tis but a scratch," wrote a lawyer on the society's website. But there was no denying that this was part of a broader ambition: "this modest tweak to how ALJs are selected is a step in the right direction towards the perhaps somewhat more ambitious goal of re-constitutionalizing the administrative state."[146] Other reactions were less sanguine. The Association of Administrative Law Judges pulled no punches, predicting that the move would "lead to cronyism and replace independent and impartial adjudicators with those who do the bidding of political appointees."[147] Congress expressed concerns as well. Senator Susan Collins (R-ME) introduced a bill to restore the ALJs to the competitive service.[148]

Whatever the arguments for and against this shift in the method of ALJ appointments, the change fits the pattern of stripping away depth in executive branch operations. Trump's assault on the ALJs was largely free of the fireworks that characterized his approach to appointments more generally, but it was part of the same campaign to elevate unitary concerns for political responsiveness and hierarchical control over traditional concerns for insulation and neutrality. A mere scratch to some, the movement on this front stands out as part of a long game for tearing at the soft underbelly of administrative authority. Its advocates have laid the groundwork for a bolder, more sweeping campaign against any civil service protections for policy-making personnel. They now have an elaborated theory of the Constitution and a new slate of sympathetic Article III judges at their back.

The final frontier: Of all of Congress's administrative improvisations, the most insulting to the idea of a unitary executive are the independent boards and commissions. These agencies place enormous power outside the "regular" executive branch. Their directors are removable only for cause, thus operating beyond the president's direct control. As Brett Kavanaugh, Trump's second appointment to the Supreme Court, put it, the way to ensure that these agencies are "more accountable to the people [is] by giving the elected and accountable President greater control over the agency (by making the heads of agencies removable at will, not for cause)."[149]

The irritation at this interface has flared since the New Deal, when the Court affirmed Congress's authority to appoint officers for fixed terms, and when, in response, Franklin Roosevelt's Committee on Administrative Management tried unsuccessfully to overhaul the independent agencies and transfer their policy-making authority into the regular department structure.[150] This remains the final frontier for unitary ambitions. The Trump administration took a big step toward increasing presidential influence over the independent agencies by making those agencies' proposed rules subject to review by OMB's Office of Information and Regulatory Affairs.[151] But the removal power remains a sticking point. The fixed and staggered terms of service at these agencies limit presidential influence even when, through sequential appointments, the president's people eventually gain control.

This is a lesson that presidents have had to learn time and again in interactions with the Federal Reserve Board (the Fed), the most powerful of these agencies. The Fed's control over the money supply and interest rates can make or break a presidency. Still, Congress has managed to resist pressures to subject the Fed to more direct presidential control. In a struggle with Roosevelt over the Banking Act of 1935, Congress granted the Board sweeping new powers, but it drew a line against the administration's proposal to make the chair and vice chair serve at the pleasure of the president.[152] The 1970s—the decade of stagflation—ramped up the friction between presidents and Fed chairs.[153] As a presidential candidate in 1976, Jimmy Carter called for a new settlement. Believing the president should "have a Chairman of the Federal Reserve whose economic views are compatible with his own," he proposed giving the Fed chair a four-year term coterminous with the term of the president. To make his proposal more palatable, Carter agreed to Senate confirmation of the chairman.[154] Still, his initiative was seen as an untoward bid for presidential influence. Once again, the Senate derailed it. It not only rejected the idea of coterminous appointment; it added the requirement for Senate confirmation for good measure.[155]

President Trump raised tensions with the Federal Reserve chairman to a new level. Never was the case for executive branch unity and democratic accountability quite so candidly arrayed against the case for administrative insulation and political independence. Trump used his opportunity to appoint the Fed chair as a way to send a message of intent. Breaking with a precedent set by the three previous presidents, he declined to reappoint the incumbent. He replaced Obama's Fed chairwoman, Janet Yellen, with another Fed governor, Jerome Powell. Powell was the first Fed chair in decades without a degree in economics. Nonetheless, he was deemed a safe and competent choice. His nomination had been vouched for by Treasury Secretary Steven Mnuchin, a former chief information officer at Goldman Sachs. The Fed's core constituency, Wall Street, was satisfied.[156]

But Trump quickly learned the lesson of his predecessors. Fed chairs have their own views, and their independence gives them the authority to resist presidential preferences. Angry at the Fed's decisions to begin incrementally raising interest rates back to pre-2008 levels, Trump launched a public campaign to bend the Fed chairman to his will. While acknowledging the "theory" of Fed independence, Trump intimated a betrayal of his expectations in appointing Powell: "He was supposed to be a low interest-rate guy. It's turned out that he's not."[157] Moreover, the president explicitly contrasted his own economic instincts with the qualifications of Fed officials in judging what to do about interest rates: "They're making a mistake because I have a gut, and my gut tells me more sometimes than anybody else's brain can ever tell me."[158] Fearing that Powell would turn him "into Hoover," Trump began to muse about finding a way to fire or replace the Fed chair.[159]

Unsurprisingly, Trump's unitary pretensions evoked strong claims of independence from his adversary. "Nothing will deter us from doing what we think is the right thing to do," Powell asserted when raising rates at the end of 2018. "Political considerations have played no role whatsoever in our discussions and decisions."[160] When reports surfaced that the president had considered trying to replace him, Powell cited his statutory protections for independence. Asked whether the president could fire him, Powell replied, "Well, the law is clear that I have a four-year term. And I fully intend to serve it." To put a fine point on it, Powell connected those protections to the Fed's great power: "Our decisions on rates can't be reversed by any other part of government."[161]

The Fed chair bolstered his statutory insulation from presidential ire by drawing on his support from Congress and outside interests. Powell held hundreds of meetings with lawmakers, and he made a conspicuous display of them.[162] The then-chairman of the House Financial Services Committee, Republican Jeb Hensarling, provided cover: "I am generally impressed with Chairman Powell's leadership."[163] The Senate quashed the president's attempts to change the Fed's direction with new appointments to the board, scuttling several nominees who were deemed unqualified.[164] Powell's predecessor, Janet Yellen, offered him praise as well: "He's doing extremely well."[165] Wall Street trusted Powell's qualifications and judgment far more than the instincts of the president. The chief economist at Pantheon Macroeconomics, for example, wrote to clients, "We're pretty sure that Jay Powell does not want to go down in history as the Fed Chair who was pushed around by an economically illiterate president."[166] As the economic contraction from the coronavirus pandemic set in, one policy economist likewise emphasized, "The market trusts Jerome Powell to do what monetary policy can do. Jerome Powell gets it."[167]

Yet another source of Powell's independence stemmed from the Fed's internal structure. The agency had arrangements of its own, beyond the statutory protection that prevented presidential removal of members of the board of governors. The point came up when Trump broached the possibility of demoting the Fed chair rather than removing him outright, a question of authority fraught with ambiguity and one that would have certainly been challenged in court. But, as one Fed official pointed out, the selection of the Fed chair as the chair of the Federal Open Market Committee (FOMC)—the mechanism through which the chair exercises influence in monetary policy—is not mandated by statute; it is only a norm. Thus, the official suggested, if the president demoted Powell, he could still be selected as FOMC chair, effectively leaving any new board chair powerless. Moreover, unlike the board, several members of the FOMC are not subject to presidential appointment. The New York Fed president and the presidents of four of the other eleven regional banks (on a rotating basis) comprise five votes on the FOMC, and they are selected by their banks' private boards of directors (with the final approval of the Fed board of governors).[168]

This is the final frontier for unity in the executive branch, and for now, it remains far out of reach. The Fed's insulation runs particularly deep. As Trump once admitted to Powell in a phone call, "I guess I'm stuck with you."[169] The president was reduced to blame-shifting and credit-claiming. When Powell took actions he did not like, Trump characterized an unaccountable Fed as "the biggest risk" to the nation's economy.[170] But when, in response to the coronavirus's impact on the economy, the Fed "embarked on the quickest and most massive response to a crisis in its more than 100-year history," Trump was eager to claim credit: "I really think he's caught up. He's stepped up over the last week. I called him today and I said, 'Jerome, good job.'"[171]

9
Depth in Oversight

The theory of the unitary executive leverages the presidency's many strategic advantages as an instrument of control. It has always been difficult for Congress to compete head-on with the singularity and visibility of that office, with its purview and resources, with its efficiency, hierarchy, and secrecy. Constitutional claims that elevate exclusivity over collaboration in management of a burgeoning executive branch maximize those assets. But difficult as it is for legislators to hold their own against an uncooperative president, the "first branch" is not easily sidelined.[1] Elaborating upon its oversight authority in the face of aggressive assertions of presidential power, Congress has significantly bolstered its role as an administration "watchdog." These new methods for surveillance of the executive branch are of interest to us because they clearly align Congress on the side of depth against unity, and because, in doing so, they set the underlying issues of constitutional design in the starkest possible relief.

Lawmakers have a keen interest in keeping abreast of the activities of those who administer the programs they enact and in uncovering evidence of executive branch wrongdoing. Those interests are sharpened when programmatic government expands its reach and executive branch operations become more highly politicized. But legislators do not make a very effective constabulary. They have too many other responsibilities. Surveilling the administrative sphere proactively and systematically, like "police patrols," would put an enormous strain on their time and resources. Scholars speak of Congress's preference for "fire alarms"— mechanisms that make it easy for others to alert legislators to problems demanding their attention.[2] That interest in notification has led to, among other things, Congress enlisting administrators more formally as eyes and ears—surrogate overseers—and insulating them from retribution by their political supervisors. Statutes created new positions for investigating executive branch activities and specified procedures for processing complaints. These laws invited subordinates to flag anything they observed on the job that might pose a threat to good order and the rule of law and to keep the legislature apprised of those concerns. Protections extended to administrators for this purpose now riddle the executive branch hierarchy, deepening specifically administrative forms of authority and compromising the pretensions of presidents to unitary control.

Congress's investments in new oversight capacities link two acutely unsettling events in the recent history of the executive branch: the impeachment proceedings against Richard Nixon and the first impeachment proceedings against Donald Trump.[3] The Nixon hearings were spurred by information provided covertly by an administrative informant, the person called Deep Throat.[4] They ushered in the new age of political suspicion and institutional confrontation and prompted Congress to codify a new oversight regime. The Trump impeachment put those new surveillance mechanisms on full display. Ultimately, they split the executive branch, pulling administrators into Congress's orbit and pitting them against the president more explicitly than ever before. With executive branch officers at the center of the prosecution's case, the confrontation devolved into a raw test of institutional power and political advantage, and the phantom twins took flight.

Like the Watergate scandal, Trump's Ukraine scandal presented an odd twist on the Deep State charge. In both, the president appeared the conspirator. Trump was accused of abusing his power by conducting a shadow foreign policy for personal political advantage. Pursuant to a stated government policy of countering Russian military aggression, Congress had appropriated $391 million in assistance to Ukraine. Trump withheld that aid, using it to engage in an extended, multi-front effort to pressure the Ukrainian government to open investigations into unsubstantiated rumors of Democratic interference in the 2016 election and into alleged corruption by former Vice President Joe Biden and his son Hunter. At the time, Biden was considered the most likely Democratic presidential nominee and a formidable challenger to Trump's reelection effort. During a phone call with Ukrainian president Volodymyr Zelensky on July 25, 2019, Trump appeared to make the deal—military-aid-for-political-investigations—explicit: "I would like you to do us a favor, though."[5] Following up, the EU ambassador and Trump donor Gordon Sondland and a State Department envoy, Kurt Volker, drafted a public statement for the Ukrainian president that would trigger release of the aid by committing the country to opening the investigations.[6] At the penultimate moment, the Ukrainian president made preparations to announce the investigations on CNN.[7]

This episode raised several important issues. There were questions about strong-arming an ally for domestic political purposes, about election law violations, about the president's impoundment authority (his power to withhold congressional appropriations made for an explicit purpose without notice), and about whether any of this activity ascended to the level of an impeachable offense. But the focus of our attention lies elsewhere. In fact, much of the political force behind these questions was mooted by a sudden turnaround. Just two days before he was to get exactly what he wanted, Trump released the aid, and the Ukrainian president canceled his public announcement of investigations. Congress, unaware at that time of why the funds were being withheld, had begun to ask questions, but the issue was close enough to the desired resolution to put off the discontent brewing on that front, and a post-announcement release of the funds would have remained within the budgetary window available to make the expenditure.[8] The immediate reason for the president's reversal came not from Congress, but from deep within the state. Trump had learned of the existence of a damaging whistleblower report about his activities regarding Ukraine.[9]

The president, the whistleblower, and the watchdog: Congress laid the groundwork for flagging behavior like this in 1978. The Inspector General Act and the whistleblower provisions of the Civil Service Reform Act, both enacted that year, provided legislators with greater access to activities within the executive branch. Each statute sought to counter the development of a closed administrative hierarchy and to redress perceived constitutional imbalances in the control of information. More than that, the statutes were passed concurrently and understood to work in tandem. In hearings on the IG legislation, Andrew Feinstein, testifying for the group Congress Watch, underscored this point: "we see the Inspector General bill containing the potential for fitting in very neatly with the whistle-blower protections." When Senator Thomas Eagleton (D-MO) questioned witnesses in Senate hearings about "the connection" between these two acts, they too emphasized their complementarity. The House Governmental Operations subcommittee counsel, James Naughton, explained that a whistleblower could "go to the Inspector General and present to him on a confidential basis information concerning action that needs to be taken."[10] IGs would then inform their superiors and alert Congress to any urgent concerns. Congress subsequently provided additional whistleblower protections, including its enactment of the Intelligence Community Whistleblower Protection Act (ICWPA) in 1998 to address national security policy.

The authorization of whistleblowers and IGs to advance Congress's interests in administrative oversight sat at the center of the Ukraine affair, and it immediately became a flashpoint in the contest between depth and collective control on the one side and unity and hierarchical control on the other. It was Trump's July phone call with the Ukrainian president that had prompted the whistleblower report. A CIA officer with an understanding of Ukrainian politics wrote to the inspector general of the Intelligence

Community (ICIG), drawing directly on language in the 1998 statute: "I am reporting an 'urgent concern' in accordance with the procedures outlined in 50 U.S.C. § 3033(k)(5)(A)." The officer's charge was serious: "In the course of my official duties, I have received information from multiple U.S. Government officials that the President of the United States is using the power of his office to solicit interference from a foreign country in the 2020 U.S. election." The complainant explained that the information was second-hand, coming from White House officials who had listened to the call. Those officials, the whistleblower alleged, "were deeply disturbed by what had transpired in the phone call," and said "they had witnessed the President abuse his office for personal gain."[11]

Equally alarming to the whistleblower were White House attempts to limit access to the call record by putting it on a highly classified computer system. As the complainant alleged, "I learned from multiple U.S. officials that senior White House officials had intervened to 'lock down' all records of the phone call, especially the official word-for-word transcript of the call that was produced—as is customary—by the White House situation room." That extraordinary procedure suggested a cover-up: "This set of actions underscored to me that White House officials understood the gravity of what had transpired in the call."[12] The whistleblower's appeal to the inspector general was meant to defy the White House attempt to bury the call record, but the report did not by itself complete Congress's carefully crafted information loop. Indeed, the White House intervened in an attempt to cut the legislators out.

The whistleblower report became the subject of a separation-of-powers dispute between presidential assertions of authority to hold back the administrator's complaint and Congress's statutory right to have access to it. Under the whistleblower statute, the next step was for the inspector general to determine if the whistleblower's complaint was credible and urgent. The ICIG, Michael Atkinson, who had been appointed by President Trump, acknowledged two potential weaknesses in the complaint that would soon serve as political fodder for contesting its value. First, the whistleblower had not heard the call directly (it might be dismissed as hearsay), and furthermore, there were "some indicia of an arguable political bias on the part of the Complainant in favor of a rival political candidate" (it might be dismissed as another "Witch Hunt"). Nonetheless, the ICIG reported that his own preliminary investigation "supports the Complainant's allegation." He found that "there are reasonable grounds to believe that the complaint relating to the urgent concern 'appears credible.'"[13] With that determination, Atkinson passed along the complaint to the director of national intelligence (DNI), who was then supposed to turn it over to Congress and to inform the ICIG that he had done so.

It was at this point that the Trump administration tried to quash the complaint by enlisting an opinion on the matter from the Department of Justice's Office of Legal Counsel (OLC). The OLC offers interpretations of the constitutionality of executive branch actions, but it is not a court. To some, it operates like "the president's law firm."[14] When Trump's White House counsel, Pat Cipollone, and his deputy counsel John Eisenberg told the president that they would ask OLC for an opinion on whether the law required that the complaint be forwarded to Congress, they were likely confident of the answer they would receive.[15] Indeed, that request was a textbook example of the "[White House] Counsel's office pressing the Office of Legal Counsel to generate constitutional apologias for presidential prerogative."[16] On OLC's advice, Acting DNI Joseph Maguire decided not to turn over the report or the ICIG's determination of its credibility to Congress's intelligence committees. Seemingly, this was in direct violation of the relevant statute. But OLC had an alternative view, one that drew upon the unique position of the president at the top of the executive branch hierarchy.

Echoing earlier arguments that executive branch officials cannot investigate the chief executive, the OLC came close to suggesting that no one in the executive branch could blow the whistle on a president. The "alleged misconduct," it observed, "does not involve any member of the intelligence community." It argued that the president's conduct could not be characterized as "an 'urgent concern' within the meaning of the statute because it does not concern 'the funding, administration, or operation of an intelligence activity' under the authority of the DNI." Furthermore, because the president was "not a member of the intelligence community," the whistleblower's "hearsay report" did not need to be turned over to Congress. For emphasis, the opinion concluded that the "ICIG's reporting responsibilities . . . do not concern officials outside the intelligence community, let alone the President." Instead, OLC stipulated, any complaint that was not an "urgent concern" should be resolved within the executive branch and reported to the Department of Justice, rather than the congressional intelligence committees.[17]

Congress, however, had not been left in the dark. It turned out that the whistleblower had already been in contact with House Intelligence Committee staff, asking for guidance as to what process to follow to report the complaint. Thus, the committee's chairman, Adam Schiff (D-CA), knew from the start to push for full access to the record.[18] Moreover, after DNI Maguire failed to meet the seven-day statutory deadline to report an urgent concern, Atkinson himself alerted the House and Senate Intelligence Committees to the situation and conveyed to them the existence of a report. As Atkinson stated, "my unresolved differences with the Acting DNI are affecting the execution of two of my most important duties and responsibilities" as ICIG, to wit: disclosing the whistleblower's complaint and keeping the intelligence committees fully informed. Atkinson did not, however, state what the complaint was about. He believed that he was bound by the OLC opinion that the complaint was not relevant to the statute even though he disagreed with that determination.[19]

Events unfolded swiftly. The congressional reaction was fierce. The Democratic House of Representatives immediately sought to defend its statutory prerogatives. Chairman Schiff moved for a subpoena to compel Maguire to turn over the complaint: "you do not possess the authority to withhold from the Committee a whistleblower disclosure from within the Intelligence Community that is intended for Congress." Moreover, Schiff complained that the DNI had "consulted the Department of Justice about the complaint, even though the statute does not provide you discretion to review, appeal, reverse, or countermand in any way the ICIG's independent determination, let alone to involve another entity within the Executive Branch in the handling of a whistleblower complaint."[20] At the same time, the Republican Senate voted on a resolution calling on the Trump administration to turn over the complaint. Though nonbinding, the resolution passed unanimously on a voice vote, indicating that Republicans were at least unwilling publicly to support the White House's attempt to bury it.[21] (As if to show bipartisan congressional solidarity on the point, the House voted for a similar resolution, even after the complaint was turned over.[22]) Talk of impeachment, already rippling through the Democratic caucus in the House, gained seemingly irresistible momentum, finally prompting the hitherto reluctant Speaker, Nancy Pelosi (D-CA), to announce the opening of an impeachment inquiry. With the aid already released, the administration moved to limit further damage by complying. It provided Congress the read-out of the July 25 phone call and turned over the whistleblower complaint. In the circumstances, however, that added fuel to the fire. The documents appeared to support the charge that an illicit quid pro quo deal had in fact been attempted, and that the president was cooperating only because he had been caught.[23]

It might seem that the surveillance statutes had done their job, that the oversight regimen put in place by Congress had decisively overcome the president's interest in withholding information. The whistleblower and the ICIG were invoking laws, not norms, and Congress was responding vigorously to what they had conveyed. But it is worth noting that the decisive work was not done by the law but by the administrators' improvisations. Just as the OLC ruling had offered a gloss on unitary claims in an attempt to cut off administrative collaboration with Congress, the officials who participated in Congress's regime of collective control had adhered more to the spirit than the letter of the law. Several steps taken outside the exact procedures in the whistleblower statute had proven instrumental in forcing Trump's hand. The whistleblower had contacted the House Intelligence Committee prior to submitting a complaint, and after the OLC ruled in the president's favor and the DNI refused to turn over the complaint to Congress, the ICIG had still alerted Congress to the existence of the complaint. Congress took those cues, raising a public storm in its efforts to get the president to back down, but the process was murky enough to raise the phantom twins from the muck.

Those seemingly small departures from prescribed procedures were instrumental to how the White House formulated its public defense. With its unitary assertions rebuffed, the Trump administration turned to the Deep State conspiracy to discredit the whistleblower report. In releasing the call summary, the White House accidentally emailed its talking points to House Democrats: "The case just shows another example of the 'Deep State,' the media, and the Democrats in Congress damaging our national security by leaking confidential information."[24] "I know the difference between a whistleblower and a deep state operative," White House adviser Stephen Miller declared, alleging that "this individual is a saboteur trying to undermine a democratically elected government!"[25]

Going further, Trump sought to strip away the shield of anonymity. He signaled to his allies that he wanted the whistleblower exposed: "I deserve to meet my accuser." He also charged the whistleblower's source in the White House with treason: "You know what we used to do in the old days when we were smart with spies and treason, right?"[26] The president bristled at the idea of protecting informants. The depth provided by Congress's oversight regime was, as he saw it, a cover for rogue plots against the government: "we must determine the Whistleblower's identity to determine WHY this was done to the USA."[27] Indeed, though the whistleblower was entitled to request anonymity and the ICIG could go along, the president had found a potentially devastating ambiguity in the oversight regimen: "Nothing in the ICWPA expressly protects the anonymity of a complainant, or provides sanctions for someone who discloses it."[28] And the fact that Schiff knew of the whistleblower before the complaint was submitted made anonymity all the more suspicious. The president called that interaction "Big stuff. That's a big story.... [Schiff] knew long before and helped write it, too. It's a scam."[29] Trump began to muse about firing the "disloyal" ICIG who had turned over the whistleblower report.[30]

Though the president's rage did not stop the advance of the oversight regime against unitary claims, troubling precedents had been set for defenders of statutorily provided depth. The opinion from the Justice Department's OLC that the whistleblower complaint could not apply to the president was not withdrawn. A group of more than sixty inspectors general from across the executive branch, led by the Justice Department's own IG, Michael Horowitz, and National Science Foundation IG Allison Lerner, protested the OLC ruling's broad implications. Implicitly impugning the objectivity of the OLC, they charged that the office had "substituted its judgment and reversed a determination the statute specifically entrusted to the ICIG because of its independence, objectivity, and expertise to credibly assess the information." More significantly, they warned that this was a troubling precedent that threatened the long-envisioned relationship between whistleblowers and IGs. First, the opinion "could seriously undermine the critical role whistleblowers play in coming forward to report waste, fraud, abuse, and misconduct across the federal government." Second, they suggested that the opinion "has the potential to undermine IG independence across the federal government."[31] As the IGs saw it, the "executive constitutionalism" undertaken by the president's legal team was on a collision course with the administrative depth provided by Congress.[32]

Impeached by depth: Impeachment is a political process. There is an element of character assassination inherent in it, and partisans are likely to wield the sharpest daggers. The impeachment proceedings against Bill Clinton and Donald Trump both indicate how quickly the partisan animosities of the current era drive toward the ultimate judgment on acceptable presidential behavior. But the Trump case gave an interesting spin to issues of partisanship and character. It was triggered and carried along by the actions of administrative subordinates. Of course, the House Democrats hungrily took the cue, but it was the administrators who had prompted them to act. More than that, the House Democrats recognized that their charges against the president were vulnerable to dismissal as a partisan character assassination. Their case hinged on bringing forward a very different sort of character from deep within the executive branch and placing it on full public view. Putting faces on distinctly administrative conventions and norms of public service, they made the depth of the executive branch central to their case against the president. Before they were done, two very different conceptions of executive branch management had been drawn out, and administrators had been held up as the better representatives of the national interest.

In announcing its impeachment inquiry, the House pointedly dismissed the constitutionality of Trump's unitary claims. Speaker Pelosi, who had helped draft the 1998 national security whistleblower act, opened the probe with a broadside against the president's expansive understanding of Article II: "The actions taken to date by the president have seriously violated the Constitution especially when the president says Article II says, 'I can do whatever I want.'" Casting that claim as a threat to fundamentals, Pelosi concluded with what would become the prosecution's recurrent refrain: "The president must be held accountable. No one is above the law."[33] On the other side was the president's refrain: his call with

the Ukrainian president had been "perfect."[34] Acting Chief of Staff
Mick Mulvaney was equally blunt and dismissive. As if operating
in a different system altogether, he all but admitted the quid pro
quo: "Did [the president] also mention to me in passing the corruption related to the D.N.C. server? . . . Absolutely. No question
about that. . . . That's why we held up the money." Mulvaney saw
no reason to apologize for that. Trump was the president. There
was an electoral warrant for his actions: "I have news for every-
body: Get over it. There's going to be political influence in foreign
policy. . . . Elections have consequences."[35]

If the Trump impeachment proceedings stand out as distinctive, it is because the president would never acknowledge any question about the propriety of his actions or credit any controversy
over norms, let alone concede a violation of the law. That meant
that this impeachment would put the standards of good government themselves on trial. In that test, the House found itself locked
in an interdependent relationship with administrators willing to
show their faces and to stigmatize the president's pretensions by
their testimony and their example. The inquiry transformed executive branch subordinates into fact witnesses. The proceedings provided them strong ground on which to defy blanket presidential
directives not to appear, and to elaborate their case for conducting
the affairs of state through official roles and regular processes.

Just as bureaucratic resistance to the unitary executive ultimately
relied on Congress for its legitimacy, the obverse was equally true.
Faced with a hostile president, Congress became reliant on executive branch subordinates to advance its own institutional claims
to oversight authority and draw the contrast with presidential
pretensions. Not only did Congress need the information these
officials had to offer, it also needed them to bring their nonpartisan,
national service credentials to the forefront.

While Congress relied on these vivid personal displays of administrative integrity, the president was eyeing those same lateral ties as prima facie evidence of the corruption of the whole

proceeding. The specter of administrative officials testifying about his administration's conduct in impeachment hearings seemed to confirm the Deep State narrative Trump had been developing all along.[36] "I am coming to the conclusion," Trump tweeted provocatively, "that what is taking place is not an impeachment, it is a COUP."[37] For the acting chief of staff, the resistance was just "career bureaucrats who are saying, 'You know what? I don't like President Trump's politics so I'm going to participate in this witch hunt.'"[38] In his mind, "career bureaucrats" was an epithet indicating institutional arrogance and political pretension.

As these competing frames were vying for public favor, the White House advanced its constitutional claims. It renounced the impeachment inquiry whole-cloth and justified the president's actions on unitary grounds. The counsel to the president, Pat Cipollone, sent a letter to House Democratic leaders outlining the administration's case. One part of Cipollone's argument drew out the plebiscitary theme, that the president is accountable not to Congress for his uses of executive authority but to the voters. House Democrats were, he charged, engaged in "unconstitutional efforts to overturn the democratic process." The claim to hierarchical control was equally blunt. Making a sweeping assertion of executive privilege to prevent executive branch officials from testifying to the House, Cipollone stated, "Current and former State Department officials are duty bound to protect the confidentiality interests of the Executive Branch." Though defied by many subordinates, the president's gag orders would not be without effect. They silenced presidential appointees higher up the chain of command and left the House with a case significantly weaker than it might have been. Cipollone's letter cited other key unitary themes. It declared that the inquiry "would inflict lasting institutional harm on the Executive Branch and lasting damage to the separation of powers." And it maintained that Trump's refusal to participate in the inquiry was part of "his obligation to preserve the rights of future occupants of his office."[39]

The Trump administration not only pushed its claims forward to protect the rights of future presidents, it also pushed them backward in time with a particularly radical twist. It denied the legal basis of the Watergate investigation and the resulting resignation of President Nixon. The Ukraine scandal had renewed the House Democrats' interest in the Russia investigation, and they sought to access redacted material and underlying evidence that the Mueller report had been based upon. Pulling this request under the umbrella of an impeachment inquiry gave it strong legal grounding. But the DOJ sought to prevent the release of this evidence, arguing that the precedent from *Haldeman v. Sirica* (1974)—granting Congress access to Watergate grand jury material in that earlier impeachment inquiry—had been wrongly decided. The DOJ's position would have placed Nixon out of the reach of impeachment by denying Congress access to critical evidence. The DC District Court Chief Judge Beryl Howell, who later ruled against DOJ, could not hide her astonishment at the implication of the DOJ's argument: "Wow, OK . . . As I said, the department is taking extraordinary positions in this case."[40] This was perhaps the furthest extension of the unitary executive theory, erasing all controversy at its point of origin. The threat that the Watergate scandal had posed to the presidency should, the administration argued, have been nipped in the bud. An inquiry should not have been allowed to proceed then and should not commence now.

The president's clampdown put most of the high-level officials out of reach of the House inquiry, but the proceedings seemed to liberate those below. Executive branch subordinates defied the gags, coming forward, one by one, to spill the beans. Their testimony detailed Trump's linkage of Ukraine aid to his domestic political concerns and elaborated its violation of norms. The National Security Council's top Ukraine expert, Lieutenant Colonel Alexander Vindman, testified in the military dress of an active-duty officer. He recounted his experience growing up in an immigrant family and his faith that American institutions protect truth-telling: "I will be fine for telling the truth." A riveting witness, the lieutenant colonel was one of the few officials to make a candid judgment of the president's conduct: "It is improper for the President of the United States to demand a foreign government investigate a U.S. citizen and political opponent."[41]

The president's directive to executive branch employees not to cooperate backfired with devastating effect at the State Department. This was a natural location for the resistance. Not only were foreign service officers privy to Ukraine relations, but their department had been at odds with the administration from the beginning. One former US ambassador in communication with State Department officials referred to this long-running tension as a source of the urge to testify in the impeachment hearings: "People are fed up. . . . There's a deep well of resentment that's just bubbled toward the top."[42] Trump had set himself at odds with State Department personnel by sidelining officials, leaving positions vacant, and demanding steep budget cuts. When the administration issued its travel ban aimed at several majority-Muslim countries in January 2017, approximately 1,000 foreign service officers and other department officials signed a "dissent cable"—a formal instrument created by Secretary of State William Rogers in 1971 to allow officials to vent concerns about the Vietnam War—expressing opposition to the order. In the words of one US diplomat in Africa, "Policy dissent is in our culture. . . . We even have awards for it."[43] That, of course, was the culture that Trump despised. When asked why he had left so many positions vacant at State, Trump dismissed the role of diplomats in foreign policy entirely: "I'm the only one that matters, because when it comes to it, that's what the policy is going to be."[44]

Congressional subpoenas to foreign service officers and other State Department officials were intended to provide "some cover so they could cooperate."[45] In turn, each witness gave a good-government seal of approval to the House's proceedings. Another character from central casting was Deputy Assistant Secretary George Kent, who was in charge of Ukraine policy in the State

Department. His sartorial bowtie complemented his personal story as "the third generation of my family to have chosen a career in public service and sworn the oath all U.S. public servants do, in defense of our Constitution." In reference to Trump's request of the Ukrainian president, Kent offered, "As a general principle, I do not believe the United States should ask other countries to engage in selective, politically associated investigations or prosecutions . . . because such selective actions undermine the rule of law."[46]

Another career official, the former ambassador to Ukraine, Marie Yovanovitch, related how the Trump administration had come to perceive her as an obstacle to its backchannel operation. Though the State Department had assured her she had "done nothing wrong," Yovanovitch was recalled from Ukraine. As she testified, "although I understood that I served at the pleasure of the president, I was nevertheless incredulous that the U.S. government chose to remove an ambassador based, as best as I can tell, on unfounded and false claims by people with clearly questionable motives."[47] This "campaign of misinformation" by Trump allies and suspect Ukrainians, alleged Yovanovitch, was a reaction to the real effort to combat corruption, her own. Yovanovitch's steely self-confidence and ability to project competence could not but impress, but her performance was countered in real time by a presidential smear. As she was testifying, Trump tweeted, "Everywhere Marie Yovanovitch went turned bad." It was a vivid reminder of the president's reputation for bullying and for disparaging women, and Yovanovitch acknowledged that intent, telling the hearing committee that she experienced it as "intimidating."[48]

The media ran with the Deep State frame. The "deep state has emerged from the shadows," reported the New York Times, and diplomats who had "been derided as a 'Deep State,'" proclaimed Politico, were "taking their revenge."[49] But career officials at odds with Trump were not the only ones to defy administration orders not to testify. Even some Trump loyalists deferred to Congress, calculating that defiance of the unitary executive was the safer course through the legal minefield. Ambassador to the EU and major Trump donor Gordon Sondland was a central figure in the drama for his help in implementing the president's Ukraine directives. In the first closed-door session of the inquiry, he asserted he had not known of the president's electoral motives, but testified that he nonetheless had disagreed with delegating Ukraine policy to Trump's personal attorney, Rudy Giuliani. He endorsed the view that "the men and women of the State Department, not the president's personal lawyer, should take responsibility for all aspects of U.S. foreign policy toward Ukraine."[50] Sondland's testimony was all the more embarrassing because Trump had tried to block it: "I would love to send Ambassador Sondland . . . to testify . . . but unfortunately he would be testifying before a totally compromised kangaroo court."[51] Later, after having "refreshed" his recollections, Sondland removed all ambiguity by admitting knowledge of a quid pro quo. Updating his testimony, he told investigators that a Ukrainian announcement of an anti-corruption investigation had been a requirement for the resumption of US aid: "I presumed that the aid suspension had become linked to the proposed anti-corruption statement."[52] And in his public testimony, Sondland answered baldly: "Was there a 'quid pro quo'? . . . the answer is yes." Furthermore, he directly implicated the president: "we followed the president's orders."[53]

All presidents set and pursue their own goals in foreign policy, and there is a long history of presidents using personal intimates, like Giuliani, to open backchannel negotiations with other countries for that purpose. Moreover, corruption in the government of Ukraine was no secret, and it presented a consequential challenge for the conduct of American policy. But Trump had little use for the State Department officers who were already dealing with the corruption problem on the ground, or with the Defense Department monitors in place to ensure that standards for American aid were met, or for the formidable investigatory apparatus at the Justice Department for dealing with charges of corruption. He was implementing his own policy and bypassing the government altogether. It was not the backchannel that rankled the administrators; it was the dueling channels.

Just as the secretary of the Navy would question whether a tweet from Trump concerning a military trial constituted a formal order, the interim ambassador to Ukraine, William Taylor, explained that, as far as he was concerned, the president's backchannel operation never really changed US policy. As Taylor saw it, the problem with the White House's direction of Ukraine affairs was that it had put the government at cross purposes: "There appeared to be two channels of U.S. policy-making and implementation, one regular and one highly irregular." The regular channel was the diplomatic process with a policy of supporting Ukraine's resistance to Russian invasion, while the irregular channel, led by Trump's personal attorney Rudy Giuliani, was pushing for political investigations. "The official foreign policy of the United States was undercut," Taylor testified, by Giuliani's "irregular efforts." While Trump was intent on getting the Ukrainian president to "publicly commit to investigations of Burisma and alleged interference in the 2016 election," Taylor viewed his own charge as carrying out the official commitments of Congress and the executive branch. He agreed with Senators Ron Johnson (R-WI) and Chris Murphy (D-CT), who had told the Ukrainian president that he "should not jeopardize . . . bipartisan support by getting drawn into U.S. domestic politics."[54] In response, the White House alleged that Taylor's testimony was part of "a coordinated smear campaign from far-left lawmakers and radical unelected bureaucrats waging war on the Constitution."[55] Ironically, the Trump administration had selected Taylor as envoy after pushing out the previous ambassador, Marie Yovanovitch, for standing in the way of its pressure campaign.

Executive branch subordinates had succeeded in the House impeachment hearings in demonstrating that the president had pursued a foreign policy in Ukraine that focused on his own political interests and that departed from the policy outlined by Congress and implemented by other executive branch officials. To the president's legal team, however, those executive branch subordinates who spoke of Trump ignoring "official policy" had missed the point entirely: they "fundamentally misunderstand the assignment of power under the Constitution." The proper constitutional understanding, they contended, was a unitary one: "Article II of the Constitution states that 'the executive Power shall be vested in a President'—not Executive Branch staff." And for the president's team, the other interpretation of "official policy" only proved that the Deep State had been real all along: "[the] theory that a purported inter-agency 'consensus' among career bureaucrats can be used to show improper motive is an affront to the tens of millions of American citizens who voted for President Trump's foreign policy and not a continuation of the Washington establishment's policy preferences."[56]

The constitutional rights of the place: The impeachment inquiry laid bare Congress's institutional interest in depth. Administrative insulation, official intermediation, professional norms, regular channels, lateral ties, the free flow of information, and the like, all serve Congress's purposes more dependably than they do those of the president. Neither side had a monopoly on arrogance in this affair, but beneath the theatrics were the deadly serious implications of stripping away depth and depriving Congress of the means of holding a president to account.

The second article of impeachment against President Trump—obstruction of Congress—spoke directly to these institutional interests. Schiff, head of the impeachment management team in the Senate trial, underscored the sheer magnitude of the president's stonewalling to truncate congressional access to pertinent information from the executive branch, and he implored the upper chamber to defend what James Madison had called "the constitutional rights of the place."[57]

If a President can obstruct his own investigation, if he can effectively nullify a power the Constitution gives solely to the Congress—indeed the ultimate power the Constitution gives—to prevent Presidential misconduct, then the President places himself beyond accountability and above the law. Cannot be indicted, cannot be impeached. It makes him a monarch, the very evil against which our Constitution and the balance of powers it carefully laid out, was designed to guard against.[58]

Acquittal, Schiff implied, would cede Congress's institutional power and ratify the president's unitary ambitions.

The president's legal team disagreed with the House Democrats' case on the merits, but their arguments affirmed that the unitary executive theory was on trial. They repeatedly referred to the vesting clause in their written briefs. Most pointedly, in the president's official written response to the two articles of impeachment, White House counsel Pat Cipollone and outside counsel Jay Sekulow invoked the clause to dismiss the House's charges:

[In] the first Article, the House attempts to seize the President's power under Article II of the Constitution to determine foreign policy. In the second Article, the House attempts to control and penalize the assertion of the Executive Branch's constitutional privileges, while simultaneously seeking to destroy the Framers' system of checks and balances. By approving the Articles, the House violated our constitutional order. . . . They sought to undermine his authority under Article II of the Constitution, which vests the entirety of "[t]he executive Power" in "a President of the United States of America."[59]

Yet again the president's legal team mixed these constitutional claims with a plebiscitary rationale. They asserted that the "conviction of a President raises particularly profound issues under our constitutional structure because it means overturning the democratically expressed will of the people in the only national election in which all eligible citizens participate."[60] Mindful of speaking to Senate Republicans and the president's base in particular, Cipollone made sure to emphasize the upcoming election in his opening public statement: "They want to remove President Trump from the ballot."[61] Toward the end of the trial, Trump's celebrity attorney Alan Dershowitz took the legal team's claims to their logical extreme. Echoing Mulvaney's "get over it" remark, he denied any binding distinction between the national interest and the president's political interest. Speaking directly to the issue of the president's electoral interference, Dershowitz opined, "If a president does something which he believes will help him get reelected—in the public interest—that cannot be the kind of quid · pro quo that results in impeachment."[62]

House Democrats had pushed this test of the constitutional rights of the place in the face of political contingencies that heavily favored their adversary. The House votes on the impeachment charges had divided starkly on partisan lines, and given the partisan alignment of power in the Senate, the prospects for conviction on the House's charges were always dim. The administrators had put on an impressive show, but it barely registered against the underlying political dynamics. Majority Leader Mitch McConnell (R-KY) put the point plainly: "The House made a partisan political decision to impeach. I would anticipate we will have a largely partisan outcome in the Senate. I'm not impartial about this at all."[63] Before it was over, a few Republican senators came forward to say that they thought the president had behaved inappropriately, but the only institutional rights affirmed in the end were those of the president.[64] Only two Republican senators supported the vote to call the high-level administration officials to testify; only one Republican senator cast a vote for the abuse of power charge; none supported the obstruction of Congress charge. No doubt, Speaker Pelosi's initial caution about opening an impeachment investigation weighed how the likely acquittal would affect the future balance of institutional prerogatives. Presented with competing systems of good government, the Senate supported unity over depth.

That was certainly Trump's takeaway. Acquittal was the perfect setup for a committed unitarian because it left executive branch depth more fully exposed. The president lost no time trumpeting the verdict as vindication for his broader war against the Deep State. In a wide-ranging assessment, he declared the situation untenable: "We've been going through this now for over three years. . . . And this should never, ever happen to another President ever." He warned of consequences for those who had sought to undermine him: "these are the crookedest, most dishonest, dirtiest people I've ever seen." He treated acquittal as a vindication of the strength of the presidential party, singling out certain congressional Republican defenders for special praise and inviting them all to the White House for a "celebration."[65]

Wasting no time, he followed through on his threats. Immediate retaliation against those whom he perceived as having aided in the inquiry sent an unmistakable signal to everyone else left in place. Trump fired Sondland, whose testimony had been central to the House's charges.[66] Vindman was removed from the NSC and transferred back to the Pentagon soon after Sondland's firing. As Trump's national security adviser Robert O'Brien saw it, "We're not some banana republic where lieutenant colonels get together and decide what the policy is or should be."[67] Later, the White House communicated to the Defense Department that Trump opposed Vindman's scheduled Army promotion to full colonel. Rather than test the president's resolve, Vindman retired from the military, citing "a campaign of bullying, intimidation and retaliation by President Trump and his allies."[68] John Rood, the undersecretary of defense for policy, also resigned under presidential pressure. His sin in the eyes of the president? He had certified to Congress that Ukraine had instituted safeguards sufficient to release the aid, undermining Trump and his defenders' conceit that the president was concerned about corruption.[69]

The retaliation took an even more aggressive turn with the firing of ICIG Michael Atkinson, who had alerted Congress to the existence of the whistleblower report even as the administration tried to withhold it. In a letter informing the House and Senate Intelligence Committee leaders of his decision, Trump wrote, "it is vital that I have the fullest confidence in the appointees serving as inspectors general. That is no longer the case with regard to this inspector general."[70] Attorney General William Barr weighed in to support the president's firing of Atkinson, saying that Trump "did the right thing." As if to ridicule Congress's regard for the "monumental laws" arrayed behind its oversight regimen, Barr accused Atkinson of overstepping a "fairly narrow statute."[71] Atkinson responded with a defense of his "faithful discharge" of his legal obligations and by urging future whistleblowers not to let recent events "silence your voices."[72]

The dismissal of Atkinson was widely renounced. Speaking on behalf of his fellow IGs, DOJ IG Michael Horowitz again countered his own department to defend his colleague: "Inspector General Atkinson is known throughout the Inspector General community for his integrity, professionalism, and commitment to the rule of law and independent oversight. That includes his actions in handling the Ukraine whistleblower complaint."[73] The firing even gave some of the president's congressional allies pause. Senator Chuck Grassley (R-IA)—the author of the Whistleblower Protection Act of 1989 and the cosponsor of a 2008 law that strengthened the reporting requirements for removing an IG—stated that the president's action "demands an explanation." For Trump, however, the explanation was obvious. Dispensing with any pretense, the president publicly stated the real reason for his displeasure: "He took this terrible, inaccurate whistleblower report and he brought it to Congress."[74] Leading a bipartisan pushback, Grassley charged that this undercut congressional intent: "Congress intended that inspectors general only be removed when there is clear evidence of wrongdoing or failure to perform the duties of the office, and not for reasons unrelated to their performance, to help preserve IG independence."[75]

But acquittal had become license for a wider offensive against IGs and congressional oversight. Trump dismissed the State Department IG who was in the midst of an investigation into misuse of government resources by the secretary of state.[76] When questioned about the move, the president made his position on IGs clear: "I have the absolute right to fire the inspectors general."[77]

When presented with a $2.2 trillion emergency relief package to counter the economic effects of the coronavirus pandemic, Trump issued a signing statement, written by the OLC, objecting to the law's provision for a new inspector general empowered to notify Congress directly of any irregularities in the use of the funds to aid businesses or agency refusals to cooperate with the IG's requests for information. The signing statement relied on the power assigned to the president in Article II to "execute the law." When questioned about Congress's interest in oversight, Trump proclaimed, "I'll be the oversight."[78]

The president went further. He removed the Pentagon's acting IG, who had been chosen by his fellow IGs to chair the Pandemic Response Accountability Committee. Trump tapped a former IG, Brian Miller, to fill the role instead, but Miller's selection raised concerns since he had more recently been a White House lawyer involved in the president's impeachment defense team.[79] Asked about a report by the acting Department of Health and Human Services IG, Christi Grimm, citing critical shortages in medical equipment at hospitals, Trump responded with disgust: "Did I hear the word 'inspector general'? Really? It's wrong." He immediately moved to replace her.[80] And when Speaker Pelosi moved to set up a House panel to oversee the crisis response, Trump referred back to the Russia probe and the impeachment proceedings to discredit any type of oversight efforts: "here we go again. . . . It's witch hunt after witch hunt after witch hunt."[81]

Administrative resistance to the unitary executive made its strongest stand in the first impeachment of Donald Trump. Invited by Congress to come out from the depths, officers put on their best case for public service and regular order. They fell short. Still, alternative outcomes under different sets of political contingencies were easy to imagine. A Republican House would never have brought charges; a Democratic Senate would, at the very least, have called the higher-ups to testify. These counterfactuals are compelling not because they bracket this episode as idiosyncratic but because they suggest the real problem: basic and pressing issues of governance are up for grabs; they are resolved by political contingencies and the institutional alignment of political power. That is no way to run a modern state. There is no good substitute for a more direct reckoning with depth.

PART III
EPILOGUE

10

A Reckoning with Depth

The Deep State versus the unitary executive has been a spectacle too vivid to ignore.[1] It should impress us all with the unsettled place of administration in contemporary American government. One might have thought that a matter of such vital importance to the effective operation of the state would have been resolved long ago. But over the past half century, questions surrounding administrative power and its political control have been growing more, not less, contentious. Trump's presidency forces a reckoning that is long overdue.

Shining a bright light at the various sites where the phantom twins confronted one another advises caution all around. Everywhere we have looked we have uncovered sobering developments. The problem was not that the president couldn't find evidence to hang on his frame; the problem was the solution intrinsic to the frame. The state Trump has asked us to embrace is every bit as menacing as the state he would have us abandon. The Deep State and the unitary executive are both distillations of ambition and fear, larger-than-life projections onto issues and arrangements that are all too real. The best that can be said of Trump's assault on depth is that it has called attention to a huge blind spot in American state formation and to structural ambiguities long finessed.

The clear-eyed choice: Trump's charge of a Deep State conspiracy operated as a blanket indictment. If not for that indictment, the counter-narrative of public-service patriotism—of administrators dutifully doing the people's business, loyal to the Constitution alone—would surely have been passed over lightly as civics-book boilerplate. Administrators are not innocents. "The Resistance" was a show of its own, one featuring high-minded propriety that did not always live up to its billing. Hubris was one of its chief vulnerabilities, and there were times when the performance left the pretensions woefully exposed. Every procedural deviation (a whistleblower consulting directly with Congress, an IG bucking the OLC, a Navy secretary ignoring a tweet) proved a self-inflicted wound. Some of the action turned downright perverse. There was sabotage by the staff at the White House. There was desperate plotting at the CFPB. There was political animus, self-righteousness, falsification of documents, and reckless disregard for protocol at the FBI.

States carry a lot of baggage. Rogue actors caught up in their own agendas are one of the real-world issues that attend administrative depth. Not the least of it is that they fuel the case for a unitary executive and lend presidentialism the appearance of a safe harbor. As it happens, the reason to hesitate in the face of that alluring, seemingly commonsensical solution has also been made plain. The presidential clampdown was itself an affront to good government. Billed as an affirmation of presidential responsibility and democratic accountability, the unitary executive turned out in practice to be a license for arbitrary action and personal impositions.

What we saw in the Trump presidency was that claims on behalf of a unitary executive put a whole range of invaluable governmental assets at risk. Consider again the worst of the excesses on the other side. Those White House saboteurs had witnessed presidential indifference to frank discussion and honest brokerage. They had spoken up for the interdependence of policies and the continuity of commitments. Hostility to reason and due deliberation seemed to them to call for desperate countermeasures. Those CFPB plotters were unwilling to sacrifice a faithful administration of the law to central command and control. A change in presidential partisanship seemed to them to call for adjustments, not for the demolition of their entire operation. That cabal at the FBI watched as credible evidence of foreign election interference was subordinated to the president's personal sensibilities and collective judgment succumbed to demands for personal loyalty.

The president's insistence that he alone held the executive power of the American state drew out these forms of resistance. Tit for tat, he and the officers of the executive branch turned the Deep State conspiracy into something of a self-fulfilling prophecy. That is why choosing sides in fights like those between Trump and Comey or Mulvaney and English is a mistake. The point to ponder is that at every site of resistance the protest was the same. It turned on the value of depth, on the wisdom of stripping administration of its own integrity and operating the executive branch as a strong arm of presidential will. The clear-eyed choice is not between the Deep State and the unitary executive. It is whether we value what depth has to offer or not.[2] If we don't, the case for the unitary executive becomes infinitely stronger; if we do, the case is weak, and we will need to find other ways to deal with the baggage that depth carries.

Trump's presidency has forced this point, and that may be its enduring significance. His administration has reminded us of the advantages of depth even in the face of all of its downsides. It has also shown us the full implications of a unitary executive. The unitary theory has no good defenses against naked instrumentalism. Adopting that theory makes it hard in practice to defend depth of any sort. The theory enables Trump-like leaders and turns electoral decisions into an iron cage in which all the rest of us are trapped.

Worlds apart: Two different conceptions of American government collided in the Trump presidency. There was surprisingly little overlap between them. It was as if their advocates were living on different planets. In one assessment, "the deck ha[d] become stacked against the Executive," and Congress was complicit: "they increasingly seek to insulate [executive power] from presidential control."[3] A unitary executive was just the thing to discipline Congress, subordinate the executive branch, redeem democracy, and restore constitutional government. In the alternative assessment, a unitary executive was an imperial presidency by another name and, as such, a threat to American democracy.[4] Presidents had been laying siege to American government for years. Congress was outflanked and in retreat. The "Steady State" was collapsing, the president "actively working to break free of the protections inherent in the American system meant to limit [his] power." This amounted to "one of the biggest challenges to our nation's checks-and-balances system in modern times."[5]

Though these people seemed to be describing wildly different worlds, they were in fact acting simultaneously within the same administration. Rival histories spun out antonymous narratives of dire threat. Together they worked to pull the government apart.

For a time during the Russia probe and the 2019 impeachment hearings, it appeared that the resistance had the president on the ropes. Administrative pushback against Trump's pretensions drew to center stage an alternative sense of good order long in political limbo. Knowledge-based authority, neutral competence, informed decision making, respect for professional expertise and judgment, rules and regular processes—all the values that depersonalize the exercise of power found a cultural resonance unrivaled since the Progressive era. For some, the mere fact that the defense of depth had gone public and found a receptive audience was evidence of its resilience.[6] Trump himself lent credence to that view. Told that he had "out-mastered the Deep State," the president demurred, saying, "We have a long way to go."[7]

Perhaps he was thinking about the Federal Reserve Board, or the National Weather Service, or Dr. Fauci. In any case, the president was too modest. The rout was impressive. Just ask all the people who were sacked or forced to resign. Conspicuous protections for depth proved to be ill-matched against the president's clamp-down. A vigorous assertion of constitutional prerogatives stripped protections away. There was, for instance, that internal guidance to the White House upholding the importance of DOJ's investigatory independence. It did not apply to the president, and Trump saw no reason to respect it. There was that thoroughgoing and quite damaging report of Trump's conduct during the Russia investigation, but an OLC opinion that a sitting president could not be indicted bent it toward equivocation. There were those rules protecting scientific integrity in agency research and decision making, but the president's political appointees altered the standards of good practice, and they lost their bite.

Statutory provisions might be thought to offer stronger protections for depth, but they too repeatedly came up short of the mark. There was the Navy's Uniform Code of Military Justice, but Trump's authority as commander in chief brushed it aside. The rescissions of presidential reorganization authority did not prevent career experts at the Department of Agriculture from being physically uprooted and shipped out of town. Statutory instructions to nominate an expert at DNI did not restrain the president from appointing a loyalist of dubious competence. The rules set out in law for using interim appointees were circumvented entirely at USCIS. Congress had provided the NSC a staff to surround the president with institutional memory and expertise, but that did not mean the president had to utilize it. Attempts by Congress to insulate the CFPB could not prevent the president from saddling the agency with a hostile acting director and packing it with political appointees committed to undermining its mission. Civil service protections were weakened by executive orders, and merit-based appointments for administrative law judges, also set out in statute, fell to a one-two punch: a successful court challenge followed up by a stroke of the presidential pen. The president's removal power cut through the statutory provision of a ten-year term for the FBI director as well as a statutory requirement for an explanation to Congress for firing an inspector general. And the president's assertions of executive privilege over documents related to the Ukraine imbroglio limited oversight and hobbled the case for impeachment.

Because these assaults on depth in administration occurred here and there, the individual episodes got more attention than the general thrust of the campaign, and the central message seemed lost in the details. All the more reason to reach for a summary view. When all is said and done, the many different sources of depth considered in this book boil down to just one. If there is a single takeaway from our survey, it is that depth ultimately depends on common understandings of what good government entails.[8] It really is all just a matter of norms.[9] Having forced a reckoning with the value of depth, the Trump administration showed there is no securing it without some agreement by the chief executive that it is worthy of respect.

The administrators who crossed paths with Trump were incredulous that a president could flagrantly disregard their sense of duty and good order. But it's hard to compel a president to accept someone else's public good. Absent some buy-in on depth, some willingness to engage what a densely articulated administrative sphere has to offer, protections provided for it will not count for much.[10] Statutes convey congressional interests and intent. Congress does not want a weak state. It has, however, consistently preferred a deep state to a strong one hierarchically controlled by the president. It provided the president with staff to promote regular order and informed decision making. It hectored the president about investigatory independence, competent officials, and the legitimacy of oversight. The rub is that presidents do not have to cooperate, that follow-through is just an expectation.

The unitary executive is their opt-out clause. The theory is, if nothing else, an elaboration of newfound skepticism of the value of depth. It promotes distinctly presidential interests in executive power, and it stigmatizes old agreements to the contrary as a betrayal of first principles. As a practical matter, the theory is a license to presidents to vent their instinctive hostility to depth, and we should expect that future presidents will use it as such.

Changing expectations reflect the change in circumstances. Presidents indulged Congress in forging a densely articulated executive branch when parties were still decentralized operations and when passing legislation was still the main chance for advancing presidential priorities. Cooperation promised both to raise the president's political profile and to promote Congress's interest in administrative depth. By the 1970s, however, the conditions that underlay those partnership agreements were unraveling. Great legislative breakthroughs had of their own accord nationalized politics and concentrated power in administration.[11] The subsequent rise of presidential parties made incumbents far more independent in political action, and the prospect of advancing political priorities through administrative control made a unitary executive a more attractive proposition for them. In the 1970s, the most republican branch saw its kingly partner begin to turn the executive into a direct extension of the presidential party. With administrative depth now a prime obstacle to presidential ambition, the choices appeared stark. Congress could accept its relegation to the sidelines, or it could try to double down on its own prerogatives.

Perhaps it will try do so again. Reactions to Trump's unitary pretensions hint at another congressional "resurgence."[12] Some legislators seek to anchor those administrative rules for scientific integrity more firmly in statute.[13] To reinforce the norm of investigatory independence, lawmakers are now calling for the administration to report all contacts between the White House and DOJ to Congress.[14] There is discussion of providing attorneys general a longer term, detached from the tenure of the president.[15] Lawmakers are also trying to figure out how to protect inspectors general from at-will removal or, failing that, how to use their own Government Accountability Office more aggressively to enhance oversight.[16] Even once prominent advocates of presidential administration are rethinking the value of independence. For instance, Cass Sunstein, a leading legal scholar and former head of Office of Information and Regulatory Affairs (OIRA), invoked the Federal

Reserve Board as a possible model for insulation at the DOJ and the FBI.[17]

But this is republicanism as whack-a-mole. It is an effort to bat down problems discretely, as they pop up, without dealing systemically with the irrepressible force behind them. The issues Congress faces are structural. A legislator with a plan does not count for much more than a sentiment. Reforms aimed at securing depth assume a Congress with a sufficiently strong sense of its own institutional interests to press them effectively. It is hardly a secret that many members are inclined to support the presidential party, and that many others anticipate a time when one of their own partisans will occupy the White House and want to cut deep.[18] Congressional reformers also need to calculate the willingness of a president to sign on to such legislation and cooperate in its implementation. The reforms of the 1970s themselves indicated the force of that constraint. Even in the post-Watergate years, with the presidency back on its heels, incumbents successfully pulled the teeth from congressional efforts to make the DOJ more independent and to insulate the IGs more securely from hierarchical control. The elaboration of the unitary theory had at that time only just begun. Presidents today are surer of their ground and far more emboldened, and they can now appeal to a Court more receptive to the constitutional and plebiscitary arguments for a unitary executive.[19]

As long as presidents push for greater separation, Congress remains limited to crafting stronger checks. That syndrome pushes the two further apart and pulls the courts into the center of political conflicts between them. One might imagine that these dynamics are consistent with the original design, but they are, for that, no less certainly a dead end. What this beleaguered republic needs is some pathway back to cooperation. Congress could parry each of the president's assaults on depth, but without a change in disposition, from confrontation back to collaboration, it will never again be much more than a watchdog. There is no good substitute for fashioning a realm of agreement.

Formality and institutional imagination: States are complicated organizations, and the American state is one of the most complicated of all.[20] Renegade administrators are nothing new to the scene, nor are conflicting purposes within and among institutions. Public tolerance for the baggage is always being tested.

Somehow, however, we managed to muddle through for a long time with these knotty issues of constitutional design and administrative control largely unresolved. Our current confrontation with depth is, in that sense, a coming of age. It could be a first, serious reckoning with what kind of state we want, or it could be our default to the syndrome now in view. The ineluctable question posed by the phantom twins is whether we are finally resigned to let go of old republican values and accept a strong, hierarchically controlled presidential democracy. That no longer seems like much of a leap; we have been taking steps in that direction for at least fifty years.

But make no mistake about it, the Constitution does not ordain this outcome. There is, in fact, something oddly contrived about today's belated push for constitutional clarity, as if only now, suddenly, the meaning of the framers' handiwork has become clear and dispositive. Stranger still is the idea that the Constitution locks us into a strong state design with all administrative power under the president's command and control. Today's unitarians are obviously uncomfortable with the depth the American state has acquired, but for all their lawyerly briefs expounding upon Article II, it is far from obvious that the best way to reckon with it is by fixating on formalities.

Our history suggests quite the contrary. The various arrangements Americans worked out in the past for dealing with administration played fast and loose with the wisdom of the Constitution. They acknowledged that the Constitution contains no unambiguous prescription for administrative control, nor any sturdy formula for national political leadership. That's why they gave it little more than a wink and a nod.

The framers had feared the development of political parties, and they designed a government that they thought would suppress them. But in the nineteenth century, locally controlled party machines seized control of their handiwork and reorganized its operations bottom to top. The parties of the early American state joined what the Constitution had separated, and they cast the president as an office broker distributing the largesse of the executive branch to the various local bosses who had elected him. In the twentieth century, American government pushed even further afield. Reformers were more intent on separating politics from administration than on separating the executive power from the legislative power. Even as they raised the president's political profile, transforming him into a policy entrepreneur and national agenda setter, they took care to instill administration with an organizational integrity of its own and to set the everyday operations of the executive branch at some distance from the chief executive officer. For those enamored of the unitary executive, all this is heresy. Nonetheless, these novel improvisations served the nation through good times and bad. One is tempted to say that constitutional heresies kept American government running effectively for most of its history.

Now, with authority contested at every site, everyone seems to be doubling down on the Constitution, intent on getting straight with the framers. Our thinking about separation and checks has become correspondingly narrow, rigid, and reactive. Little wonder that our institutional imagination has been taken over by phantoms. The republic was better served by the confidence displayed in our history to think these matters through for ourselves. The Constitution need not enclose us by its wisdom and stifle our creativity. The alternative is to follow the path charted by prior generations of reformers. They spent less time trying to resolve the structural ambiguities and more time looking for new ways to finesse them. The sturdy solutions have always been informal and extra-constitutional. They worked around written text and aimed at building institutional partnerships.

This is not a quick-fix prescription. The remedy is not likely to be found in a presidential election. It entails reimagining the system as a whole, and that is a tall order. But it has been done before, and past experience provides us some good leads as to how to do it again.

Our history points to two primary sites for a restoration of co-operation: party and administration. If there is any hope for reclaiming common ground in governing, it lies with reworking those arrangements. Currently these are both being taken over by the presidency. That is the predicament. There is no way back to a reconciliation of depth and unity so long as every significant interest is driven to get control of the presidency for itself and to use the office for its own purposes. Any redesign will have to begin by breaking our obsession with the presidency, and at this late date, it is hard to imagine who will take up that cause.

Going back to the party state of the nineteenth century is not an option, but we would do well to think again about party design and how a different kind of party organization might tie political leaders more securely to a collaborative enterprise.[21] The objective now should be to break the hold of the presidential party over the national party. A broader base and a stronger hand for coalition partners might increase the political costs of unilateral action.

For far too long, the Progressives' idea of separating politics from administration has been dismissed as naïve.[22] What the Progressives recognized was that instilling administration with an integrity of its own protects and supports the collective commitments of a programmatic government. The naïveté of our day is that the only way to jettison the baggage that attends the Progressive prescription is by empowering a political strongman at the top. It is precisely because institutional developments are now pushing hard against the Progressive formula that whack-a-mole responses will not do. Reformers will need to deal directly with why the Progressives' formulas unraveled and to replace them with a different but no less profound rearrangement. For some, interrogation along these lines will circle back to party organization and peg the current predicament to changes in the presidential selection system that took hold in the 1970s. For others, the flaw in the Progressive redesign was that the place of administration was never secured by constitutional amendments. But here again, the longing for constitutional solutions appears symptomatic of the times. The formal problems will not be solved without a political reorientation. The question is whether a consensus on the value of depth can be rebuilt.[23]

The reason to consider systemic changes along these lines is that a profound change of a different sort is already far advanced, theoretically and politically. The Nixon presidency was not a "plot that failed."[24] Nixon's bold reimagining of governing relationships was taken up by others. They turned it into a long-term project, a roadmap to the future. That future is now. It presents itself rhetorically as a choice between the Deep State and the unitary executive. It beckons us toward a strong state, hierarchically controlled by the president. Its defenders assure us that this is how it was meant to be, that the framers envisioned a plebiscitary democracy in which every incumbent cuts deep, each truly an administration unto himself. But the vesting clause was not written to empower a presidential party. That's a combination that perverts original meaning. Like a forced marriage, it's a volatile union and a practical disaster. If the goal is to rediscover the wisdom of the framers, Americans will need to break out of the syndrome in which they are currently caught and find the right balance for themselves.

Afterword

"Elections have consequences." That disarming invocation of the political upset of 2016 fueled Donald Trump's assault on the "Deep State" and bolstered his case for a unitary executive. Repeated time and again over the course of his administration, the reference fused the current system of national political mobilization to sweeping claims on behalf of presidential control of the executive branch. In the process, it crystalized a uniquely volatile formula for governing, one in which charismatic leaders get to turn the executive branch into the strong arm of a personal party.

Four years after his upset victory, Trump attempted to leverage the enhanced position he had created for himself to defy the consequences of elections. Defeated in his bid for a second term, he demanded that federal administrators and party elites in the states discredit the outcome and lay aside the verdict of the voters. Failing at that, he made a last-ditch appeal to his political base, mobilizing them for direct action. A riot ensued at the Capitol, delaying the count of the electoral votes in Congress.

Surely the most important result of the presidential contest of 2020 was that, despite it all, Trump was unseated, and his duly elected opponent was sworn in on schedule. But submerged in that rocky reaffirmation of regular order was something more. Defeat and removal shelved the portentous follow-through planned for the government's administrative arm in Trump's second term.

On his way to victory, Joe Biden had drawn a sharp contrast with Trump on these matters. He had promised to respect the independence of the Department of Justice (DOJ), to follow the science in his response to the pandemic, and to heed the experts' warnings about climate change. With Biden safely installed in office, spectacular clashes between the president and the executive branch mercifully receded from the daily news.

So, did Biden's ascendance resolve the issues we have raised about the Trump presidency? Our contention is that it did not. Biden's campaign counterpoint to Trumpism was reassuring, but it skirted some basic questions. Do presidents now get to decide for themselves whether to defer to science or to respect prosecutorial independence? Are these things they provide or not in whatever way seems politically expedient to them? Accepting Biden's style as the antidote to Trump's concedes a lot to the personal presidency. Character claims and well-intentioned overtures will take us only so far in arresting the drift toward presidentialism.

As we write, the Trump-Biden transition is still shaking out. The lingering effects of that four-year drive to transform administrative power into personal power are pervasive. More than that, Trump's assault left the Biden White House struggling to reset the boundaries of appropriate action. Biden's professed respect for the authority of administrators vies with abiding presidential interests in control of the executive branch. Notwithstanding his promises of self-restraint, the new president has not denied himself the potential for achieving results directly through presidential unilateralism, nor have administrators been lulled into complacency.

Although there is less talk these days about a "Deep State" and a "unitary executive," the phantom twins of this beleaguered republic have not been dispelled. At this writing, they have not even withdrawn to their old haunts in the shadows of the Constitution. The Trump presidency aggravated pathologies sown into the current arrangements of presidential democracy in America. Strategies may shift subtly from one president to the next, but short of some basic rearrangement, contests over the scope of the president's executive power are poised to intensify. Sampling events between the fall of 2020, when our initial analysis left off, and the fall of 2021, when this new paperback edition went to press, we follow up on a variety of issues touched upon in our original text and then go on to survey President Biden's initial efforts to lay the conflicts of the Trump era to rest.

Trump's administration: As we point out in *Phantoms*, there is little reason to think that unitary command and control will bring about a leaner federal government. The effect of maximizing presidential control over the executive branch is, rather, to personalize administration and magnify the selective impact of presidential power. Trump's record confirmed that, anti-government rhetoric notwithstanding, conservative presidents do not shrink the state. Personnel added at the Departments of Defense, Treasury, Homeland Security, and Veterans Affairs increased the overall size of the federal workforce by more than 3 percent during the Trump years.[1]

The impact of Trump's assault on the "Deep State" was profound but scattered. The nation's civil servants did not suffer lightly their status as presidential punching bags. Where they perceived that their agencies had been politicized and that political appointees had no use for their advice, they left in droves. The effect was to compound long-standing challenges to executive branch capacity. In the first nine months of Trump's presidency, nearly 80,000 federal employees left the workforce, a 40 percent increase over the losses in that timespan during the Obama administration.[2] First-year losses to the Senior Executive Service were 26 percent greater than in Obama's first year.[3] Agencies on the White House hit list were decimated, especially at the SES level.[4]

Stripping away administrative depth and tightening top-down control politicizes administration of the law and undercuts Congress's authority to set agency missions and determine national commitments.[5] The executive branch lost over 28 percent of its public health educators under Trump and nearly 20 percent of its Internal Revenue Service officers. Inspection and investigation took big hits at the Labor Department's Wage and Hour Division, at the Occupational Safety and Health Administration, and at the Bureau of Mines.[6] The departure of top careerists at Housing and Urban Development crippled the department's major divisions and wiped out its "in-house legacy knowledge." Core operations such as fair housing enforcement declined precipitously.[7] After Mick Mulvaney neutered the Consumer Financial Protection Bureau (CFPB), Trump appointed a successor, Kathy Kraninger, who shifted the bureau's focus from enforcement to "education." Kraninger prioritized "empowering consumers to help themselves" and "protect their own interests."[8]

It takes time to cultivate depth in government, and once it is stripped away, it is hard to replace. As one authority on federal personnel policy put it, "You can't recover that in one administration … When they don't have that expertise, they have to reinvent the wheel."[9] Reinvention itself will be difficult as Trump administration hostility to federal employees seriously damaged recruitment efforts.[10] For example, following upon Trump's assault on the State Department, applications to take the Foreign Service exam fell by half, from 12,000 in 2016 to under 6,000 in 2020.[11]

Vacancies in targeted agencies across the government threatened to hobble Biden administration initiatives. Take the climate agenda. We reported in our text that the Trump administration's relocation of the Department of Agriculture's Economic Research Service and National Institute of Food and Agriculture, agencies that study how climate change affects farmers, resulted in the loss of two-thirds of those workforces. It ended up around 75 percent. These were harbingers of things to come. A subsequent relocation of the headquarters of the Bureau of Land Management from Washington, DC to Grand Junction, Colorado resulted in the departure of all but 23 percent of reassigned employees. Coming on top of over a hundred preexisting vacancies, one relocated official observed, "Everything's broken down." The Biden administration plans to move the BLM's headquarters back to Washington, but recovery is a long-term proposition and the demand for scientific expertise to meet the administration's climate goals is immediate.[12] The US Geological Survey lost nearly three hundred of its scientists and other technical experts, diminishing its capacity to model future climate change impacts. The Environmental Protection Agency (EPA) saw a 24 percent decline in the number of its environmental protection specialists. Staff at the agency speculated that new climate rules and regulations could be delayed for years. A perception that scientific work would continue to be whipsawed by presidential politics threatened to prolong the impact of the "brain drain" in the executive branch.[13]

Biden was hobbled not only by offices that were vacated during the Trump years, but also by offices that were filled. For example, by tightening his hold over the immigration bureaucracy, Trump handed Biden a "Deep State" problem of his own.[14] The Trump Department of Justice appointed 323 new immigration judges (IJs), filling over two-thirds of these career positions. The sheer pace of the hiring raised concerns about qualifications. The American Bar Association warned that the hiring process might have resulted in "underqualified or potentially biased judges," and the Government Accountability Office opened an investigation into whether the administration had deliberately hired partisan judges. The administration ramped up the effect of these appointments by ordering each IJ to decide at least 700 cases a year, and by appointing those with the lowest approval rates for asylum seekers to the Board of Immigration Appeals.[15] Biden has been left to figure out how to counter, or at least circumvent, the effects of these actions. IJs are not invulnerable to reassignment or removal.[16] Initial actions by the Biden administration reassigned the head of the Executive Office of Immigration Review and suspended the Trump administration's quotas.[17] Pressed to act more aggressively, Biden proposed hiring his own slate of judges and sought a vast expansion of appointments to US Citizenship and Immigration Services.[18]

In our assessment of Trump's handling of the coronavirus pandemic, we argued that crisis management entails power sharing and that a unitary executive is a poor substitute for teamwork.

Trump's performance on this score did not improve during his last months, and that may be where his impact on administrative assets will remain most durable. No doubt, the public's patience was strained during the prolonged crisis by the ongoing reexamination of evidence by public health experts and by serial revisions of their guidance. Still, Trump's hostility did lasting damage to their credibility, and that came at a terrible price. The president's personal brush with Covid-19 in October 2020 might have prompted a reset in his public relations with the government's medical advisers, but it did not. Indeed, one might have thought that Trump would want to tout his administration's stunning, late-breaking success in the development of vaccines and burnish his post-defeat reputation with a national campaign of his own to get people immunized. Instead, he watched from the sidelines as his acolytes ramped up the politicization of policy responses to the pandemic. Trump allowed a program that he himself had fast-tracked to become mired in innuendo and misinformation. His lasting legacy echoed in a political campaign against "Fauci-ism" and in dangerously distorted public perceptions of government policies and advice.[19] During Biden's first year, political resistance to Covid-19 vaccines concentrated in Trump-voting counties, leading to a disproportionate rise in deaths among his supporters.[20]

Trump was stopped before he could consolidate his gains in a second term, and that has left the long-term prospects of Trumpism in limbo. Taking a broad view of the matter, however, it would appear that Trump, whether consciously or not, followed pretty closely the path of the presidents who have had the most durable success in reconstructing American government: he eviscerated the institutional supports for the programmatic commitments of his opponents; he built a new, formidable party committed to his own priorities; and he packed the courts with judges sympathetic to his new dispensation.[21] Even without a second term, Trump had an extraordinary impact on the judiciary. Three Supreme Court justices, nearly a third of federal appellate judges, more than a quarter of the total number of active judges—this will reshape American government long into the future.[22] Trump's picks skewed younger.[23] Many are ardent supporters of the unitary theory. Their approach to presidential power is, as we shall see, already rearranging the executive branch.

Near misses: Forty-four thousand votes spread over three states sealed Trump's defeat.[24] His reelection was a near miss. Before he lost, his administration was on the brink of some transformative actions. Here we follow up on five initiatives flagged in our book.

Timing sealed the fate of the Trump administration's effort to use "transparency" policy to hobble the EPA. Going into Election Day, the administration was still rushing to complete work on its new "meta rule" restricting the use of protected data in promulgating environmental regulations.[25] When Trump's EPA issued the final version in early January 2021, it described the new rule as "procedural" rather than "substantive." The designation was purposeful. It would have allowed the policy to take effect right away, and more to the point, it would have exempted the rule from repeal by the new Democratic majority under the Congressional Review Act. But drawing this distinction was a gamble and a long shot at that. A district court judge determined that the rule was, in fact, substantive in nature and that it had not gone through all the notice-and-comment requirements for such actions under the Administrative Procedure Act.[26] Reversed on a technicality, the administration would surely have redoubled its efforts on behalf of this priority in a second term. With Biden's election, the latest (but certainly not the last) round in the transparency wars went to the scientists.

As our text reported, the personalization of power over the Intelligence Community had long been part of Trump's preparation for the 2020 campaign. With the installation of Robert O'Brien as national security adviser and John Ratcliffe as director of national intelligence (DNI), the displacement of professional competence and credibility by political interest and personal loyalty was well advanced. The new team dealt with election issues accordingly. Reliable reports that Russia was interfering in the election to support Trump again were deflected, redirected, and diluted. "China is using a massive and sophisticated influence campaign that dwarfs anything that any other country is doing," Ratcliffe asserted. "First you have China, which has the most massive program to influence the United States politically, [then] you have Iran and you have Russia," echoed O'Brien. After the election, the China angle was picked up by other Trump allies to try to persuade congressional Republicans that the presidential vote was invalid. A later public report from the Intelligence Community on all foreign interference in the election concluded that China was not a factor. On the other hand, Russian support for Trump over Biden was found to be substantial and sustained.[27] In addition, a whistleblower reported that acting appointees at DHS, Chad Wolf and Ken Cuccinelli, had directed career officers to downplay intelligence assessments of the Russian effort as well as assessments about the threat posed by white supremacists in the United States.[28] There was nothing to indicate that the president might return leadership of the Intelligence Community to more experienced hands after the election. On the contrary, Trump planned to start his second term by consolidating his hold over the narrative and clearing out the remaining voices for competence and credibility. CIA Director Gina Haspel and FBI Director Christopher Wray were both on the chopping block.[29]

Trump was also pursuing major change through the Census Bureau, an agency that was just coming to our attention as work on *Phantoms* neared completion. In July 2020, the president issued a memorandum mandating the exclusion of undocumented immigrants in the United States from the population count, and new political overseers were installed to supervise the production of the state-by-state estimates.[30] At stake were the apportionment of seats in the House of Representatives and the distribution of federal tax dollars. The changes would have been a significant boon for the Republican Party. A challenge to the plan was deferred by the Supreme Court, but bureau careerists raised concerns of their own. Facing a demand from Trump's appointed director, Steven

Dillingham, to provide the tally of unauthorized immigrants, senior officials questioned the validity of the estimates and stipulated that they would have to accompany the requested numbers with an explanation indicating that they were not reliable. Other careerists complained to the Commerce Department's inspector general, leaning into a rule akin to a scientific integrity policy. Facing questions from the IG and eying his exit with the outgoing administration, Dillingham dropped the matter. The administration would not have been given up so easily with a different election outcome and more time to finalize the estimates. In fact, the episode left the bureau's personnel so anxious about their political exposure that they began circulating new ideas for insulating their agency more deeply from interference. Meanwhile, President Biden issued an executive order rescinding Trump's directive on his first day in office.[31]

A similar dynamic played out in another late-breaking initiative at the Postal Service, this one implicating the election itself. During the summer of 2020, with the election season in full view, the administration's newly appointed postmaster general, Louis DeJoy, began issuing drastic cost-cutting orders, among other things dismantling mail sorting machines, removing mail collection boxes, and curtailing overtime pay. Postal employees pushed back. Support for their cause was amplified by the vastly expanded use of mail-in voting during the pandemic. If the cutbacks produced delays in the delivery of ballots, they might have seriously affected the vote count.[32] Coming under scrutiny from Congress and the courts, DeJoy agreed to a temporary rollback of some of his most draconian directives. Questions about the residual impact of his cuts persisted after Election Day, but they were no longer potent enough to prove decisive.[33] After the canvass, DeJoy moved ahead with his plans, and mail delivery slowed noticeably once again. Biden's efforts to oust DeJoy were complicated by protections against removal of members of the USPS Board of Governors, which holds the power to fire the postmaster general but remains packed with Trump appointees.[34]

Perhaps the most portentous near miss of all was the failure to implement Trump's executive order creating a Schedule F in the civil service. Issued in October 2020, the order would have removed job protections from any civil servant with a policy advising role. Potentially affecting thousands of careerists, this action promised to be "the most substantive change to the US civil service system since its creation in 1883."[35] The order followed through on James Sherk's memo, early in Trump's term, outlining the "Constitutional Option" for marginalizing civil service resistance to presidential direction. It also took advantage of sympathetic signals in recent rulings by the Supreme Court. In the end, the initiative fell to timing and logistics. Trump's defeat sealed its fate, as it was simply not possible to put the order into effect before inauguration day.[36] Biden not only rescinded the order, he also directed agencies to roll back other orders that had taken aim at civil service employee unionization and weakened their protections against removal.[37] Of course, orders rescinding orders underscores administrative depth's now-precarious dependence on presidential discretion. As one public administration scholar notes, if "Congress fails to directly respond, there is little reason to believe that such an attempt to assert control of the bureaucracy will not happen again."[38]

Resistance: Those who dismiss the Trump administration as bumbling and ineffective point to its low win rate against judicial challenges to agency actions. Administrations usually win about 70 percent of these challenges; the Trump administration prevailed less than 23 percent of the time. Many of these administrative actions were set aside by the courts on procedural grounds, indicating slipshod or rushed preparation.[39] Procedural deflections like that seldom extend to the substance of the proposed actions and thus leave open the potential for a redo. Moreover, the administration's reactions to these adverse rulings often mocked the judicial push-back. Failing to reverse some Obama-era regulations, Trump-era administrators stymied their implementation by stretching out the legal process, or by issuing delays in implementation, or by pressing ahead again with full rule withdrawals.[40] Nonetheless, the administration's general disregard for procedural requirements, requirements that the courts were bound to respect, proved self-defeating and testified to the enduring significance of administrative depth.

The contest between unity and depth at Trump's Justice Department was as fierce and murky in the endgame as it was prior to the 2020 election. On one track, the FBI remained in the crosshairs of Trump's efforts to expose a Deep State conspiracy. After the election, Attorney General William Barr designated US Attorney John Durham as a "special counsel," ensuring that Durham's investigation into the origins of the FBI's Russia probe would continue into the Biden administration. Following upon his indictment of FBI lawyer Kevin Clinesmith, Durham indicted a cybersecurity lawyer who, while raising concerns in a meeting with the FBI about potential links between the Trump Organization and a Russian bank, allegedly hid from the bureau his association with the Hillary Clinton campaign.[41] Durham then indicted the primary source behind the infamous Steele dossier for lying to the FBI. The special counsel found that Igor Danchenko too had hidden his ties to Democratic operatives and even fabricated one of his allegations. At this writing, Durham is still at work. Nothing revealed in his actions thus far has impugned the Senate Intelligence Committee's bipartisan findings about the Trump campaign's connections to Russian interference in the election. Moreover, an early inspector general report that excoriated the FBI for sloppiness had found that the bureau had adequate reasons to open the Russia investigation quite apart from the Steele dossier. Still, the revelation of these connections to the Democratic Party did little to silence allegations of FBI complicity or to instill confidence in the agency's credibility. The bureau had, after all, cited portions of the Steele dossier in its FISA warrant applications.[42]

While Durham had the FBI under scrutiny, pressures on the Justice Department were building along several other fronts. The primary challenge for the DOJ had always been the president's hostility to norms of investigatory independence. That grew more pointed after the election. Trump blew past even Barr's efforts to minimize the effects of the Mueller probe. Setting aside the work of the department altogether, the president pardoned Roger Stone, Paul Manafort, and Michael Flynn, ensuring that the alleged "Witch Hunt" came to nothing at all.[43] More disturbing still was Trump's effort during his final days to pressure government officials to validate his charges of election fraud. At first, resistance was equivocal. Before the election, Barr seemed sympathetic to the president's key talking point. He echoed the assertion that mail-in voting was prone to significant electoral fraud even as it was adopted more widely amid the Covid-19 pandemic.[44] After the election, Barr appeared again to bow to the president's demands. He directed prosecutors to investigate potential irregularities in the election, even though there had been little suggestive evidence. In protest, the director of DOJ's Elections Crimes Branch resigned his position.[45]

Ultimately, however, Trump's demands proved too much for Barr to bear. He himself resigned in December 2020, but not before announcing that his department's investigations had turned up no evidence of widespread voter fraud. Trump would later explain this stiff public rebuke to his charges as Barr's attempt to prove that he was not in the president's pocket: "Bill Barr was being portrayed as a puppet of mine. They said he's my 'personal lawyer,' 'he'll do anything,' and I said, 'Here we go...' He got more and more difficult, and I knew it." Trump went on to complain that there had been no DOJ charges of election fraud, no criminal charges against James Comey or Andrew McCabe, no announcement of an investigation into Hunter Biden, and no conclusion to Durham's probe before the election.[46] As Trump saw things, it was Deep State deflection across the board.

After Barr's resignation, Trump intensified his demands on DOJ. The president pressured the acting attorney general, Jeffrey Rosen, to open investigations into claims of election fraud in states decisive to the election's outcome.[47] When Rosen resisted, Trump sought to replace him with another DOJ official, Jeffrey Clark, who was disposed to pursuing the fraud claims. Specifically, Clark appeared willing to have the DOJ send warnings to officials in the key states about "irregularities" in voting and to suggest that the state legislatures needed to question the election results. The acting deputy attorney general, Richard Donoghue, joined Rosen in refusing to support these moves. As Donoghue wrote, Trump told the DOJ to publicly refer to the 2020 election as "corrupt" and then to "leave the rest to me and the [Republican] Congressmen."[48] An Oval Office confrontation ensued on January 3, 2021. As a Senate Judiciary Committee report later explained, Donoghue told the president that all DOJ assistant attorneys general "would resign if Trump replaced Rosen with Clark." More than that, he speculated "that U.S. Attorneys and other DOJ officials might also resign en masse."[49] The threat of open resistance carried the day. The president appeared isolated.

But again, not completely. Congressional defenders of the president's conduct later echoed unitary claims and castigated the work of the "Deep State" in the affair. Republicans on the Senate Judiciary Committee argued that Trump's behavior was fully within the scope of his constitutional duties: "President Trump's actions were consistent with his responsibilities as President to faithfully execute the law and oversee the Executive Branch." They suggested that it was "reasonable that President Trump maintained substantial skepticism concerning the DOJ's and FBI's neutrality and their ability to adequately investigate election fraud allegations in a thorough and unbiased manner."[50] Representative Jim Jordan (R-OH) argued that the problem was not that Trump or Chief of Staff Mark Meadows pressed DOJ officials to investigate election fraud; rather, "When the chief of staff to the president of the United States asks someone in the executive branch to do something, and they basically give him the finger, I think that's the problem we should be looking into."[51]

Trump's post-election demands on administrators raised alarms at the Pentagon as well as at DOJ. Here again, the pretenses of a unitary executive tested administrative deference, turning the "Deep State" conspiracy into something of a self-fulfilling prophecy. In fact, relations between the president and Defense Department personnel had already been strained by the administration's response to a Black Lives Matter protest near the White House in June 2020. Facing demands from Trump to invoke the Insurrection Act and use the military in response to the protests, Secretary of Defense Mark Esper recoiled. Trump responded to the insubordination with outrage: "You took away my authority! . . . You're not the president! I'm the goddamn president!"[52] Esper's relationship with Trump never recovered, and Trump fired him soon after the November election.[53] Still, the Insurrection Act was never invoked.

Relations between Trump and the chairman of the Joint Chiefs of Staff, General Mark Milley, deteriorated in this period also. Officers in this position have been cutting a higher political profile since the Goldwater-Nichols reforms of the Reagan era, and the effects have often proven controversial.[54] Milley had appeared in his combat fatigues walking next to Trump to St John's Episcopal Church to rebuke the Black Lives Matter protesters. The perception conveyed by that incident—that the military was being enlisted in domestic politics—prompted the general to a quick public apology.[55] But then, after the election, concerns about Trump's judgment swelled within the national security establishment. Milley and CIA Director Gina Haspel began to worry about the defeated president's stability, thinking that he might do something precipitous, even launch a war, over his bruised ego. In the wake of the January 6 riot, Milley reportedly took action to ensure that he could intercede on any Trump choice to launch nuclear weapons or undertake other significant military actions. The general went so far as to assure House Speaker Nancy Pelosi (D-CA) that he would vet any order.[56] The prospect that military officers might actively resist directives from the commander in chief became new fodder for the Deep State charge and put Milley in a tough spot. Even Alexander Vindman, no fan of Trump after serving as a star witness against the president in the first impeachment hearings, suggested Milley should resign for having circumvented civilian control of the armed forces.[57]

Eventually, "the resistance" extended all the way up to the vice president. When he rebuffed the president's demand that he use his role in counting the electoral votes in Congress to reject the certification of several states' slates of electors, Mike Pence became the improbable, last symbol of Deep State treachery. The president's call for redress at the "Stop the Steal" rally for his supporters put the onus squarely on his hitherto loyal vice president. The rioters who breached the Capitol and delayed the electoral count chanted "Hang Mike Pence." In response to the siege and the threat of violence against Pence and members of Congress, the House of Representatives invoked the ultimate sanction: they impeached the president again, this time for inciting an insurrection.[58] In the Senate trial (which took place after Trump left office), seven Republican senators voted to convict, the most bipartisan conviction vote in American history. But a majority of Republican senators stuck with the former president, and he was acquitted.[59]

Signposts: The election, the pandemic, and the post-election crisis all compounded the intensity of Trump's final months in office. New lines were crossed under those pressures, and new connections, both conceptual and practical, were forged. Although Trump ultimately departed, these signposts should not pass unnoticed. They point the way to presidentialism, a future now all-too-clearly in view.

Complaints about violations of the Hatch Act, prohibiting the mixing of official business with political advocacy on government property, have become more common in recent administrations. On that score, the Trump presidency was no exception. But there was a notable difference in this administration's response to these complaints. Affirmation of the rules in and around the White House is largely up to the president, and in this case, the usual apologies from presidential aides who overstepped the line were conspicuous for their absence. In November 2021, the agency charged with investigating such complaints, the Office of Special Counsel, released a stinging report detailing a string of violations in the final months of the Trump presidency by thirteen high ranking officials. Written by a Trump appointee, Henry Kerner, the report did not just document the wrongdoing, it pointed to the administration's "willful disregard" for the law. Several of the violations involved the use of White House grounds as a backdrop for the Republican National Convention and the use of other federal offices to stage campaign events. Presidential approval magnified the brazenness of the defiance.[60]

Kerner's report is a marker. On reflection, it connected all the dots: insulation stripped away and government exposed directly to the president's personal political interests; management fused to mobilization; the collapse of even the pretense of a distinction between politics and administration. But this was just one of many developments lending clarity to the emergent synthesis in those final days. Another that stands out to us as especially noteworthy was lodged in arguments by those who rose to defend the president's mobilization of his supporters on January 6. The issue concerned a lawsuit brought by Representative Eric Swalwell (D-CA), accusing the president of inciting an insurrection. Seeking dismissal of the lawsuit, Trump's lawyer rested his case firmly in Article II's vesting clause.

The memorandum claimed that a president's right to free speech, unlike a citizen's right, is not subject to boundaries or limitations. Political mobilization, it asserted, was an integral part of the president's job description: "a political speech by the President is not at the 'outer perimeter' of his duties—it is at the dead center." Then, pushing this remarkable interpretation of Article II further, the memorandum argued that this "duty" was expansively protected by the Constitution, that any attempt to regulate presidential speech—even incitement—infringed on the executive power: "the adjudication of any injunction or declaration based upon the words or action of the then-President would improperly regulate the executive department, in violation of Article II, § 1, which requires the executive power be exercised solely by the President." Not only was this claim at odds with the framers' obvious discomfort with a politicized, mobilizing president, it suggested that the Constitution freed the president to mobilize his followers however he pleased. The memo was unequivocal that unitary claims could, in fact, be utilized against electoral accountability and in pursuit of narrow partisan advantage: "The executive power rests with the President and him alone. . . . While holding that office, former President Trump was free to advocate for the appointment and certification of electors."[61]

The lines crossed and the conceptual connections forged in those final days did not materialize out of the blue. They capitalized on current institutional arrangements and the emergent claims about "the executive power" to which they correspond. These claims and arrangements merge management of the executive branch with political mobilization of a personal party. They cut through the alternative understandings and informal configurations of power that American government has long relied upon for its ballast.

*   *   *   *

Biden's bind: Joe Biden came to the presidency offering experience and competence, respect for government and its capacities, steady hands and a concern for sound management. He set out to prove that administrative assets could be harnessed constructively and that he could make the state work effectively. But demonstrating that know-how has proven difficult. Over the course of his first year, the new president repeatedly found himself at cross purposes, and in no small measure, he was brought up short by his own branding. The president had changed, but not the presidency, and when an experienced advocate for government stumbles on the follow-through, it's the institutional issues that come more clearly into focus.

Management values just don't fare very well when placed at the mercies of today's presidential politics. Consider Biden's campaign pledge to reverse Trump-era immigration policies. The incoming administration saw immediately the implications of its promise to move quickly on this commitment, but it was already too late to slow things down. The ensuing rush of migrants precipitated a crisis at the southern border and made short work of the president's boast that he was the one who knew how to solve problems.[62]

Biden occupied an office pressured to "act now," to "move faster," to "go bold," to "think big," and to "show results." These incentives cut strongly toward unitary command and control. The president had promised to listen to the experts and lead with the science, but he had also pledged decisive action on "Day 1." The administration opened with a stunning display of personal administration. There was a record-breaking round of executive unilateralism, carefully orchestrated to impress the public with presidential resolve.[63] The White House Office expanded rapidly, giving the new president the most expensive personal entourage in history. White House policy "czars" were hired to turn the executive branch into an extension of Biden priorities.[64] The Office of Information and Regulatory Affairs (OIRA) was similarly directed. Biden's remarkable memorandum to OIRA reads as if it was ripped from a campaign speech. He demanded "concrete suggestions on how the regulatory review process can promote public health and safety, economic growth, social welfare, racial justice, environmental stewardship, human dignity, equity, and the interests of future generations."[65] The president's base watched impatiently for that directive to deliver the goods.[66]

The Biden administration may be more conflicted than the Trump administration over how to navigate between mobilization and management, but the issues that present themselves are anchored in the current arrangements of our presidential democracy. The anticipated return to "normal" has thus simmered in irresolution, the new president tripping repeatedly over the fault lines in this structure. The search for agreeable lines of authority has been unsteady, and through it all, the phantom twins have continued their tussle.

Biden and the Deep State: Perception that "the resistance" was a reaction to the unique threat posed by Donald Trump fed an expectation that the new president and the executive branch would find themselves on the same page. But the structural realities became clear as soon as Biden asserted his authority. When he tilted toward the restoration of norms, his base called him out for failing to use his office more aggressively. When he put himself out front, boldly advancing his position as the nation's political leader, his administrative assets made hash of his pretensions.

Biden repeatedly signaled his respect for administrative independence. To underscore his commitment to restoring the credibility of the DOJ, he selected a circuit court judge, Merrick Garland, as attorney general. The new AG followed the script: "I don't want the department's career people to think that a new group comes in and immediately applies a political lens." But what Garland saw as even-handedness, the president's supporters saw as trimming. They expected a quick, decisive reversal of course. They charged the new AG with "running [the DOJ] like it's a chambers," with failing to "make a clean break from the Trump era" or to "come clean about what happened."[67] Biden restored another norm by reappointing Jerome Powell, his predecessor's choice, as chairman of the Federal Reserve Board. For the president this was an affirmation of "stability and independence at the Federal Reserve," but for many of his followers it was a missed opportunity. They wanted a political ally at the Fed, one who would advance the cause of banking regulation and fight against climate change.[68] Next to renewed faith in administrators, the "return to normal" featured confidence in Congress to deliver promised reforms. But when efforts to enact the president's agenda through statutes stalled, legislators pressed the case for presidential unilateralism to new heights: "It is now incumbent on President Biden to keep his promise to us and to the

American people by using the ultimate tool in his toolbox of executive action in every arena immediately."[69]

When heeding the call to move faster, Biden has encountered
pushback on the other side. An early scuffle implicating his pledge
to "follow the science" in his response to the pandemic offers one
example. At issue was how this vow would inform the president's
efforts to take charge of the crisis. Could he enlist the government's
scientists in a demonstration of steely resolve to stamp out the
plague? As it happened, Biden's resolve got out ahead of "the science." Operatives deep within the executive branch pounced on his
overreach, and his bid for public confidence fizzled in confusion.

The story unfolded in the summer of 2021. When the White
House learned that vaccine efficacy tended to wane over time, it determined that all Americans should be eligible for booster shots.
The president announced a booster program that would commence
on September 20, in time to head off a spike in cases during the
colder months. To be sure, scientists had been advising the White
House about the need for such a program. It was the White House,
however, that set the pace. In response, two top vaccine regulators at
the Food and Drug Administration announced their resignations.
They charged the White House with assaulting the autonomy of
their agency in formulating any booster program. According to
one member of the FDA's vaccine advisory committee, this was "the
administration's booster plan; it wasn't the FDA's booster plan." In
rushing to meet its September deadline, "the administration has
kind of backed themselves up against the wall." The Biden team
tried to smooth over differences by expressing confidence that
they would "have enough information and enough data" before the
deadline. But the dissonance in the president's leadership stance
was glaring. One former Trump official had the audacity to assert
that it was "unprecedented" for Biden to announce a rollout date for
boosters before the regulators had weighed in.[70]

Administrators schooled in resistance by their experience under
Trump gave Biden no quarter. The two FDA regulators who had

decided to retire pressed the issue by publishing a research paper in *The Lancet*. They concluded that there was no support for giving most Americans a booster shot: "Careful and public scrutiny of the evolving data will be needed to assure that decisions about boosting are informed by reliable science more than by politics."[71] The FDA's advisory committee overwhelmingly rejected the president's plan days before his self-imposed deadline.[72] A public, nationwide debate among the experts over the value of boosters tore into the president's credibility. Biden's determination to show that he was on top of the crisis backfired as questions about who should get the shots and when took control of the narrative. Soon the states began to go their own way on the matter, and both the FDA and CDC found themselves playing catch up. No one looked good. When, in November, the agencies did finally authorize and recommend booster shots for all adults, they did so without convening their advisory committees. Leading with the science proved to be anything but straightforward.[73]

Biden's resolve came back to bite him more severely when he bucked his military advisers and ended US involvement in the "forever war" in Afghanistan. Withdrawing from Afghanistan was one commitment made by both candidates in the 2020 campaign, and Biden was determined to make good on that pledge at the outset of his term. In drawing a hard line against the professionals on this issue, he appeared on solid ground, both constitutionally and politically. But in standing firm on his authority as commander in chief and making good on a popular promise, he accepted great risks, in particular the risks of defying his own self-professed respect for expertise and of acting on his own.

The new president had good reason to be skeptical of military advisers advocating another extension of the US commitment. No one was telling him that a positive outcome was in the offing. Moreover, as vice president, Biden had witnessed the pressures placed on Barack Obama at the outset of that administration to increase the troop commitment to Afghanistan. In the course of those labored negotiations, Biden advised Obama to be wary of generals "trying to box in a new president." "Don't let them jam you," he warned.[74] Biden had also observed the erratic course of the Trump administration, first allowing itself to get "jammed" by the military and then virtually capitulating to the Taliban insurgents in negotiations over the withdrawal of US troops. These experiences steeled Biden's determination to be different. After rejecting the importunities from his military advisers to keep the existing troops in the country and insisting on a complete pullout, he assured the nation that the long-awaited withdrawal was in steady hands and that it would be carried out in a secure and orderly way.[75]

The main objective was accomplished by the end of August 2021, but not without a very public display of chaos. The US-backed Afghan army failed to pick up the fight from the departing Americans, the government quickly collapsed, and an evacuation effort had to be organized hastily under hostile conditions. It proved difficult to locate all the Americans left stranded in the country. Desperate Afghan allies converged on the airport in Kabul hoping to redeem American promises of a passage to safety. A deadly terrorist attack shook the effort to its core. Biden was left to stew in his assurances of competence and the consequences of his resolve.

The Pentagon brass provided no cover. General Milley, chairman of the Joint Chiefs of Staff, and General Kenneth "Frank" McKenzie, head of US Central Command, publicly contradicted the president's claim that he had not been urged to keep troops in the country. They testified to Congress that the president had been forewarned of the risks of a government collapse and that he had been advised to continue to provide support. When Secretary of Defense Lloyd Austin assured Congress that US credibility with its allies "remains solid," Milley demurred: "Damage is one word that could be used." Asked why he did not resign in protest, Milley pressed his point backhandedly as an act of deference to the president's control over the military: "It would be an incredible act of political defiance for a commissioned officer to just resign because my advice is not taken."[76]

Foreign policy and security experts magnified the critique, calling the president's competence into question even more directly. Ryan Crocker, a retired ambassador to Afghanistan under Obama and Iraq under George W. Bush, called the withdrawal "a self-inflicted wound" and questioned Biden's "ability to lead our nation as commander in chief." Former Secretary of Defense Leon Panetta was equally blunt: "It just struck me that they were crossing their fingers and hoping chaos would not result. And it doesn't work that way."[77] Retired General David Petraeus described the withdrawal as "disastrous" and suggested that "an undesirable policy outcome" should not just be chalked up as an "intelligence failure."[78] Richard Haas, the president of the Council on Foreign Relations, ripped into Biden: not only had he "implement[ed] the Trump policy he had inherited; his administration did so in a Trumpian way, consulting minimally with others and leaving NATO allies to scramble."[79] As one commentator noted, "the Blob"—the foreign policy and national security establishment—"couldn't achieve any of their stated war aims, but they've proven they can absolutely wreck you politically."[80]

Biden got his booster program, and he ended the "forever war" in Afghanistan. But he most assuredly did not resolve the tensions between the chief executive and the executive branch. Fair to say, these episodes have a snafu-like character that contrasts markedly with the sensational conflicts of the Trump era. Most obvious is the fact that Biden did not return fire. Even when the administration bypassed the experts, there was no public challenge to their standing or loyalty. The president did not turn administrative pushback into an occasion to force a confrontation. In the face of resistance, he moved on. The fault lines, however, remain unmistakable. The depth of the executive branch poses risks for presidents. Protective of their agencies' missions and reputations, administrators and their allies extracted a significant price for Biden's initiative. They turned his professed respect for administrative depth and his boast of competence against him.

Biden's example brings us back to the critical questions. Does depth, with all its baggage, harbor values still worth protecting? If so, how much do we want to rely on presidents, with all their competing incentives, to defend those values?

Biden and the unitary executive: Biden was not alone in his promise to restore good government values in the wake of the Trump administration. Democrats in Congress announced their own commitment to this goal in the Protecting Our Democracy Act (PODA). Invoking the post-Watergate reforms, they sought to curb executive power on a wide variety of fronts. The act would, for example, bolster protections for whistleblowers, enact clearer limits on the appointment of "acting" officials to positions normally requiring Senate confirmation, make it more difficult for presidents to grant pardons in a corrupt manner, restrict a president's ability to spend or freeze money in a manner inconsistent with congressional appropriations, strengthen a ban on emoluments, impose new limits on presidential emergency declarations, prevent statutes of limitations on criminal acts from expiring during a president's term, and strengthen the ability of the Office of Special Counsel to enforce the Hatch Act. A Biden spokesperson lent administration support to the initiative, dubbing it a sweeping repudiation of Trumpism: "The prior administration's routine abuse of power and violation of longstanding norms posed a deep threat to our democracy. . . . We strongly support efforts to restore guardrails and breathe life back into those longstanding norms."[81]

But for all the talk of restoration and cooperation, several aspects of the legislation gave the administration pause. Reforms that threatened executive branch unity and hierarchy tested the limits of the administration's interest in collaboration. This reaction was reminiscent of the Carter administration's mixed response to the post-Watergate reforms. Provisions that would provide Congress information about White House-DOJ interactions and provisions that would prevent inspectors general from being fired without cause were particular sore points.[82] Just before the House passed the legislation in December 2021, the administration gave the move a pointedly cautious endorsement: it would "continue to work with Congress . . . to pass a bill that is grounded in constitutional principles . . . including by upholding the longstanding interests of the Executive Branch. . . . [and] ensur[ing] that no branch of government is able to abuse its authority or undermine a co-equal branch's constitutional prerogatives."[83] At this writing, the Senate seems likely to break up the bill, and the prospects of each of its several parts is uncertain.

The administration was not only wary of relinquishing prerogatives, it was also quick to embrace new powers for clamping down on administrators. The Supreme Court, now dominated by conservatives, has been advancing the doctrine of executive branch unity with newfound fervor. It has doubled down on its earlier decisions. Extending the logic in *Lucia v. SEC* (holding that administrative law judges were "inferior officers"), *U.S. v. Anthrex* held that "the unreviewable executive power exercised by [administrative patent judges] was incompatible with their status as inferior officers" and stipulated that the director of the patent office must have discretion to review and alter the APJs' decisions in order for the president to exercise proper supervision over the executive branch. Once again, the principle of unity cut through depth. As Chief Justice Roberts wrote, "The Constitution. . . forbids the enforcement of statutory restrictions on the Director [of the patent office] that insulate the decisions of APJs from his direction and supervision. . . . What matters is that the Director have the discretion to review decisions rendered by APJs. In this way, the President remains responsible for the exercise of executive power—and through him, the exercise of executive power remains accountable to the people."[84] The Court also reaffirmed the logic of *Seila Law v. CFPB* (holding that the director of the Consumer Financial Protection Bureau could not be protected from presidential removal). In *Collins v. Yellen*, the Court held that a statutory restriction on the president's authority to remove the director of the

Federal Housing Finance Authority (FHFA) "violates the separation of powers." In his opinion for the Court, Justice Samuel Alito
pointed to a series of cases articulating a unitary jurisprudence: "a
straightforward application of our reasoning in *Seila Law* dictates
the result here."[85]

Hinting at larger stakes, a *Collins* footnote listed other vulnerable targets in the executive branch: "*Amicus* warns that if the
Court holds that the Recovery Act's removal restriction violates
the Constitution, the decision will 'call into question many other
aspects of the Federal Government.' . . . *Amicus* points to the
Social Security Administration, the Office of Special Counsel,
the Comptroller, 'multi-member agencies for which the chair is
nominated by the President and confirmed by the Senate to a fixed
term,' and the Civil Service." While the Court refused to take the
bait, its demur was nonetheless ominous: "None of these agencies
is before us, and we do not comment on the constitutionality of any
removal restriction that applies to their officers."[86]

Different as Biden is from Trump, he was not about to disavow
newfound powers of unitary command and control. His too is
a personal administration, one that deploys a political calculus
in dealing with administrative authority. Employing the powers
now at his disposal to advance his political priorities, Biden has,
in effect, sustained the drive toward a unitary executive. Acting on
the Court's earlier decision in *Seila Law*, he removed the Trump-
appointed CFPB director years before her statutory term was set to
expire.[87] After the Court's ruling in *Collins*, he fired the director of
the FHFA.[88]

And Biden went further, extending the Court's logic on his
own. It is a telling irony that a political determination to undo the
"damage" of the Trump administration has tightened the grip of the
unitary executive. The new president dismissed Trump holdovers
who had "burrowed in" to protected civil service status.[89] He fired
the National Labor Relation Board's general counsel ten months before his designated term expired. At the CFPB, the administration

used substantial separation incentives and launched investigations to sideline senior career officials and make room for the new president's own people.[90] Biden affirmed Trump's designation of the DNI as a cabinet position, notwithstanding Congress's concerns in setting up that office that cabinet membership would politicize intelligence and subordinate it to policy priorities.[91] Biden even continued a Trump policy made possible by the *Lucia* ruling on administrative law judges. Bolstering Trump's actions, he issued an executive order confirming that ALJs would be exempt from merit hiring.[92] This in the face of House Democrats who were seeking legislation to restore merit-based hiring to the ALJs.[93]

Putting an even finer point on it, Biden fired the Social Security Administration commissioner, a Trump holdover whose designated term was to expire in 2025.[94] Needless to say, the president did not want an official hostile to his agenda in place at that agency. Still, he might have feigned a plausible "for cause" reason for the removal. Instead, the Justice Department's Office of Legal Counsel elaborated the Court's recent unitary-executive jurisprudence to justify the action: "We think the best reading of *Collins* and *Seila Law* leads to the conclusion that, notwithstanding the statutory limitation on removal, the President can remove the SSA Commissioner at will." The OLC referred to the Court's unitary boilerplate directly: "The Constitution vests the executive power and other specific authorities in a President on whom it imposes a duty to 'take Care that the Laws be faithfully executed.'"[95]

Like the Court, the OLC limited the implications of this finding with a coy demur, and that itself spoke volumes. Begging off any broader claims, it echoed the *Collins* footnote and listed the dominos yet to fall: "[our opinion] does not imply any similar determination with respect to the validity of tenure protections conferred on other executive officials—for example the Special Counsel, another single-member agency head whose removal restrictions implicate different considerations. . . . Nor does our conclusion speak to the constitutionality of existing or hypothetical tenure protections for any other agency heads, including multi-member commissions, that do not share the specific combination of features identified here."[96]

Claims on behalf of a unitary executive are now pushing against an open door. The Court has signaled fair game in the drive to strip away administrative depth and politicize the executive branch. No president, not even one professing good government values, is going to decline the invitation to personalize control and create an administration all his own.

* * * *

Rearrangement: Reducing executive branch exposure to presidential politics isn't easy. Neither is it costless or without risk. Presidents resist the addition of depth, and with good reason: often they end up paying a political price for it. But depth supports collective goods. It promotes a steady administration of the laws, underwriting continuity, consistency, and collaboration in governance. It cultivates expertise, protects scientific integrity, and promotes investigatory independence. We should think twice before we squander those values in service to overwrought conceptions of democratic accountability and the constitutional division of powers.

For all the evidence of continued administrative resistance, presidential democracy in America is currently arranged to cut through administrative insulation and promote the transformation of the executive branch into an arm of the presidential party. Not only is government management tightly fused to political mobilization, but both have been presidentialized and personalized. Trump's "Deep State" frame brought these trends into focus. Combining constitutional conjectures and democratic pretensions, his presidency provided a playbook for future strongmen who want to cut deep. [97]

Presidents like Biden, who profess different standards, are unlikely to arrest these trends on their own. Acting within current arrangements, they may, in fact, advance them. We cannot count on presidents, even well-meaning presidents, to counter the drift toward presidentialism. Neither can we count on the Constitution or the will of the people. The danger of democratic backsliding in America lies in the current arrangement of those touchstones of legitimacy.

The good news is that Americans have a long history of inventing new ways to govern. Time and again, we have altered the relationship between government management and political mobilization, reconfiguring constitutional relationships in the process. More often than not, we have done so without constitutional amendments. Rearrangement need not be hostile to presidential power. Well into the twentieth century, serial reconfigurations accommodated progressively more vigorous forms of presidential leadership. Simultaneously, however, they strengthened interbranch collaboration in managing the commitments lodged in the executive branch. The tradition to be recovered is the one that refused to lock presidential power into a zero-sum relationship with collective responsibility in administration.

It is not presidential power per se that needs to be arrested; it is the personalization of presidential power. A strong presidency can operate safely and effectively in service to others if it is properly institutionalized. The objective in rearranging things should not be to instill unity in the executive branch but to incentivize a more unified mode of operations in the government as a whole. This has been done before. It entails relaxing the formal separation of powers, bolstering the institutions that surround the presidency, and enlisting the nation's political leader, so far as possible, in collaborative governing arrangements.

As things stand, this will require a radical change of course. The current vogue of constitutional formalism has all but stifled creativity in rethinking institutional relationships. A rigid prioritization of the separation of powers heavily favors a personalized presidency, especially so under the current system of selection and political mobilization. For its part, the Supreme Court is fast at the work of facilitating personalization through its promotion of the unitary executive.[98] That has left administrative depth exposed and made inter-branch collaboration more difficult.

One desperate but notable reminder of the alternative path forward was provided by a dissenting opinion in *Seila Law*. Justice Elena Kagan took direct aim at the Court's new formalism. Though renowned for her scholarly advocacy of "presidential administration," she seized this opportunity to reassert Congress's historic role as a design innovator. Congress, Kagan averred, has significant latitude "to organize all the institutions of American governance," and she urged the Court to support novel arrangements: "Throughout the Nation's history, this Court has left most decisions about how to structure the executive branch to Congress and the President, acting through legislation they both agree to."[99]

Kagan's dissent is notable not just for its focus on Congress, but for its departure from the now-familiar call to double down on the separation of powers and prevent Congress from delegating so much its policy-making authority to administrators in the executive branch. As she recognized, creativity in delegation is essential to Congress's full participation in modern governance. It is precisely because crafting complex legislation is difficult that Congress's ability to innovate in the design of administrative institutions is crucial. Constraining that ability in the name of a cleaner separation of powers is unlikely to strengthen democracy, or produce better policy, or return Congress to its former glory as the premier lawmaker. On the contrary, the prospect is to hobble the legislature even more.

Kagan was dissenting from a decision that preempted congressional innovation in administrative design. The PODA is Congress's most recent effort to reassert itself. The bill includes a lot of useful correctives, but even if they are enacted and pass judicial muster, they remain a collection of whack-o-mole responses to Trump era transgressions. Like the post-Watergate reforms, they do more to respond to the prior mobilization than to anticipate the next one. Resolving the thorny problems before us will require more.

Ideas for a more thoroughgoing redesign are not hard to come by. Congress might reassert its partnership role more effectively by reviving the use of multi-member independent boards. It could limit the number and reach of political overseers in the agencies and bolster protections for career administrators.[100] It could depoliticize key administrative positions by assigning the appointment of some "inferior officers," like administrative law judges, to the courts.[101] It could create a congressional regulation office, mirroring the president's Office of Information and Regulatory Affairs, to engage executive branch agencies in a more cooperative process of rule-making.[102] Whatever the merits of these various proposals, they share an interest in countering the personalization of administrative management.

Reviving Congress's traditional interest in governmental design, and in particular in protecting administrative depth, will be critical, but it will not be enough. Bolstering bureaucracy without at the same time strengthening democracy is unlikely to produce a durable, much less a responsible settlement. To insulate administration from presidential impositions without at the same time rearranging the institutions through which American democracy is mobilized could just compound the problems posed by administrative depth. More than that, without democracy reforms, both congressional incentives to insist on greater collaboration in control of the executive branch and presidential incentives to cooperate are likely to remain weak.

Currently, American democracy is undergoing a profound rearrangement, much of which is subversive. Gerrymandering, voting rights restrictions, stripping away the authority of state election officials, and weakening campaign finance regulations—these are locking in patterns of mobilization that further the personalization of political power at all levels. Here again, reversing course will be difficult. The general idea behind a constructive reform program is, however, the same. Rearrangement should seek so far as possible to institutionalize popular will more effectively and to strengthen the hand of actors surrounding the presidency.

The drive toward a unitary executive coincided with the demise of the convention system of nominations and the rise of candidate-centered campaigns.[103] The result has been an odd combination of weak parties with fierce partisanship.[104] Among the many effects, this combination has hobbled the cause of collective responsibility in administrative management. By the same token, changing the mode of candidate selection and national mobilization can have a profound impact on the way the government is managed. The objective on this front would be to make presidents more accountable to strong and independent party organizations, and beyond that, to ensure that the parties themselves maintain broad and diverse coalitions at all levels.[105] Reforms along these lines would reverberate throughout the constitutional system, reconfiguring inter-branch relations.

The current agitation to protect voting rights and expand American democracy is largely a reaction to the stiffening of constraints.[106] It has yet to speak directly, in its own voice, to a revised formula for governance. A more thoroughgoing democratization of the polity has traditionally been an opportunity to rethink how this state will operate. To be effective, reforms that ease constraints on political mobilization need to be related—conceptually, organizationally, and institutionally—to a new understanding of executive branch management. At present, unfortunately, populism is driving both sides of the debate over electoral reform, and serious talk of institutional mediation and collective control is all but squeezed out. That does not bode well for the future of presidential democracy in America.

Notes

Foreword for the Paperback Edition

1. Jack Balkin, "Depth and Unity," *Balkinization*, July 12, 2021, https://balkin. blogspot.com/2021/07/depth-and-unity.html.
2. E.g., Balkin, "Depth and Unity"; Blake Emerson, "Going Deeper," *Balkinization*, July 9, 2021, https://balkin.blogspot.com/2021/07/going-deeper.html; Anya Bernstein and Cristina Rodríguez, "Are the Phantoms Real?" *Balkinization*, July 14, 2021, https://balkin.blogspot.com/2021/07/are-phantoms-real.html.
3. John A. Dearborn, Desmond S. King, and Stephen Skowronek, "How to Tame the Presidency after Trump," *New York Times*, March 16, 2021, https://www.nytimes.com/2021/03/16/opinion/congress-presidency-trump.html.
4. Philip A. Wallach, "How Deep Is Your State?" *Law & Liberty*, June 23, 2021, https://lawliberty.org/book-review/how-deep-is-your-state/.
5. Steven Gow Calabresi, "'A Shining City on a Hall': The Unitary Executive and the Deep State," *Balkinization*, July 11, 2021, https://balkin.blogspot.com/2021/07/a-shining-city-on-hill-unitary.html. On this point, see also, William Howell, "Populism, the Deep State, and the Unitary Executive," *New Rambler*, April 15, 2021, https://newramblerreview.com/book-reviews/political-science/populism-the-deep-state-and-the-unitary-executive.

Chapter 1

1. On the origins of the term "Deep State," see Jean Pierre-Filiu, *From Deep State to Islamic State: The Arab Counter-Revolution and Its Jihadi Legacy* (New York: Oxford University Press, 2015), ch. 1.
2. See, for example, David A. Graham, "There Is No American 'Deep State,'" *The Atlantic*, February 20, 2017, https://www.theatlantic.com/international/archive/2017/02/why-its-dangerous-to-talk-about-a-deep-state/517221/.
3. Anonymous, "I Am Part of the Resistance Inside the Trump Administration," *New York Times*, September 5, 2018, https://www.nytimes.com/2018/09/05/opinion/trump-white-house-anonymous-resistance.html.

4. Anonymous, "I Am Part of the Resistance Inside the Trump Administration."

5. Stephen Skowronek, *The Politics Presidents Make: Leadership from John Adams to Bill Clinton* (Cambridge, MA: Belknap Press of Harvard University Press, 1997).

6. Blake Emerson, "The Departmental Structure of Executive Power: Subordinate Checks from Madison to Mueller," *Yale Journal on Regulation* 38, no. 1 (January 2021).

7. Hugh Heclo, *On Thinking Institutionally* (Boulder, CO: Paradigm, 2008), 55.

8. See, for example, James MacGregor Burns, *Presidential Government: The Crucible of Leadership* (Boston: Houghton Mifflin, 1965).

9. Malcolm Byrne, *Iran-Contra: Reagan's Scandal and the Unchecked Abuse of Presidential Power* (Lawrence: University Press of Kansas, 2014).

10. Paul C. Light, *Thickening Government: Federal Hierarchy and the Diffusion of Accountability* (Washington, DC: Brookings Institution, 1995).

11. James W. Fesler, "The Higher Civil Service in Europe and the United States," in *The Higher Civil Service in Europe and Canada: Lessons for the United States*, ed. Bruce L. R. Smith (Washington, DC: Brookings Institution, 1984), 87–92.

12. *An Investigation into the Removal of Nine U.S. Attorneys in 2006*, Office of the Inspector General and Office of Professional Responsibility, U.S. Department of Justice, September 2008, https://oig.justice.gov/special/s0809a/final.pdf.

13. James Risen, "If Donald Trump Targets Journalists, Thank Obama," *New York Times*, December 30, 2016, https://www.nytimes.com/2016/12/30/opinion/sunday/if-donald-trump-targets-journalists-thank-obama.html.

14. Jeffrey Crouch, Mark J. Rozell, and Mitchel A. Sollenberg, "The Unitary Executive Theory and President Donald J. Trump," *Presidential Studies Quarterly* 47, no. 3 (September 2017): 561–573.

15. For an overview of this literature, see Desmond King and Robert C. Lieberman, "The American State," in *The Oxford Handbook of American Political Development*, eds. Richard M. Valelly, Suzanne Mettler, and Robert C. Lieberman (New York: Oxford University Press, 2016), 231–258.

16. On the clash of "intercurrent" systems, see Karen Orren and Stephen Skowronek, *The Search for American Political Development* (New York: Cambridge University Press, 2004). On "multiple orders," see Desmond S. King and Rogers M. Smith, "Racial Orders in American Political Development," *American Political Science Review* 99, no. 1 (February 2005): 75–92.

Chapter 2

1. J. P. Nettl, "The State as a Conceptual Variable," *World Politics* 20, no. 4 (July 1968): 559–592.

2. Samuel P. Huntington, *Political Order in Changing Societies* (New Haven, CT: Yale University Press, 1968), 98–99.

3. Richard E. Neustadt, *Presidential Power: The Politics of Leadership* (New York: Wiley, 1960), 33.

4. Marver H. Bernstein, *Regulating Business by Independent Commission* (Westport, CT: Greenwood Press, 1955); Grant McConnell, *Private Power and American Democracy* (New York: Alfred A. Knopf, 1966). For a recent engagement, see Daniel Carpenter and David A. Moss, eds., *Preventing Regulatory Capture: Special Interest Influence and How to Limit It* (New York: Cambridge University Press, 2014).

5. Theodore J. Lowi, "How the Farmers Get What They Want," *Reporter*, May 21, 1964, 34–37; Theodore J. Lowi, *The End of Liberalism: The Second Republic of the United States* (New York: W. W. Norton, 1979).

6. Steven G. Calabresi and Nicholas Terrell, "The Fatally Flawed Theory of the Unbundled Executive," *Minnesota Law Review* 93, no. 5 (May 2009): 1696–1740, at 1700. See also Cass R. Sunstein and Lawrence Lessig, "The President and the Administration," *Columbia Law Review* 94, no. 1 (January 1994): 1–123; Elena Kagan, "Presidential Administration," *Harvard Law Review* 114, no. 8 (June 2001): 2245–2385.

7. Jody Freeman, "Collaborative Governance in the Administrative State," *UCLA Law Review* 45, no. 1 (October 1997): 1–98.

8. Desmond King and Robert C. Lieberman, "Ironies of State Building: A Comparative Perspective on the American State," *World Politics* 61, no. 3 (July 2009): 547–588.

9. Dwight D. Eisenhower, "Farewell Radio and Television Address to the American People," January 17, 1961, *The American Presidency Project*, https://www.presidency.ucsb.edu/documents/farewell-radio-and-television-address-the-american-people.

10. Lowi, *End of Liberalism*.

11. Lawrence R. Jacobs and Desmond King, *Fed Power: How Finance Wins* (New York: Oxford University Press, 2016).

12. Peter Dale Scott, *The American Deep State: Big Money, Big Oil, and the Attack on US Democracy* (Lanham, MD: Rowman and Littlefield, 2015).

13. Blake Emerson, *The Public's Law: Origins and Architecture of Progressive Democracy* (New York: Oxford University Press, 2019).

14. B. Dan Wood, *The Myth of Presidential Representation* (New York: Cambridge University Press, 2009); Douglas L. Kriner and Andrew

Reeves, *The Particularistic President: Executive Branch Politics and Political Inequality* (New York: Cambridge University Press, 2015).

15. John A. Dearborn, *Power Shifts: Congress and Presidential Representation* (Chicago: University of Chicago Press, 2021), Part II.

16. James N. Druckman and Lawrence R. Jacobs, *Who Governs? Presidents, Public Opinion, and Manipulation* (Chicago: University of Chicago Press, 2015).

17. "Executive Branch Employment by Gender and Race/National Origin," September 2006–September 2017, Federal Employment Reports, Data, Analysis & Documentation, Office of Personnel Management, https://www.opm.gov/policy-data-oversight/data-analysis-documentation/federal-employment-reports/reports-publications/executive-branch-employment-by-gender-and-racenational-origin/.

18. Joel D. Aberbach, Robert D. Putnam, and Bert A. Rockman, *Bureaucrats and Politicians in Western Democracies* (Cambridge, MA: Harvard University Press, 1981), 64, 73; Jon D. Michaels, "The American Deep State," *Notre Dame Law Review* 93, no. 4 (2018): 1653–1670, at 1658–1663.

19. Herbert Kaufman, *The Forest Ranger: A Study in Administrative Behavior* (Baltimore: Johns Hopkins University Press, 1960); Daniel P. Carpenter, *The Forging of Bureaucratic Autonomy: Reputations, Networks, and Policy Innovation in Executive Agencies, 1862–1928* (Princeton, NJ: Princeton University Press, 2001).

20. "Americans' Trust in Military, Scientists Relatively High; Fewer Trust Media, Business Leaders, Elected Officials," *Pew Research Center*, March 22, 2019, https://www.pewresearch.org/ft_19-03-21_scienceconfidence_americans-trust-in-military/. However, the high public regard for the military should not mask the racialized hierarchy present in the armed forces. Desmond King, *Separate and Unequal: African Americans and the US Federal Government*, rev. ed. (New York: Oxford Univeristy Press, 2007), ch. 4. Despite past successes at integration, by 2020, the representation of communities of color in the senior levels of the military had collapsed. People of color constituted 43% of the forces' 1.3 million members, but held only 2 of the 41 most senior leadership positions, according to data in Helene Cooper, "African Americans Are Highly Visible in the Military, but Almost Invisible at the Top," *New York Times*, May 25, 2020, https://www.nytimes.com/2020/05/25/us/politics/military-minorities-leadership.html. Cooper reports the reversal in earlier advances toward integration.

21. Neustadt, *Presidential Power*, ch. 2.

22. For a more recent example, consider Defense Secretary James Mattis's resignation from the Trump administration: Helene Cooper, "Jim Mattis,

Defense Secretary, Resigns in Rebuke of Trump's Worldview," *New York Times*, December 20, 2018, https://www.nytimes.com/2018/12/20/us/politics/jim-mattis-defense-secretary-trump.html.

23. Ronald Kessler, *The Secrets of the FBI* (New York: Crown, 2011), 40–41.

24. Bruce Ackerman, *The Decline and Fall of the American Republic* (Cambridge, MA: Belknap Press of Harvard University Press, 2010), 60.

25. Daniel J. Sargent, *A Superpower Transformed: The Remaking of American Foreign Relations in the 1970s* (New York: Oxford University Press, 2015), 46.

26. William J. Novak, "The Myth of the 'Weak' American State," *American Historical Review* 113, no. 3 (June 2008): 752–772.

27. Suzanne Mettler, *The Submerged State: How Invisible Government Policies Undermine American Democracy* (Chicago: University of Chicago Press, 2011); Adam Sheingate, "Why Can't Americans See the State?" *The Forum* 7, no. 4 (2009): 1–14; Ursula Hackett, *America's Voucher Politics: How Elites Learned to Hide the State* (New York: Cambridge University Press, 2020).

28. Brian Balogh, *A Government out of Sight: The Mystery of National Authority in Nineteenth-Century America* (New York: Cambridge University Press, 2009).

29. Paul Frymer, *Building an American Empire: The Era of Territorial and Political Expansion* (Princeton, NJ: Princeton University Press, 2017).

30. Michael Mann, "The Autonomous Power of the State: Origins, Mechanisms and Results," *European Journal of Sociology* 25, no. 2 (1984): 185–213.

31. Ira Katznelson, "Flexible Capacity: The Military and Early American Statebuilding," in *Shaped by War and Trade: International Influences on American Political Development*, eds. Ira Katznelson and Martin Shefter (Princeton, NJ: Princeton University Press, 2002), 82–110; Jonathan Obert, *The Six-Shooter State: Public and Private Violence in American Politics* (New York: Cambridge University Press, 2018).

32. See, for example, Rogers M. Smith, *Civic Ideals: Conflicting Visions of Citizenship in US History* (New Haven, CT: Yale University Press, 1997); King, *Separate and Unequal*; Karen Orren and Stephen Skowronek, *The Policy State: An American Predicament* (Cambridge, MA: Harvard University Press, 2017), 23–24.

33. James Willard Hurst, *Law and the Conditions of Freedom in the United States Nineteenth Century* (Madison: University of Wisconsin Press, 1956), ch. 1.

34. Franz Neumann, *The Democratic State and the Authoritarian State: Essays in Political and Legal Theory* (New York: Free Press, 1964).

35. Frank Dobbin and John Sutton, "The Strength of a Weak State: The Rights Revolution and the Rise of Human Resources Management Divisions,"

American Journal of Sociology 104, no. 2 (September 1998): 441–476, at 441.

36. Gerald Berk, Dennis C. Galvan, and Victoria Hattam, eds. *Political Creativity: Reconfiguring Institutional Order and Change* (Philadelphia: University of Pennsylvania Press, 2013).

37. Michael McFaul, "The Deeply Dedicated State," *New York Review of Books*, October 31, 2019, https://www.nybooks.com/daily/2019/10/31/the-deeply-dedicated-state/.

Chapter 3

1. On the idea that a mandate can derive from an electoral surprise, see Lawrence A. Grossback, David A. M. Peterson, and James A. Stimson, *Mandate Politics* (New York: Cambridge University Press, 2007), 189.

2. Donald J. Trump, "Remarks by President Trump before Marine One Departure," July 12, 2019, White House, https://www.whitehouse.gov/briefings-statements/remarks-president-trump-marine-one-departure-52/.

3. Michael Brice-Saddler, "While Bemoaning Mueller Probe, Trump Falsely Says the Constitution Gives Him 'the Right to Do Whatever I Want," *Washington Post*, July 23, 2019, https://www.washingtonpost.com/politics/2019/07/23/trump-falsely-tells-auditorium-full-teens-constitution-gives-him-right-do-whatever-i-want/.

4. Jason Zengerle, "How the Trump Administration Is Remaking the Courts," *New York Times*, August 22, 2018, https://www.nytimes.com/2018/08/22/magazine/trump-remaking-courts-judiciary.html. See also Amanda Hollis-Brusky, *Ideas with Consequences: The Federalist Society and the Conservative Counterrevolution* (New York: Oxford University Press, 2015).

5. Jed Shugerman, "Brett Kavanaugh's Legal Opinions Show He'd Give Donald Trump Unprecedented New Powers," *Slate*, July 19, 2018, https://slate.com/news-and-politics/2018/07/brett-kavanaugh-would-give-donald-trump-unprecedented-new-powers.html; Mark Sherman, "Kavanaugh: Watergate Tapes Decision May Have Been Wrong," *Associated Press*, July 21, 2018, https://apnews.com/3ea406469d344dd8b2527aed9 2da6365/High-court-nominee-gets-started-answering-questions.

6. Neomi Rao, "The Administrative State and the Structure of the Constitution," Heritage Foundation, Lecture No. 1288, June 15, 2018 [Delivered October 4, 2017], 4, https://www.heritage.org/sites/default/files/2018-06/HL1288_0.pdf.

7. Bob Woodward, *Fear: Trump in the White House* (New York: Simon and Schuster, 2018), 326.

8. Letter from Marc E. Kasowitz to Robert S. Mueller, June 23, 2017. "The Trump Lawyers' Confidential Memo to Mueller, Explained," *New York Times*, June 2, 2018, https://www.nytimes.com/interactive/2018/06/02/us/politics/trump-legal-documents.html#june-23-2017.

9. Emily Bazelon, "Who Is Bill Barr?" *New York Times*, October 26, 2019, https://www.nytimes.com/interactive/2019/10/26/opinion/william-barr-trump.html.

10. Adam Liptak, "Supreme Court to Rule on Trump's Power to Fire Head of Consumer Bureau," *New York Times*, October 18, 2019, https://www.nytimes.com/2019/10/18/us/politics/supreme-court-trump-consumer-bureau.html.

11. John Yoo, "Beware of Impeaching Trump. It Could Hurt the Presidency," *New York Times*, September 24, 2019, https://www.nytimes.com/2019/09/24/opinion/ukraine-trump.html; Justine Coleman, "Trump, New Legal Guru Meet at White House," *The Hill*, August 2, 2020, https://thehill.com/homenews/administration/510202-trump-new-legal-guru-meet-at-white-house-report.

12. Peter Strauss, "The Trump Administration and the Rule of Law," *Revue française d'administration publique* no. 170 (2019): 443–446; Peter M. Shane, *Madison's Nightmare: How Executive Power Threatens American Democracy* (Chicago: University of Chicago Press, 2009).

13. @realDonaldTrump, October 17, 2019, 11:06 PM, Twitter, https://twitter.com/realDonaldTrump/status/1185029472132698113.

14. Peter Baker, Lara Jakes, Julian E. Barnes, Sharon LaFraniere, and Edward Wong, "Trump's War on the 'Deep State' Turns against Him," *New York Times*, October 23, 2019, https://www.nytimes.com/2019/10/23/us/politics/trump-deep-state-impeachment.html.

15. Julie Hirschfeld Davis, "Rumblings of a 'Deep State' Undermining Trump?: It Was Once a Foreign Concept," *New York Times*, March 6, 2017, https://www.nytimes.com/2017/03/06/us/politics/deep-state-trump.html.

16. Michelle Cottle, "They Are Not the Resistance. They Are Not a Cabal. They Are Public Servants," *New York Times*, October 20, 2019, https://www.nytimes.com/2019/10/20/opinion/trump-impeachment-testimony.html.

17. Jefferson Morley, "The 'Deep State' Is a Political Party," *New Republic*, November 8, 2019, https://newrepublic.com/article/155629/deep-state-political-party.

18. Quoted in James B. Stewart, *Deep State: Trump, the FBI, and the Rule of Law* (New York: Penguin Press, 2019), 324.

19. Alexander Hamilton, "The Federalist No. 69" [March 14, 1788], in *The Federalist*, ed. Terence Ball (New York: Cambridge University Press, 2003),

335; Charles C. Thach Jr., *The Creation of the Presidency, 1775–1789: A Study in Constitutional History* (Baltimore: Johns Hopkins University Press, 1923), 138–139.

20. *Morrison v. Olson*, 487 U.S. 654, 705 (1988) (Scalia, J., dissenting). Emphasis in original.

21. Saikrishna Bangalore Prakash, *Imperial from the Beginning: The Constitution of the Original Executive* (New Haven, CT: Yale University Press, 2015), 196.

22. See, for example, the different perspectives in the following: Steven G. Calabresi and Kevin H. Rhodes, "The Structural Constitution: Unitary Executive, Plural Judiciary," *Harvard Law Review* 105, no. 6 (April 1992): 1153–1216; John Yoo, *The Powers of War and Peace: The Constitution and Foreign Affairs after 9/11* (Chicago: University of Chicago Press, 2005); Prakash, *Imperial from the Beginning*; Cass R. Sunstein and Lawrence Lessig, "The President and the Administration," *Columbia Law Review* 94, no. 1 (January 1994): 1–123; and Vicki Divoll, "Transcript: Eight Things I Hate about the Unitary Executive Theory," *Vermont Law Review* 38, no. 1 (Fall 2013): 147–154.

23. Steven G. Calabresi and Christopher S. Yoo, *The Unitary Executive: Presidential Power from Washington to Bush* (New Haven, CT: Yale University Press, 2008).

24. Stephen Skowronek, "The Conservative Insurgency and Presidential Power: A Developmental Perspective on the Unitary Executive," *Harvard Law Review* 122, no. 8 (June 2009): 2070–2103; Daphna Renan, "The President's Two Bodies," *Columbia Law Review* 120, no. 5 (June 2020): 1119–1214.

25. Bazelon, "Who Is Bill Barr?"

26. Jeremy D. Bailey, *The Idea of Presidential Representation: An Intellectual and Political History* (Lawrence: University Press of Kansas, 2019), ch. 5.

27. Edward Rubin, "The Myth of Accountability and the Anti-administrative Impulse," *Michigan Law Review* 103, no. 8 (August 2005): 2073–2136; Heidi Kitrosser, *Reclaiming Accountability: Transparency, Executive Power, and the U.S. Constitution* (Chicago: University of Chicago Press, 2015).

28. Andrew Kent, Ethan J. Leib, and Jed Handelsman Shugerman, "Faithful Execution and Article II," *Harvard Law Review* 132, no. 8 (June 2019): 2111–2192.

29. William P. Barr, "Attorney General William P. Barr Delivers the 19th Annual Barbara K. Olson Memorial Lecture at the Federalist Society's 2019 National Lawyers Convention," November 15, 2019, Office of Public Affairs,

Department of Justice, https://www.justice.gov/opa/speech/attorney-general-william-p-barr-delivers-19th-annual-barbara-k-olson-memorial-lecture.

30. David Brian Robertson, *The Original Compromise: What the Constitution's Framers Were Really Thinking* (New York: Oxford University Press, 2013), ch. 10–11; Jonathan Gienapp, *The Second Creation: Fixing the American Constitution in the Founding Era* (Cambridge, MA: Belknap Press of Harvard University Press, 2018), ch. 3.

31. Terry M. Moe, "The Politicized Presidency," in *New Directions in American Politics*, eds. John E. Chubb and Paul E. Peterson (Washington, DC: Brookings Institution, 1985), 235–271.

32. Calabresi and Yoo, *Unitary Executive*.

33. Nicholas F. Jacobs, Desmond King, and Sidney M. Milkis, "Building a Conservative State: Partisan Polarization and the Redeployment of Administrative Power," *Perspectives on Politics* 17, no. 2 (June 2019): 453–469; Matt Welch, "No, Donald Trump Did Not 'Shrink' Government," *Reason*, August 27, 2020, https://reason.com/2020/08/27/no-donald-trump-did-not-shrink-government/.

34. Arthur M. Schlesinger Jr., *The Imperial Presidency* (Boston: Houghton Mifflin, 1973).

35. Stuart E. Eizenstat, *President Carter: The White House Years* (New York: Thomas Dunne Books, 2018), 697.

36. Joel D. Aberbach and Bert A. Rockman, *In the Web of Politics: Three Decades of the US Federal Executive* (Washington, DC: Brookings Institution Press, 2000), 32–35.

37. *Removing Politics from the Administration of Justice*, Hearings before the Subcommittee on Separation of Powers of the Committee on the Judiciary, United States Senate, 93rd Congress, 2nd Session (Washington, DC: Government Printing Office, 1974); Calabresi and Yoo, *Unitary Executive*, 363–366.

38. Andrew Rudalevige, "Beyond Structure and Process: The Early Institutionalization of Regulatory Review," *Journal of Policy History* 30, no. 4 (October 2018): 577–608.

39. Shane, *Madison's Nightmare*, 154–155.

40. "Democrats historically have been as reluctant to work with careerists as Republicans, not because of the ideology but because of the desire for speed." Paul Light, quoted in Charles S. Clark, "Deconstructing the Deep State," *Government Executive*, August 15, 2017, https://www.govexec.com/feature/gov-exec-deconstructing-deep-state/.

41. Karen Orren and Stephen Skowronek, *The Policy State: An American Predicament* (Cambridge, MA: Harvard University Press, 2017), 123–138.

42. Alexander Hamilton, "The Federalist No. 72" [March 19, 1788], in *The Federalist*, 352–353.
43. Alexander Hamilton, "The Federalist No. 77" [April 4, 1788], in *The Federalist*, 373.
44. Hamilton, "Federalist No. 72," 352.
45. James W. Ceaser, *Presidential Selection: Theory and Development* (Princeton, NJ: Princeton University Press, 1979), ch. 1.
46. Gary C. Jacobson, *Presidents and Parties in the Public Mind* (Chicago: University of Chicago Press, 2019).

Chapter 4

1. Steven G. Calabresi and Christopher S. Yoo, *The Unitary Executive: Presidential Power from Washington to Bush* (New Haven, CT: Yale University Press, 2008).
2. Stephen Skowronek, "The Conservative Insurgency and Presidential Power: A Developmental Perspective on the Unitary Executive," *Harvard Law Review* 122, no. 8 (June 2009): 2071–2103.
3. Mel Laracey, "Jefferson's Unitary Executive Theory, as Expressed in His Presidential Newspaper," Paper Presented at the 2019 Annual Meeting of the American Political Science Association, Washington, DC.
4. Noble E. Cunningham Jr., *The Jeffersonian Republicans in Power: Party Operations, 1801–1809* (Chapel Hill: University of North Carolina Press, 1963), 29, 39, 60–63.
5. Leonard White, *The Jeffersonians: A Study in Administrative History* (New York: Macmillan, 1951), 52–53.
6. Representative William Gaston (F-NC) criticized the caucus method in congressional floor debate in 1814: "How hideous the deformity of the practice! The *first* step made in the election is by those whose interference the Constitution prohibits." *Annals of Congress*, 13th Congress, 2nd Session (January 3, 1814), 842. Cited in M. Ostrogorski, "The Rise and Fall of the Nominating Caucus, Legislative and Congressional," *American Historical Review* 5, no. 2 (December 1899): 253–283.
7. White, *Jeffersonians*, 54.
8. Andrew Jackson, "Veto Message [of the Re-authorization of the Bank of the United States]," July 10, 1832, *The American Presidency Project*, https://www.presidency.ucsb.edu/documents/veto-message-the-re-authorization-bank-the-united-states.

9. Andrew Jackson, "Message Read to the Cabinet on Removal of the Public Deposits," September 18, 1833, *The American Presidency Project*, https:// www.presidency.ucsb.edu/documents/message-read-the-cabinet-removal-the-public-deposits.

10. *Kendall v. Stokes*, 38 U.S. 607 (1838); Leonard White, *The Jacksonians: A Study in Administrative History, 1829–1861* (New York: Macmillan, 1954), 38–39.

11. Daryl J. Levinson and Richard H. Pildes, "Separation of Parties, Not Powers," *Harvard Law Review* 119, no. 8 (June 2006): 2311–2386.

12. White, *Jacksonians*, 45.

13. Letter from James K. Polk to Cave Johnson, December 21, 1844, in "Letters of James K. Polk to Cave Johnson, 1833–1848," *Tennessee Historical Magazine* 1, no. 3 (September 1915): 209–256, at 254. Emphasis in original.

14. James K. Polk, "Inaugural Address," March 4, 1845, *The American Presidency Project*, https://www.presidency.ucsb.edu/documents/ inaugural-address-30.

15. The party system "made each branch [of government] more dependent on the other." White, *Jacksonians*, 554.

16. John A. Dearborn, "The 'Proper Organs' for Presidential Representation: A Fresh Look at the Budget and Accounting Act of 1921," *Journal of Policy History* 31, no. 1 (January 2019): 1–41.

17. Stephen Skowronek, "Twentieth-Century Remedies," *Boston University Law Review* 94, no. 3 (May 2014): 795–805; John A. Dearborn, *Power Shifts: Congress and Presidential Representation* (Chicago: University of Chicago Press, 2021), Part I.

18. M. J. C. Vile, *Constitutionalism and the Separation of Powers* (Oxford: Oxford University Press, 1967), ch. 10.

19. *Humphrey's Executor v. United States*, 295 U.S. 602 (1935).

20. Sidney M. Milkis, *The President and the Parties: The Transformation of the American Party System* (New York: Oxford University Press, 1993), ch. 5–6; John A. Dearborn, "The Foundations of the Modern Presidency: Presidential Representation, the Unitary Executive Theory, and the Reorganization Act of 1939," *Presidential Studies Quarterly* 49, no. 1 (March 2019): 185–203. For an analysis putting some distance between FDR's proposals and the unitary executive theory, see Noah A. Rosenblum, "The Antifascist Roots of Presidential Administration," NYU School of Law, working paper.

21. Speaking to the Federalist Society, Trump's attorney general William Barr complained about Congress's attempts to "insulate" agencies from

presidential authority: "This phenomenon first arose in the wake of the Great Depression, as Congress created a number of so-called 'independent agencies' and housed them, at least nominally, in the Executive Branch." William P. Barr, "Attorney General William P. Barr Delivers the 19th Annual Barbara K. Olson Memorial Lecture at the Federalist Society's 2019 National Lawyers Convention," November 15, 2019, Office of Public Affairs, Department of Justice, https://www.justice.gov/opa/speech/attorney-general-william-p-barr-delivers-19th-annual-barbara-k-olson-memorial-lecture.

22. Sean Gailmard and John W. Patty, *Learning While Governing: Expertise and Accountability in the Executive Branch* (Chicago: University of Chicago Press, 2013), ch. 6.

23. Karen Orren and Stephen Skowronek, *The Policy State: An American Predicament* (Cambridge, MA: Harvard University Press, 2017), 108–109.

24. Richard E. Neustadt, *Presidential Power: The Politics of Leadership* (New York: Wiley, 1960).

25. *Youngstown Sheet & Tube Co. v. Sawyer*, 343 U.S. 579, 635 (1952) (Jackson, J., concurring).

26. Gene Sperling, director of the National Economic Council, quoted in James Bennet and Robert Pear, "How a Presidency Was Defined by the Thousand Parts of Its Sum," *New York Times*, December 8, 1997, https://www.nytimes.com/1997/12/08/us/how-a-presidency-was-defined-by-the-thousand-parts-of-its-sum.html.

27. Jeffrey Hart, "The Presidency: Shifting Conservative Perspectives?" *National Review*, November 22, 1974, 1351–1355, at 1353.

28. William M. Lunch, *The Nationalization of American Politics* (Berkeley and Los Angeles: University of California Press, 1987); Gary Gerstle, *Liberty and Coercion: The Paradox of American Government from the Founding to the Present* (Princeton, NJ: Princeton University Press, 2015); Bryan D. Jones, Sean M. Theriault, and Michelle Whyman, *The Great Broadening: How the Vast Expansion of the Policymaking Agenda Transformed American Politics* (Chicago: University of Chicago Press, 2019); Stephen Skowronek and Karen Orren, "The Adaptability Paradox: Constitutional Resilience and Principles of Good Government in Twenty-First Century America," *Perspectives on Politics* 18, no. 2 (June 2020): 354–369.

29. Elena Kagan, "Presidential Administration," *Harvard Law Review* 114, no. 8 (June 2001): 2245–2385, at 2309.

30. Sam Rosenfeld, *The Polarizers: Postwar Architects of Our Partisan Era* (Chicago: University of Chicago Press, 2018), 177.

31. Samuel Beer to Senator George McGovern, 1969, quoted in Rosenfeld, *Polarizers*, 139.

32. Ronald Reagan at Conservative Political Action Conference, 1975, quoted in Rosenfeld, *Polarizers*, 188.

33. Sidney M. Milkis, "The Progressive Party and the Rise of Executive-Centered Partisanship," in *The Progressives' Century: Political Reform, Constitutional Government, and the Modern American State*, eds. Stephen Skowronek, Stephen M. Engel, and Bruce Ackerman (New Haven, CT: Yale University Press, 2016), 174–196; Sidney M. Milkis and John Warren York, "Barack Obama, Organizing for Action, and Executive-Centered Partisanship," *Studies in American Political Development* 31, no. 1 (April 2017): 1–23.

34. Kagan, "Presidential Administration," 2335.

35. Skowronek, "Conservative Insurgency," 2099.

36. Richard P. Nathan, *The Plot That Failed: Nixon and the Administrative Presidency* (New York: Wiley, 1975); Joel D. Aberbach and Bert A. Rockman, "Clashing Beliefs within the Executive Branch: The Nixon Administration Bureaucracy," *American Political Science Review* 70, no. 2 (June 1976): 456–468.

37. Richard J. Ellis, *The Development of the American Presidency* (New York: Routledge, 2012), 284.

38. Michael Koncewicz, "The GOP Appointees Who Defied the President," *The Atlantic*, November 19, 2019, https://www.theatlantic.com/ideas/archive/2019/11/the-gop-appointees-who-defied-the-president/602230/.

39. Karen M. Hult and Charles E. Walcott, *Empowering the White House: Governance under Nixon, Ford, and Carter* (Lawrence: University Press of Kansas, 2004).

40. Ellis, *Development of the American Presidency*, 284–287.

41. Daniel J. Galvin, *Presidential Party Building: Dwight D. Eisenhower to George W. Bush* (Princeton, NJ: Princeton University Press, 2010), ch. 4; Rosenfeld, *Polarizers*, 173–178.

42. "'I have impeached myself': Edited transcript of David Frost's interview with Richard Nixon Broadcast in May 1977," *Guardian*, September 7, 2007, https://www.theguardian.com/theguardian/2007/sep/07/greatinterviews1.

43. Paul C. Light, *Monitoring Government: Inspectors General and the Search for Accountability* (Washington, DC: Brookings Institution Press, 1993),

51. On Congress increasingly focusing on oversight over lawmaking, see Jones, Theriault, and Whyman, *Great Broadening*, 276.

44. Keith E. Whittington, *Constitutional Construction: Divided Power and Constitutional Meaning* (Cambridge, MA: Harvard University Press, 1999), ch. 5.

45. "The right of employees, individually or collectively, to petition Congress or a Member of Congress, or to furnish information to either House of Congress, or to a committee or Member thereof, may not be interfered with or denied." 5 U.S.C. § 7211.

46. *Improving Congressional Budget Control*, Hearings before the Joint Study Committee on Budget Control, 93rd Congress, 1st Session (Washington, DC: Government Printing Office, 1973), 42, 73.

47. Light, *Monitoring Government*, 67.

48. *Congressional Record*, 95th Congress, 2nd Session (September 27, 1978), 32032, 32029.

49. *Establishment of Offices of Inspector General*, Hearings before a Subcommittee of the Committee on Government Operations, House of Representatives, 95th Congress, 1st Session (Washington, DC: Government Printing Office, 1977), 165.

50. Scott Shane, "Recent Flexing of Presidential Powers Had Personal Roots in Ford White House," *New York Times*, December 30, 2006, https://www.nytimes.com/2006/12/30/washington/30roots.html.

51. President Gerald Ford, quoted in Louis Fisher, *Presidential War Power*, 3rd ed. (Lawrence: University Press of Kansas, 2013), 156.

52. Quoted in Light, *Monitoring Government*, 60.

53. Department of Justice, "Memorandum on the Constitutional Issues Presented by H.R. 2819," reprinted in *Establishment of Offices of Inspector General*, Hearings, 844.

54. *Establishment of Offices of Inspector General*, Hearings, 22–23.

55. *Establishment of Offices of Inspector General*, Hearings, 238.

56. "Separation of Powers: Legislative-Executive Relations," and cover memo from Stephen J. Markham, Assistant Attorney General for the Office of Legal Policy, to Edwin Meese III, re: "Separation of Powers," April 30, 1986, 38, 14, 19. Posted by Charlie Savage, *New York Times*, at https://www.documentcloud.org/documents/6561980-Meese-Separation-of-Powers-Report.html.

57. On the incentives of parties in Congress, see, for example, Frances E. Lee, *Insecure Majorities: Congress and the Perpetual Campaign* (Chicago: University of Chicago Press, 2016).

58. Calabresi and Yoo, *Unitary Executive*, 400–404.

59. Andrew Rudalevige, *The New Imperial Presidency: Renewing Presidential Power after Watergate* (Ann Arbor: University of Michigan Press, 2005).

Phantoms Unleashed: Introduction

1. E.g., *Department of Homeland Security. v. Regents of the University of California*, 591 U.S. ___ (2020), which halted the Trump administration's efforts to unilaterally end the Deferred Action for Childhood Arrivals (DACA) program; *Trump v. Vance*, 591 U.S. ___ (2020), which allowed the District Attorney of New York County to subpoena Trump's tax records; *Committee on the Judiciary of the United States House of Representatives v. Donald F. McGahn, II*, No. 19-5331 (D.C. Cir. 2020) (en banc), which stated that the House had legal standing to turn to the courts to compel former White House counsel Donald McGahn to testify in response to a subpoena from the House Judiciary Committee.

2. John R. Commons, *The Legal Foundations of Capitalism* (New York: Macmillan, 1924), 123.

3. Dave Philipps, "Trump Clears Three Service Members in War Crimes Cases," *New York Times*, November 15, 2019, https://www.nytimes.com/2019/11/15/us/trump-pardons.html.

4. Philipps, "Trump Clears Three Service Members in War Crimes Cases."

5. Jimmy Carter, "Proclamation 4483—Granting Pardon for Violations of the Selective Service Act, August 4, 1964 to March 28, 1973," January 21, 1977, *The American Presidency Project*, https://www.presidency.ucsb.edu/documents/proclamation-4483-granting-pardon-for-violations-the-selective-service-act-august-4-1964.

6. Ron Soodalter, *Hanging Captain Gordon: The Life and Trial of an American Slave Trader* (New York: Washington Square Press, 2006), 159.

7. Richard Spencer, "Richard Spencer: I Was Fired as Navy Secretary. Here's What I've Learned Because of It," *Washington Post*, November 27, 2019, https://www.washingtonpost.com/opinions/richard-spencer-i-was-fired-as-navy-secretary-heres-what-ive-learned-because-of-it/2019/11/27/9c2e58bc-1092-11ea-bf62-eadd5d11f559_story.html.

8. Maggie Haberman, Helene Cooper, and Dave Philipps, "Navy Is Said to Proceed with Disciplinary Plans against Edward Gallagher," *New York Times*, November 23, 2019, https://www.nytimes.com/2019/11/23/us/politics/navy-discipline-edward-gallagher.html.

9. Helene Cooper, Maggie Haberman, and Dave Philipps, "Esper Demands Resignation of Navy Secretary over SEAL Case," *New York Times*, November 24, 2019, https://www.nytimes.com/2019/11/24/us/politics/navy-secretary-richard-spencer-resign.html.

10. Jeremy Diamond, "Trump Defends Military Pardons over Objections from 'Deep State' at Florida Rally," *CNN*, November 26, 2019, https://www.cnn.com/2019/11/26/politics/trump-eddie-gallagher-rally/index.html.

11. @realDonaldTrump, November 21, 2019, 8:30 AM, Twitter, https://twitter.com/realdonaldtrump/status/1197507542726909952.

12. Spencer, "I Was Fired as Navy Secretary."

13. Cooper, Haberman, and Philipps, "Esper Demands Resignation of Navy Secretary over SEAL Case."

14. E.g., Eric Schmitt, Helene Cooper, Thomas Gibbons-Neff, and Maggie Haberman, "Esper Breaks with Trump on Using Troops against Protesters," *New York Times*, June 3, 2020, https://www.nytimes.com/2020/06/03/us/politics/esper-milley-trump-protest.html; Helene Cooper, "Milley Apologizes for Role in Trump Photo Op: 'I Should Not Have Been There,'" *New York Times*, June 11, 2020, https://www.nytimes.com/2020/06/11/us/politics/trump-milley-military-protests-lafayette-square.html; Lara Seligman, "Trump Skirts Senate to Install Nominee under Fire for Islamophobic Tweets in Pentagon Post," *Politico*, August 2, 2020, https://www.politico.com/news/2020/08/02/donald-trump-anthony-tata-pentagon-390851.

Chapter 5

1. President's Committee on Administrative Management (PCAM), *Report of the Committee with Studies of Administrative Management in the Federal Government*, 74th Congress, 2nd Session (Washington, DC: US Government Printing Office, 1937), 5.

2. Patrick R. O'Brien, "A Theoretical Critique of the Unitary Executive Framework: Rethinking the First Mover Advantage, Collective Action Advantage, and Informational Advantage," *Presidential Studies Quarterly* 47, no. 1 (March 2017): 169–185.

3. PCAM, *Report*, 5. Emphasis added.

4. PCAM, *Report*, 52.

5. Daphna Renan, "The President's Two Bodies," *Columbia Law Review* 120, no. 5 (June 2020): 1119–1214.

6. Katie Zezima, Dan Balz, and Chris Cillizza, "Reince Priebus Named Trump's Chief of Staff," *Washington Post*, November 13, 2016, https://www.washingtonpost.com/news/post-politics/wp/2016/11/13/reince-priebus-named-as-trumps-chief-of-staff/.

7. Ana Swanson, "Trump's America First Trade Agenda Roiled by Internal Divisions," *New York Times*, October 20, 2017, https://www.nytimes.com/2017/10/20/us/politics/trumps-america-first-trade-agenda-roiled-by-internal-divisions.html.

8. Deborah B. Solomon, "Who Is Peter Navarro?: He Said There's a 'Special Place in Hell' for Trudeau," *New York Times*, June 11, 2018, https://www.nytimes.com/2018/06/11/business/who-is-peter-navarro.html.

9. Bob Woodward, *Fear: Trump in the White House* (New York: Simon and Schuster, 2018), 140.

10. Woodward, *Fear*, 141, 143.

11. Philip Rucker and Carol Leonnig, *A Very Stable Genius: Donald J. Trump's Testing of America* (London: Bloomsbury, 2020), 130–132.

12. Rucker and Leonnig, *Very Stable Genius*, 133.

13. Woodward, *Fear*, 223.

14. Rucker and Leonnig, *Very Stable Genius*, 138.

15. Woodward, *Fear*, 155–158.

16. Woodward, *Fear*, 264, xvii–xix.

17. Woodward, *Fear*, xix.

18. Woodward, *Fear*, 298.

19. Ben White, "How Trump's Trade War Finally Broke Gary Cohn," *Politico*, March 6, 2018, https://www.politico.com/story/2018/03/06/gary-cohn-trump-backstory-trade-tariffs-443857.

20. Tim Alberta, *American Carnage: On the Front Lines of the Republican Civil War and the Rise of President Trump* (New York: Harper, 2019), 495–497, 558–559.

21. Ana Swanson, "Peter Navarro, a Top Trade Skeptic, Is Ascendant," *New York Times*, February 25, 2018, https://www.nytimes.com/2018/02/25/us/politics/peter-navarro-trade.html.

22. Quoted in Philip Bump, "Objective Information Has Less of a Place in an Intuition-Based Presidency," *Washington Post*, March 13, 2018, https://www.washingtonpost.com/news/politics/wp/2018/03/13/objective-information-has-less-of-a-place-in-an-intuition-based-presidency/.

23. Quoted in Sanya Mansoor, "Former White House Chief Economic Advisor to Trump Says Tariffs 'Hurt the US'," *Time*, January 19, 2020, https://time.com/5767999/former-white-house-economic-advisory-tariffs/.

24. Dion Rabouin, "US Farmers Could Really Use Some Help," *Axios*, November 5, 2019, https://www.axios.com/us-china-trade-war-farmers-struggle-58ae9a18-9482-4b0e-8b85-524b7e7e6b90.html; Dion Rabouin, "The End of Trump's Manufacturing Renaissance," *Axios*, December 5, 2019, https://www.axios.com/trump-tariffs-manufacturing-job-losses-6c4841de-0c01-4c4f-99c5-6e2bf26d670e.html.

25. Daniel J. Galvin, "Party Domination and Base Mobilization: Donald Trump and Republican Party Building in a Polarized Era," *The Forum* 18, no. 2 (2020): 135–168.

26. David Shribman, "Rising with a Network of Contacts," *New York Times*, April 27, 1983, A22.

27. Robert E. Lighthizer, "The Venerable History of Protectionism," *New York Times*, March 6, 2008, https://www.nytimes.com/2008/03/06/opinion/06iht-edlighthizer.1.10774536.html.

28. Matt Peterson, "The Making of a Trade Warrior," *The Atlantic*, December 29, 2018, https://www.theatlantic.com/politics/archive/2018/12/robert-lighthizers-bid-cut-chinas-trade-influence/578611/.

29. Quoted in Andrew Rustuccia and Megan Cassella, "'Ideological Soulmates': How a China Skeptic Sold Trump on a Trade War," *Politico*, December 26, 2018, https://www.politico.com/story/2018/12/26/trump-lighthizer-china-trade-war-1075221.

30. Adam Behsudi and Doug Palmer, "Labor Unions Win, Drug Companies Lose in New Trade Deal," *Politico*, December 10, 2019, https://www.politico.com/news/2019/12/10/labor-unions-drug-companies-trade-deal-081230.

31. Doug Palmer, "Trade Rep: China Will Determine Success of Trade Deal," *Politico*, December 15, 2019, https://www.politico.com/news/2019/12/15/lighthizer-china-success-trade-deal-085597.

32. Brian Bennett, "Inside Jared Kushner's Unusual White House Role," *Time*, January 16, 2020, https://time.com/5766186/jared-kushner-interview/.

33. Jill Colvin and Zeke Miller, "Where's Mick?: Trump Acting Chief of Staff Has Low-Key Style," *Associated Press*, March 16, 2019, https://apnews.com/b4a6ecfaed224a5cafdf2e6188a6483f.

34. Nancy Cook, "Mick Mulvaney as Chief of Staff: Let Trump Be Trump," *Politico*, December 19, 2018, https://www.politico.com/story/2018/12/19/mick-mulvaney-trump-white-house-chief-of-staff-1070785.

35. John Bresnahan, Jake Sherman, and Nancy Cook, "Trump Taps Key Hill Ally Mark Meadows to Be Chief of Staff," *Politico*, March 6, 2020,

https://www.politico.com/news/2020/03/06/mark-meadows-white-house-chief-staff-123210.

Chapter 6

1. Daphna Renan, "Presidential Norms and Article II," *Harvard Law Review* 131, no. 8 (June 2018): 2187–2282.
2. Stephen Skowronek, *Building a New American State: The Expansion of National Administrative Capacities, 1877–1920* (New York: Cambridge University Press, 1982), 47, 51.
3. *Congressional Globe*, 41st Congress, 2nd Session (April 27, 1870), 3036.
4. Jed Handelsman Shugerman, "The Creation of the Department of Justice: Professionalization without Civil Rights or Civil Service," *Stanford Law Review* 66, no. 1 (January 2014): 121–172, at 171.
5. Shugerman, "Creation of the Department of Justice," 165.
6. *Congressional Globe*, 41st Congress, 2nd Session (April 27, 1870), 3036.
7. Shugerman, "Creation of the Department of Justice," 156.
8. Jed Handelsman Shugerman, "Professionals, Politicos, and Crony Attorneys General: A Historical Sketch of the US Attorney General as a Case for Structural Independence," *Fordham Law Review* 87, no. 5 (April 2019): 1965–1994.
9. Steven G. Calabresi and Christopher S. Yoo, *The Unitary Executive: Presidential Power from Washington to Bush* (New Haven, CT: Yale University Press, 2008), 363–366.
10. "An Address by the Honorable Griffin B. Bell, Attorney General of the United States, before Department of Justice Lawyers," US Department of Justice, Washington, DC, September 6, 1978, 5, https://www.justice.gov/sites/default/files/ag/legacy/2011/08/23/09-06-1978b.pdf. Emphasis added.
11. Renan, "Presidential Norms and Article II," 2210. On the exception for the president, see Donald F. McGahn II, Counsel to the President, Memorandum to all White House Staff re: "Communications Restrictions with Personnel at the Department of Justice," January 27, 2017, https://www.politico.com/f/?id=0000015a-dde8-d23c-a7ff-dfef4d530000.
12. *Ten-Year Term for FBI Director*, Report to accompany S. 2106, Report No. 93-1213, United States Senate, 93rd Congress, 2nd Session (October 2, 1974), 1.

13. Bruce A. Green and Rebecca Roiphe, "May Federal Prosecutors Take Direction from the President?," *Fordham Law Review* 87, no. 5 (April 2019): 1817–1858.

14. James Comey, *A Higher Loyalty: Truth, Lies, and Leadership* (New York: Flatiron Books, 2018), 96–98. Emphasis added.

15. Barack Obama, "Remarks on the Resignation of Robert S. Mueller III as Director of the Federal Bureau of Investigation and the Nomination of James B. Comey, Jr., to Be Director of the Federal Bureau of Investigation," June 21, 2013, *The American Presidency Project*, https://www.presidency. ucsb.edu/documents/remarks-the-resignation-robert-s-mueller-iii-director-the-federal-bureau-investigation-and.

16. See, for example, Dennis Halcoussis, Anton D. Lowenberg, and G. Michael Phillips, "An Empirical Test of the Comey Effect on the 2016 Presidential Election," *Social Science Quarterly* 101, no. 1 (January 2020): 161–171.

17. Memorandum from Attorney General Michael Mukasey to All Department Employees re: "Election Year Sensitivities," Office of the Attorney General, Department of Justice, March 5, 2008, 1, https://www. justice.gov/sites/default/files/ag/legacy/2009/02/10/ag-030508.pdf.

18. Comey, *Higher Loyalty*, 169–172.

19. Matt Apuzzo, Adam Goldman, and Nicholas Fandos, "Code Name Crossfire Hurricane: The Secret Origins of the Trump Investigation," *New York Times*, May 16, 2018, https://www.nytimes.com/2018/05/16/us/politics/crossfire-hurricane-trump-russia-fbi-mueller-investigation.html.

20. James B. Comey, "Statement for the Record," Senate Select Committee on Intelligence, June 8, 2017, 3–4, https://www.intelligence.senate.gov/sites/default/files/documents/os-jcomey-060817.pdf.

21. Comey, "Statement," 5.

22. James B. Stewart, *Deep State: Trump, the FBI, and the Rule of Law* (New York: Penguin Press, 2019), 174–176; Comey, "Statement," 6–7.

23. David Alistair Yalof, *Prosecution among Friends: Presidents, Attorneys General, and Executive Branch Wrongdoing* (College Station: Texas A&M University Press, 2012).

24. Bob Woodward, *Fear: Trump in the White House* (New York: Simon and Schuster, 2018), 166.

25. Special Counsel Robert S. Mueller III, *Report on the Investigation into Russian Interference in the 2016 Presidential Election*, Vol. II, US Department of Justice, March 2019, 73, https://www.justice.gov/storage/report_volume2.pdf.

26. Woodward, *Fear*, 162.

27. Stewart, *Deep State*, 12, 204.

28. Philip Rucker and Carol Leonnig, *A Very Stable Genius: Donald J. Trump's Testing of America* (London: Bloomsbury, 2020), 61, 65.

29. Comey, *Higher Loyalty*, 269–270.

30. Stewart, *Deep State*, 243.

31. Mueller, *Report*, Vol. II, 78.

32. Mueller, *Report*, Vol. II; Katy J. Harriger, "'Witch Hunts' and the Rule of Law: Trump, the Special Counsel, and the Department of Justice," *Presidential Studies Quarterly* 50, no. 1 (March 2020): 176–192.

33. Confidential Memo from John M. Dowd and Jay A. Sekulow to Robert S. Mueller III, January 29, 2018. "The Trump Lawyers' Confidential Memo to Mueller, Explained," *New York Times*, June 2, 2018, https:// www.nytimes.com/interactive/2018/06/02/us/politics/trump-legal-documents.html.

34. Woodward, *Fear*, 333.

35. Woodward, *Fear*, 350.

36. William P. Barr, "Attorney General William P. Barr Delivers the 19th Annual Barbara K. Olson Memorial Lecture at the Federalist Society's 2019 National Lawyers Convention," November 15, 2019, Office of Public Affairs, Department of Justice, https://www.justice.gov/opa/speech/ attorney-general-william-p-barr-delivers-19th-annual-barbara-k-olson-memorial-lecture.

37. Stewart, *Deep State*, 245.

38. Confidential Memo from John M. Dowd and Jay A. Sekulow to Robert S. Mueller III, January 29, 2018.

39. Woodward, *Fear*, 327. Fusion GPS was commissioned by the Democrats to investigate candidate Trump's Russian connections, resulting in the notorious Steele dossier, the contents of which are still being disputed.

40. *Report of Investigation of Former Federal Bureau of Investigation Director James Comey's Disclosure of Sensitive Investigative Information and Handling of Certain Memoranda*, Office of the Inspector General, US Department of Justice, August 2019, 57, https://oig.justice.gov/reports/ 2019/o1902.pdf.

41. *A Review of Various Actions by the Federal Bureau of Investigation and Department of Justice in Advance of the 2016 Election*, Office of the Inspector General, US Department of Justice, June 2018, x, https://www. justice.gov/file/1071991/download.

42. Stewart, *Deep State*, 96, 137, 299.

43. Michael S. Schmidt, Matt Apuzzo, and Adam Goldman, "Mueller Removed Top Agent in Russia Inquiry over Possible Anti-Trump Texts," *New York Times*, December 2, 2017, https://www.nytimes.com/2017/12/02/us/politics/mueller-removed-top-fbi-agent-over-possible-anti-trump-texts.html.

44. *A Review of Various Actions by the Federal Bureau of Investigation and Department of Justice in Advance of the 2016 Election*, xii.

45. *Review of Four FISA Applications and Other Aspects of the FBI's Crossfire Hurricane Investigation*, Office of the Inspector General, US Department of Justice, December 2019, iii, viii, 362, https://www.justice.gov/storage/120919-examination.pdf.

46. Charlie Savage, "Problems in FBI Wiretap Applications Go beyond Trump Aide Surveillance, Review Finds," *New York Times*, March 31, 2020, https://www.nytimes.com/2020/03/31/us/politics/fbi-fisa-wiretap-trump.html.

47. Jack Goldsmith, "Independence and Accountability at the Department of Justice," *Lawfare*, January 30, 2018, https://www.lawfareblog.com/independence-and-accountability-department-justice.

48. David Rohde, "William Barr, Trump's Sword and Shield," *New Yorker*, January 13, 2020, https://www.newyorker.com/magazine/2020/01/20/william-barr-trumps-sword-and-shield.

49. Stewart, *Deep State*, 279.

50. Stewart, *Deep State*, 313.

51. "Attorney General William P. Barr Delivers Remarks on the Release of the Report on the Investigation into Russian Interference in the 2016 Presidential Election," April 18, 2019, Office of Public Affairs, Department of Justice, https://www.justice.gov/opa/speech/attorney-general-william-p-barr-delivers-remarks-release-report-investigation-russian.

52. Mueller, *Report*, Vol. II, 158.

53. Jeffrey Toobin, "Why the Mueller Investigation Failed," *New Yorker*, June 29, 2020, https://www.newyorker.com/magazine/2020/07/06/why-the-mueller-investigation-failed; Michael S. Schmidt, "Justice Dept. Never Fully Examined Trump's Ties to Russia, Ex-Officials Say," *New York Times*, August 30, 2020, https://www.nytimes.com/2020/08/30/us/politics/trump-russia-justice-department.html.

54. Rucker and Leonnig, *Very Stable Genius*, 250, 376.

55. Mueller, *Report*, Vol. II, 181–182.

56. Stewart, *Deep State*, 311.

57. Stewart, *Deep State*, 329.

58. Quoted in Stewart, *Deep State*, 330.

59. Quint Forgey, "Barr Taps US Attorney to Investigate 'Unmasking' as Part of Russia Probe Review," *Politico*, May 28, 2020, https://www.politico.com/news/2020/05/28/barr-russia-probe-attorney-286920.

60. Adam Goldman and William K. Rashbaum, "Review of Russia Inquiry Grows as FBI Witnesses Are Questioned," *New York Times*, October 19, 2019, https://www.nytimes.com/2019/10/19/us/politics/durham-review-fbi-witnesses.html.

61. Adam Goldman, Julian E. Barnes, and Katie Benner, "Durham Inquiry Includes Scrutiny of a Media Leak," *New York Times*, April 24, 2020, https://www.nytimes.com/2020/04/24/us/politics/john-durham-ignatius-column.html.

62. Katie Benner, "Barr and Durham Publicly Disagree with Horowitz Report on Russia Inquiry," *New York Times*, December 9, 2019, https://www.nytimes.com/2019/12/09/us/politics/barr-durham-ig-report-russia-investigation.html.

63. Josh Gerstein and Natasha Bertrand, "Horowitz Pushes Back at Barr over Basis for Trump-Russia Probe," *Politico*, December 11, 2019, https://www.politico.com/news/2019/12/11/horowitz-barr-trump-russia-probe-082448.

64. Joint statement of Representatives Adam Schiff (D-CA) and Jerrold Nadler (D-NY), quoted in Ana Radelat, "Escalation of Durham Probe Ratchets Up Political Bickering," *Connecticut Mirror*, October 25, 2019, https://ctmirror.org/2019/10/25/escalation-of-durham-probe-ratchets-up-political-bickering/.

65. Katelyn Polantz and Veronica Stracqualursi, "Barr Defends Trump's Firing of Intel Community Watchdog as 'Right Thing' to Do," *CNN*, April 10, 2020, https://www.cnn.com/2020/04/10/politics/william-barr-john-durham-russia-investigation/index.html.

66. *Russian Active Measures Campaigns and Interference in the 2016 U.S. Election*, Vol. 5: *Counterintelligence Threats and Vulnerabilities*, Report of the Select Committee on Intelligence, United States Senate, 116th Congress, 1st Session (August 2020), https://www.intelligence.senate.gov/sites/default/files/documents/report_volume5.pdf; Karoun Demirjian, Ellen Nakashima, and Matt Zapotosky, "Senate Panel Told Justice Dept. of Suspicions over Trump Family Members' Russia Testimony," *Washington Post*, August 15, 2020, https://www.washingtonpost.com/national-security/senate-intelligence-committee-donald-trump-jr-jared-kushner-stephen-bannon-erik-prince/2020/08/15/a7905a84-def5-11ea-b205-ff838e15a9a6_story.html.

· 67. Adam Goldman, "Ex-F.B.I. Lawyer Expected to Plead Guilty in Review of Russia Inquiry," *New York Times*, August 14, 2020, https://www.nytimes.com/2020/08/14/us/politics/kevin-clinesmith-durham-investigation.html. Maria Bartiromo interview on "*Sunday Morning Futures*" with Senate Judiciary Chairman Lindsay Graham (R-SC), "Graham Shares Newly Declassified FBI Docs Showing 'Clear' Bias toward Trump," *Fox News*, YouTube, August 23, 2020, https://www.youtube.com/watch?v=9OGgyYSOkGg.

68. Reported in Brooke Singman, "Trump Lays Down Gauntlet for Barr on Durham Probe: Either 'Greatest Attorney General' or 'Average Guy'," *Fox News*, August 13, 2020, https://www.foxnews.com/politics/trump-barr-durham-probe-gauntlet.

69. Stewart, *Deep State*, 256.

70. Mueller, *Report*, Vol. II, 78.

71. Anne Flaherty, "Barr Blasts Trump's Tweets on Stone Case: 'Impossible for Me to Do My Job'," *ABC News*, February 13, 2020, https://abcnews.go.com/Politics/barr-blasts-trumps-tweets-stone-case-impossible-job/story?id=68963276.

72. Mark Sherman, "Trump Says He's the Nation's Top Cop, a Debatable Claim," *Associated Press*, February 19, 2020, https://apnews.com/7f48f53276aa0f4070dfb34e977c10d4.

73. Carol E. Lee, Ken Dilanian, and Peter Alexander, "Barr Takes Control of Legal Matters of Interest to Trump, Including Stone Sentencing," *NBC News*, February 11, 2020, https://www.nbcnews.com/politics/justice-department/barr-takes-control-legal-matters-interest-trump-including-stone-sentencing-n1135231.

74. "DOJ Alumni Statement on the Events Surrounding the Sentencing of Roger Stone," *Medium*, February 16, 2020, https://medium.com/@dojalumni/doj-alumni-statement-on-the-events-surrounding-the-sentencing-of-roger-stone-c2cb75ae4937.

75. Nicholas Fandos, Katie Benner, and Charlie Savage, "Justice Dept. Officials Outline Claims of Politicization under Barr," *New York Times*, June 24, 2020, https://www.nytimes.com/2020/06/24/us/politics/justice-department-politicization.html.

76. Josh Gerstein, "Barr Reignites Charge He Is Conducting Mueller Cleanup for Trump," *Politico*, May 8, 2020, https://www.politico.com/news/2020/05/08/barr-flynn-trump-mueller-244043.

77. Mary B. McCord, "Bill Barr Twisted My Words in Dropping the Flynn Case. Here's the Truth," *New York Times*, May 10, 2020, https://www.nytimes.com/2020/05/10/opinion/bill-barr-michael-flynn.html.

78. "DOJ Alumni Statement on Flynn Case," *Medium*, May 11, 2020, https://medium.com/@dojalumni/doj-alumni-statement-on-flynn-case-7c38a9a945b9.

79. Sherman, "Trump Says He's the Nation's Top Cop."

80. Peter Baker, "In Commuting Stone's Sentence, Trump Goes Where Nixon Would Not," *New York Times*, July 11, 2020, https://www.nytimes.com/2020/07/11/us/politics/trump-roger-stone-nixon.html.

81. Robert S. Mueller III, "Robert Mueller: Roger Stone Remains a Convicted Felon, and Rightly So," *Washington Post*, July 11, 2020, https://www.washingtonpost.com/opinions/2020/07/11/mueller-stone-oped/.

82. @realDonaldTrump, July 9, 2020, 10:38 AM, Twitter, https://twitter.com/realDonaldTrump/status/1281236214646034432. Trump's full tweet stated: "The Supreme Court sends case back to Lower Court, arguments to continue. This is all a political prosecution. I won the Mueller Witch Hunt, and others, and now I have to keep fighting in a politically corrupt New York. Not fair to this Presidency or Administration!"

83. *In Re: Michael T. Flynn*, No. 20-5143 (D.C. Cir. 2020) (Rao, Circuit Judge, opinion of the court), 8, https://www.cadc.uscourts.gov/internet/opinions.nsf/79798A0FA0633B7985258591004DD3E7/$file/20-5143-1848728.pdf.

84. Renan, "Presidential Norms and Article II," 2193, 2281.

Chapter 7

1. Vannevar Bush, *Science: The Endless Frontier*, A Report to the President (Washington, DC: Government Printing Office, 1945), 11.

2. 5 U.S.C. § 706.

3. Sheila Jasanoff, *The Fifth Branch: Science Advisers as Policymakers* (Cambridge, MA: Harvard University Press, 1990).

4. *Whistleblower Protection Enhancement Act of 2012*, Report 112–155 to Accompany S. 743, Committee on Homeland Security and Governmental Affairs, United States Senate, 112th Congress, 2nd Session (Washington, DC: Government Printing Office, 2012), 24.

5. Rachel Augustine Potter, *Bending the Rules: Procedural Politicking in the Bureaucracy* (Chicago: University of Chicago Press, 2019), 116–118.

6. Brad Plumer and Coral Davenport, "Science under Attack: How Trump Is Sidelining Researchers and Their Work," *New York Times*, December 28, 2019, https://www.nytimes.com/2019/12/28/climate/trump-administration-war-on-science.html.

7. Potter, *Bending the Rules*, 117.

8. Lisa Friedman and Coral Davenport, "Trump Administration Rolls Back Clean Water Protections," *New York Times*, September 12, 2019, https://www.nytimes.com/2019/09/12/climate/trump-administration-rolls-back-clean-water-protections.html.

9. Plumer and Davenport, "Science under Attack."

10. Jason Ross Arnold, *Secrecy in the Sunshine Era: The Promises and Failures of U.S. Open Government Laws* (Lawrence: University Press of Kansas, 2014), 219–220.

11. *Massachusetts v. Environmental Protection Agency*, 549 U.S. 497 (2007).

12. Barack Obama, "Inaugural Address," January 20, 2009, *The American Presidency Project*, https://www.presidency.ucsb.edu/documents/inaugural-address-5.

13. Barack Obama, "Memorandum on Scientific Integrity," March 9, 2009, *The American Presidency Project*, https://www.presidency.ucsb.edu/documents/memorandum-scientific-integrity.

14. Office of Science and Technology Policy, "Scientific Integrity," Obama White House, https://obamawhitehouse.archives.gov/administration/eop/ostp/library/scientificintegrity; Heidi Kitrosser, "Scientific Integrity: The Perils and Promise of White House Administration," *Fordham Law Review* 79, no. 6 (May 2011): 2395–2424.

15. Albert C. Lin, "President Trump's War on Regulatory Science," *Harvard Environmental Law Review* 43, no. 2 (2019): 247–306, at 287.

16. Arnold, *Secrecy in the Sunshine Era*, 363–366.

17. Jackie Calmes and Gardiner Harris, "Obama Endorses Decision to Limit Morning-After Pill," *New York Times*, December 8, 2011, https://www.nytimes.com/2011/12/09/us/obama-backs-aides-stance-on-morning-after-pill.html.

18. Tim Dickinson, "The Spill, the Scandal and the President," *Rolling Stone*, June 8, 2010, https://www.rollingstone.com/politics/politics-news/the-spill-the-scandal-and-the-president-193093/.

19. Lisa Friedman, "A War against Climate Science, Waged by Washington's Rank and File," *New York Times*, June 15, 2020, https://www.nytimes.com/2020/06/15/climate/climate-science-trump.html.

20. Oliver Milman, "Trump Administration's War on Science Has Hit 'Crisis Point', Experts Warn," *Guardian*, October 3, 2019, https://www.theguardian.com/science/2019/oct/03/science-trump-administration-crisis-point-report.

21. @realDonaldTrump, September 1, 2019, 10:51 AM, Twitter, https://twitter.com/realDonaldTrump/status/1168174613827899393.

22. Lisa Friedman and Mark Walker, "Hurricane Tweet That Angered Trump Wasn't about Trump, Forecasters Say," *New York Times*, November 7, 2019, https://www.nytimes.com/2019/11/07/climate/trump-alabama-sharpie-hurricane.html.

23. Caitlin Oprysko, "An Oval Office Mystery: Who Doctored the Hurricane Map?" *Politico*, September 4, 2019, https://www.politico.com/story/2019/09/04/donald-trump-sharpie-hurricane-map-1481733.

24. *Evaluation of NOAA's September 6, 2019, Statement about Hurricane Dorian Forecasts*, Report No. OIG-20-032-1, Office of Inspector General, US Department of Commerce, June 26, 2020, 19, 35, https://www.oig.doc.gov/OIGPublications/OIG-20-032-I.pdf.

25. Andrew Freedman, Josh Dawsey, Juliet Eilperin, and Jason Samenow, "Trump Pushed Staff to Deal with NOAA Tweet That Contradicted His Inaccurate Hurricane Claim, Officials Say," *Washington Post*, September 11, 2019, https://www.washingtonpost.com/weather/2019/09/11/lawmakers-commerce-department-launch-investigations-into-noaas-decision-back-presidents-trump-over-forecasters/; *Evaluation of NOAA's September 6, 2019, Statement about Hurricane Dorian Forecasts*, 43–44.

26. Christopher Flavelle, Lisa Friedman, and Peter Baker, "Commerce Chief Threatened Firings at NOAA after Trump's Dorian Tweets, Sources Say," *New York Times*, September 9, 2019, https://www.nytimes.com/2019/09/09/climate/hurricane-dorian-trump-tweet.html.

27. Flavelle, Friedman, and Baker, "Commerce Chief Threatened Firings at NOAA after Trump's Dorian Tweets, Sources Say."

28. Caitlin Oprysko, "Government Scientists Blast Trump Weather Wars after NOAA Defends His Hurricane Forecast," *Politico*, September 9, 2019, https://www.politico.com/story/2019/09/09/scientists-trump-noaa-hurricane-alabama-1487628.

29. Reported in Nicholas Bogel-Burroughs, Christopher Flavelle, and Lisa Friedman, "NOAA Chief, Defending Trump on Dorian, Also Tries to Buoy Scientists," *New York Times*, September 10, 2019, https://www.nytimes.com/2019/09/10/climate/neil-jacobs-noaa-hurricane-dorian.html.

30. Zahra Hirji and Jason Leopold, "'HELP!!!!' Internal #SharpieGate Emails Show Government Officials Freaked Out over Trump's 'Doctored' Hurricane Map," *BuzzFeed News*, February 1, 2020, https://www.buzzfeednews.com/article/zahrahirji/sharpiegate-fake-hurricane-map-emails.

31. "NAO 202-735D: Scientific Integrity," December 7, 2011, National Oceanic and Atmospheric Administration, https://www.corporateservices.noaa. gov/ames/administrative_orders/chapter_202/202-735-D.html.

32. Andrew Freedman and Jason Samenow, "NOAA Leaders Violated Agency's Scientific Integrity Policy, Hurricane Dorian 'Sharpiegate' Investigation Finds," *Washington Post*, June 15, 2020, https://www.washingtonpost.com/ weather/2020/06/15/noaa-investigation-sharpiegate/.

33. *Evaluation of NOAA's September 6, 2019, Statement about Hurricane Dorian Forecasts*, 45.

34. Stephen Skowronek, *Building a New American State: The Expansion of National Administrative Capacities, 1877–1920* (New York: Cambridge University Press, 1982), 70.

35. One area in which the Trump administration received congressional cooperation was at the Department of Veterans Affairs. In June 2017, Congress passed legislation making it easier to fire employees there, seeking to address poor performance by that agency. Legislators expected to hold senior executives accountable. However, within months (by March 2018), the VA had fired over 1,700 mostly rank-and-file employees, sometimes for minor infractions, leading some lawmakers to regret their support for the move. Since then, Congress has been more skeptical of Trump administration requests to weaken the rules. Isaac Arnsdorf, "The Trump Administration's Campaign to Weaken Civil Service Ramps Up at the VA," *ProPublica*, March 12, 2018, https://www.propublica.org/article/veterans-affairs-the-trump-administration-campaign-to-weaken-civil-service-ramps-up.

36. Mihir Zaveri, "Trump's NOAA Pick, Barry Myers, Asks to Withdraw Nomination," *New York Times*, November 21, 2019, https://www.nytimes. com/2019/11/21/us/politics/barry-myers-noaa-nomination.html.

37. Andrew Freedman and Jason Samenow, "As NOAA Leaders Take Fall for 'Sharpiegate,' Commerce Department Officials Have So Far Escaped Scrutiny," *Washington Post*, June 18, 2020, https://www.washingtonpost.com/weather/ 2020/06/18/sharpiegate-commerce-staff-duck-investigations/.

38. 15 U.S.C. § 313; "Role of the National Weather Service and Selected Legislation in the 114th Congress," Report 44583, *Congressional Research Service*, August 8, 2016, 1; Christopher Flavelle and Lisa Friedman, "As Election Nears, Trump Makes a Final Push Against Climate Science," *New York Times*, October 27, 2020, https://www.nytimes.com/2020/10/27/climate/trump-election-climate-noaa.html.

39. Scott Detrow, "Scott Pruitt Confirmed to Lead Environmental Protection Agency," *NPR*, February 17, 2017, https://www.npr.org/2017/02/17/515802629/ scott-pruitt-confirmed-to-lead-environmental-protection-agency.

40. Friedman, "A War Against Climate Science, Waged by Washington's Rank and File."

41. Coral Davenport, "Trump's Environmental Rollbacks Find Opposition Within: Staff Scientists," *New York Times*, March 27, 2020, https://www.nytimes.com/2020/03/27/climate/trumps-environmental-rollbacks-staff-scientists.html.

42. Lisa Friedman, "Cost of New EPA Coal Rules: Up to 1,400 More Deaths a Year," *New York Times*, August 21, 2018, https://www.nytimes.com/2018/08/21/climate/epa-coal-pollution-deaths.html.

43. Davenport, "Trump's Environmental Rollbacks Find Opposition Within."

44. *Policy Assessment for the Review of the National Ambient Air Quality Standards for Particulate Matter*, External Review Draft, September 2019, US Environmental Protection Agency, Office of Air Quality Planning and Standards, Health and Environmental Impacts Division, Research Triangle Park, NC, 1–2, https://www.epa.gov/sites/production/files/2019-09/documents/draft_policy_assessment_for_pm_naaqs_09-05-2019.pdf.

45. *Regulatory Impact Analysis for the Proposed Emission Guidelines for Greenhouse Gas Emissions from Existing Electric Utility Generating Units; Revisions to Emission Guideline Implementing Regulations; Revisions to New Source Review Program*, August 2018, US Environmental Protection Agency, Office of Air Quality Planning and Standards, Health and Environmental Impact Division, Research Triangle Park, NC, ES-1, https://www.epa.gov/sites/production/files/2018-08/documents/utilities_ria_proposed_ace_2018-08.pdf.

46. Davenport, "Trump's Environmental Rollbacks Find Opposition Within."

47. Davenport, "Trump's Environmental Rollbacks Find Opposition Within."

48. Nadja Popovich, Livia Albeck-Ripka, and Kendra Pierre-Louis, "The Trump Administration Is Reversing 100 Environmental Rules. Here's the Full List," *New York Times*, July 15, 2020, https://www.nytimes.com/interactive/2020/climate/trump-environment-rollbacks.html.

49. Danny Hakim and Eric Lipton, "Pesticide Studies Won EPA's Trust, Until Trump's Team Scorned 'Secret Science,'" *New York Times*, August 24, 2018, https://www.nytimes.com/2018/08/24/business/epa-pesticides-studies-epidemiology.html.

50. "CLA Petitions EPA to Stop Using Studies That Are Not Backed by Sound Science or Quality Data," *CropLife America*, December 2, 2016, http://www.croplifeamerica.org/news/2017/10/26/cla-petitions-epa-to-stop-using-studies-that-are-not-backed-by-sound-science-or-quality-data.

51. Hakim and Lipton, "Pesticide Studies."

52. Hakim and Lipton, "Pesticide Studies."

53. Eric Niiler, "The EPA's Anti-Science 'Transparency' Rule Has a Long History," *Wired*, November 13, 2019, https://www.wired.com/story/the-epas-anti-science-transparency-rule-has-a-long-history/.

54. Donald J. Trump, "Executive Order 13777—Enforcing the Regulatory Reform Agenda," February 24, 2017, *The American Presidency Project*, https://www.presidency.ucsb.edu/documents/executive-order-13777-enforcing-the-regulatory-reform-agenda.

55. Lorraine Chow, "Trump Gives Pen to Dow Chemical CEO after Signing Executive Order to Eliminate Regulations," *EcoWatch*, February 24, 2017, https://www.ecowatch.com/trump-executive-order-regulations-2282814216.html.

56. "EPA Administrator Pruitt Proposes Rule to Strengthen Science Used in EPA Regulations," News Releases, Environmental Protection Agency, April 24, 2018, https://www.epa.gov/newsreleases/epa-administrator-pruitt-proposes-rule-strengthen-science-used-epa-regulations.

57. Hakim and Lipton, "Pesticide Studies."

58. Liz Crampton, "EPA Will Not Ban Chlorpyrifos," *Politico*, July 18, 2019, https://www.politico.com/story/2019/07/18/epa-will-not-ban-chlorpyrifos-1603479.

59. Ellie Kaufman, "Senate Confirms Former Coal Lobbyist Andrew Wheeler to Lead EPA," *CNN*, February 28, 2019, https://www.cnn.com/2019/02/28/politics/andrew-wheeler-confirmation/index.html.

60. Lisa Friedman, "EPA to Limit Science Used to Write Public Health Rules," *New York Times*, November 11, 2019, https://www.nytimes.com/2019/11/11/climate/epa-science-trump.html.

61. Friedman, "EPA to Limit Science Used to Write Public Health Rules."

62. US Environmental Protection Agency Science Advisory Board Draft Report, "SAB Consideration of the Scientific and Technical Basis of EPA's Proposed Rule Titled *Strengthening Transparency in Regulatory Science*," October 16, 2019, 1–2, https://yosemite.epa.gov/sab/sabproduct.nsf/ea5d9a9b55cc319285256cbd005a472e/8a4dabc3b78f4106852584e100541a03/$FILE/Science%20and%20Transparency%20Draft%20Review_10_16_19_.pdf.

63. Lisa Friedman, "EPA Updates Plan to Limit Science Used in Environmental Rules," *New York Times*, March 4, 2020, https://www.nytimes.com/2020/03/04/climate/trump-science-epa.html.

64. Rebecca Beitsch, "EPA Looks to Other Statutes to Expand Scope of Coming 'Secret Science' Rule," *The Hill*, July 29, 2020, https://thehill.com/policy/energy-environment/509663-epa-looks-to-other-statutes-to-expand-scope-of-coming-secret.

65. Lisa Friedman, "Coronavirus Doesn't Slow Trump's Regulatory Rollbacks," *New York Times*, March 25, 2020, https://www.nytimes.com/2020/03/25/climate/coronavirus-environmental-regulations-trump.html; Don Jenkins, "Federal judges rehear case for banning chlorpyrifos," *Capital Press*, July 28, 2020, https://www.capitalpress.com/state/oregon/federal-judges-rehear-case-for-banning-chlorpyrifos/article_c026e40e-d0fa-11ea-b59a-b3c391a93c48.html.

66. "Policy on EPA Scientific Integrity," US Environmental Protection Agency, https://www.epa.gov/osa/policy-epa-scientific-integrity.

67. Maggie Koerth, "Trump Finds the Weak Spot in Obama's Protections for Scientists," *FiveThirtyEight*, January 24, 2017, https://fivethirtyeight.com/features/trump-finds-the-weak-spot-in-obamas-protections-for-scientists/.

68. Office of the Chief Scientist, "Scientific Integrity," Departmental Regulation 1074-001, Office of the Chief Information Officer, US Department of Agriculture, https://www.ocio.usda.gov/document/departmental-regulation-1074-001.

69. Jeffrey Hart, "The Presidency: Shifting Conservative Perspectives?," *National Review*, November 22, 1974, 1351–1355, at 1353.

70. *INS v. Chadha*, 462 U.S. 619 (1983).

71. *Ratification of Reorganization Plans*, Hearing before a Subcommittee of the Committee on Government Operations, House of Representatives, 98th Congress, 2nd Session (Washington, DC: Government Printing Office, 1985 [1984]), 3.

72. Dwight D. Eisenhower, "Special Message to the Congress Transmitting Reorganization Plan 2 of 1953 Concerning the Department of Agriculture," March 25, 1953, *The American Presidency Project*, https://www.presidency.ucsb.edu/documents/special-message-the-congress-transmitting-reorganization-plan-2-1953-concerning-the.

73. Liz Crampton and Ryan McCrimmon, "Trump Administration to Move USDA Researchers to Kansas City Area," *Politico*, June 13, 2019, https://www.politico.com/story/2019/06/13/usda-kansas-city-area-1529072.

74. Ryan McCrimmon, "Economists Flee Agriculture Dept. after Feeling Punished under Trump," *Politico*, May 7, 2019, https://www.politico.com/story/2019/05/07/agriculture-economists-leave-trump-1307146.

75. Crampton and McCrimmon, "Trump Administration to Move USDA Researchers to Kansas City Area."

76. Derrick Z. Jackson, "A Stealth Move to Undermine Science at the US Department of Agriculture," Union of Concerned Scientists, November 14, 2018, https://blog.ucsusa.org/derrick-jackson/a-stealth-move-to-undermine-science-at-the-us-department-of-agriculture.

77. Liz Crampton, "USDA Farms Out Economists Whose Work Challenges Trump Policies," *Politico*, May 22, 2019, https://www.politico.com/story/2019/05/22/usda-agriculture-economists-trump-policies-1340168.

78. Plumer and Davenport, "Science under Attack."

79. Ryan McCrimmon, "Farm Spending Bill Set for House Markup," *Politico*, July 9, 2020, https://www.politico.com/newsletters/morning-agriculture/2020/07/09/farm-spending-bill-set-for-house-markup-789049.

80. "Interior Set to Move BLM Headquarters to Colorado," *FEDWeek*, January 22, 2020, https://www.fedweek.com/fedweek/interior-set-to-move-blm-headquarters-to-colorado/.

81. James MacGregor Burns, *Leadership* (New York: Harper and Row, 1978); Archie Brown, *The Myth of the Strong Leader: Political Leadership in the Modern Age* (New York: Basic Books, 2014).

82. Arjen Boin, Paul 't Hart, Eric Stern, and Bengt Sundelius, *The Politics of Crisis Management: Public Leadership under Pressure* (New York: Cambridge University Press, 2005).

83. Eric A. Posner and Adrian Vermeule, "Crisis Governance in the Administrative State: 9/11 and the Financial Meltdown of 2008," *University of Chicago Law Review* 76, no. 4 (2009): 1613–1681, at 1614. See also Clinton Rossiter, *Constitutional Dictatorship: Crisis Government in the Modern Democracies* (Princeton, NJ: Princeton University Press, 1948).

84. National Emergencies Act of 1976 (P.L. 94-412, 90 Stat. 1255, September 14, 1976).

85. That is not to say that the influence of private interests was absent in this episode. For example, the White House's efforts to secure more personal protective equipment for medical providers, led by Trump's son-in-law Jared Kushner, prioritized tips about finding such supplies from "VIPs"—the president's political allies. Yasmeen Abutaleb and Ashley Parker, "Kushner Coronavirus Efforts Said to Be Hampered by Inexperienced Volunteers," *Washington Post*, May 5, 2020, https://www.washingtonpost.com/politics/kushner-coronavirus-effort-said-to-be-hampered-by-inexperienced-volunteers/2020/05/05/6166ef0c-8e1c-11ea-9e23-6914ee410a5f_story.html.

86. Boin, Hart, Stern, and Sundelius, *Politics of Crisis Management*, 49.

87. Plumer and Davenport, "Science under Attack."

88. Deb Riechmann, "Trump Disbanded NSC Pandemic Unit That Experts Had Praised," *Associated Press*, March 14, 2020, https://apnews.com/ce014d94b64e98b7203b873e56f80e9a.

89. Dan Diamond and Nahal Toosi, "Trump Team Failed to Follow NSC's Pandemic Playbook," *Politico*, March 25, 2020, https://www.politico.com/news/2020/03/25/trump-coronavirus-national-security-council-149285.

90. *Worldwide Threat Assessment of the US Intelligence Community*, Daniel R. Coats, Director of National Intelligence, Statement for the Record, Senate Select Committee on Intelligence, January 29, 2019, 21, https://www.dni.gov/files/ODNI/documents/2019-ATA-SFR---SSCI.pdf.

91. David E. Sanger, Eric Lipton, Eileen Sullivan, and Michael Crowley, "Before Virus Outbreak, a Cascade of Warnings Went Unheeded," *New York Times*, March 19, 2020, https://www.nytimes.com/2020/03/19/us/politics/trump-coronavirus-outbreak.html.

92. Marisa Taylor, "Exclusive: US Slashed CDC Staff inside China Prior to Coronavirus Outbreak," *Reuters*, March 25, 2020, https://www.reuters.com/article/us-health-coronavirus-china-cdc-exclusiv/exclusive-u-s-slashed-cdc-staff-inside-china-prior-to-coronavirus-outbreak-idUSKBN21C3N5.

93. Marisa Taylor, "Exclusive: US Axed CDC Expert Job in China Months before Virus Outbreak," *Reuters*, March 22, 2020, https://www.reuters.com/article/us-health-coronavirus-china-cdc-exclusiv/exclusive-u-s-axed-cdc-expert-job-in-china-months-before-virus-outbreak-idUSKBN21910S.

94. Emily Baumgaertner and James Rainey, "Trump Administration Ended Pandemic Early-Warning Program to Detect Coronaviruses," *Los Angeles Times*, April 2, 2020, https://www.latimes.com/science/story/2020-04-02/coronavirus-trump-pandemic-program-viruses-detection.

95. Yasmeen Abutaleb, Josh Dawsey, Ellen Nakashima, and Greg Miller, "The US Was Beset by Denial and Dysfunction as the Coronavirus Raged," *Washington Post*, April 4, 2020, https://www.washingtonpost.com/national-security/2020/04/04/coronavirus-government-dysfunction/.

96. Dan Diamond, "Trump's Mismanagement Helped Fuel Coronavirus Crisis," *Politico*, March 7, 2020, https://www.politico.com/news/2020/03/07/trump-coronavirus-management-style-123465.

97. Greg Miller and Ellen Nakashima, "President's Intelligence Briefing Book Repeatedly Cited Virus Threat," *Washington Post*, April 27, 2020, https://www.washingtonpost.com/national-security/presidents-intelligence-briefing-book-repeatedly-cited-virus-threat/2020/04/27/ca66949a-8885-11ea-ac8a-fe9b8088e101_story.html.

98. David Nakamura, "'Maybe I Have a Natural Ability': Trump Plays Medical Expert on Coronavirus by Second-Guessing the Professionals," *Washington Post*, March 6, 2020, https://www.washingtonpost.com/politics/maybe-i-have-a-natural-ability-trump-plays-medical-expert-on-coronavirus-by-second-guessing-the-professionals/2020/03/06/3ee0574c-5ffb-11ea-9055-5fa12981bbbf_story.html.

99. Thomas Frank, "Trump Says the Coronavirus Is the Democrats' 'New Hoax,'" *CNBC*, February 28, 2020, https://www.cnbc.com/2020/02/28/trump-says-the-coronavirus-is-the-democrats-new-hoax.html.

100. Diamond, "Trump's Mismanagement Helped Fuel Coronavirus Crisis."

101. Luciana Borio and Scott Gottlieb, "Act Now to Prevent an American Epidemic," *Wall Street Journal*, January 28, 2020, https://www.wsj.com/articles/act-now-to-prevent-an-american-epidemic-11580255335.

102. Aaron Blake, "'It Will Go Away': A Timeline of Trump Playing Down the Coronavirus Threat," *Washington Post*, March 12, 2020, https://www.washingtonpost.com/politics/2020/03/12/trump-coronavirus-timeline/.

103. Natasha Bertrand, Daniel Lippmann, Meredith McGraw, and Lara Seligman, "American's National Security Machine Stares Down Viral Threat," *Politico*, March 12, 2020, https://www.politico.com/news/2020/03/12/america-national-security-viral-threat-126574.

104. Abutaleb, Dawsey, Nakashima, and Miller, "The US Was Beset by Denial and Dysfunction as the Coronavirus Raged."

105. Elizabeth Chuck, "'It Is a Failing. Let's Admit It,' Fauci Says of Coronavirus Testing Capacity," *NBC News*, March 12, 2020, https://www.nbcnews.com/health/health-news/it-failing-let-s-admit-it-fauci-says-coronavirus-testing-n1157036.

106. On the alleged connection between a unitary executive and more effective coordination, see Steven G. Calabresi and Nicholas Terrell, "The Fatally Flawed Theory of the Unbundled Executive," *Minnesota Law Review* 93, no. 5 (May 2009): 1696–1740, at 1717. Caitlyn Oprysko, "'I Don't Take Responsibility at All': Trump Deflects Blame for Coronavirus Testing Fumble," *Politico*, March 13, 2020, https://www.politico.com/news/2020/03/13/trump-coronavirus-testing-128971.

107. Eric Lipton, David E. Sanger, Maggie Haberman, Michael D. Shear, Mark Mazzetti, and Julian E. Barnes, "He Could Have Seen What Was Coming: Behind Trump's Failure on the Virus," *New York Times*, April 11, 2020, https://www.nytimes.com/2020/04/11/us/politics/coronavirus-trump-response.html.

108. Brianna Ehley, "US Coronavirus Outbreak Inevitable, CDC Official Says," *Politico*, February 25, 2020, https://www.politico.com/news/2020/02/25/us-coronavirus-outbreak-inevitable-cdc-117389.

109. Lipton, Sanger, Haberman, Shear, Mazzetti, and Barnes, "He Could Have Seen What Was Coming."

110. Charles Duhigg, "Seattle's Leaders Let Scientists Take the Lead. New York's Did Not," *New Yorker*, April 26, 2020, https://www.newyorker.com/magazine/2020/05/04/seattles-leaders-let-scientists-take-the-lead-new-yorks-did-not.

111. "Mike Pence Coronavirus Update Transcript: Pence & Task Force Hold Briefing," *Rev*, March 2, 2020, https://www.rev.com/blog/transcripts/mike-pence-coronavirus-update-transcript-pence-task-force-hold-briefing.

112. "Press Briefing by Vice President Pence and Members of the Coronavirus Task Force," White House, Press Briefings, March 10, 2020, https://www.whitehouse.gov/briefings-statements/press-briefing-vice-president-pence-members-coronavirus-task-force/.

113. Sarah Owermohle, "'You Don't Want to Go to War with a President,'" *Politico*, March 3, 2020, https://www.politico.com/news/2020/03/03/anthony-fauci-trump-coronavirus-crisis-118961; Alexander Bolton, "GOP Senators Tell Trump to Make Fauci Face of Government's Coronavirus Response," *The Hill*, March 10, 2020, https://thehill.com/homenews/senate/486870-gop-senators-tell-trump-to-make-fauci-face-of-governments-coronavirus.

114. Sheryl Gay Stolberg, "Top Coronavirus Official for US Has Fought an Epidemic Before," *New York Times*, March 6, 2020, https://www.nytimes.com/2020/03/06/us/politics/coronavirus-trump-deborah-birx.html.

115. Michael D. Shear, Noah Weiland, Eric Lipton, Maggie Haberman, and David E. Sanger, "Inside Trump's Failure: The Rush to Abandon Leadership Role on the Virus," *New York Times*, July 18, 2020, https://www.nytimes.com/2020/07/18/us/politics/trump-coronavirus-response-failure-leadership.html.

116. David E. Sanger and Maggie Haberman, "Does the Coronavirus Task Force Even Matter for Trump?," *New York Times*, May 7, 2020, https://www.nytimes.com/2020/05/07/us/politics/coronavirus-task-force-trump.html.

117. "15 Days to Slow the Spread," March 16, 2020, White House, https://www.whitehouse.gov/articles/15-days-slow-spread/; Kevin Liptak, "White House Advises Public to Avoid Groups of More than 10, Asks People to Stay Away from Bars and Restaurants," *CNN*, March 16, 2020, https://www.cnn.com/2020/03/16/politics/white-house-guidelines-coronavirus/index.html.

118. @realDonaldTrump, March 22, 2020, 11:50 PM, Twitter, https://twitter.com/realDonaldTrump/status/1241935285916782593; Thomas Heath and Jacob Bogage, "Dow Caps Its Worst First Quarter with a Slide of More than

400 Points," *Washington Post*, March 31, 2020, https://www.washingtonpost.com/business/2020/03/31/stocks-markets-today-coronavirus/.

119. Quint Forgey, "Trump Says He'll 'Rely on' Public Health Experts on Social Distancing Decisions," *Politico*, March 30, 2020, https://www.politico.com/news/2020/03/30/trump-social-distancing-decisions-public-health-experts-155406.

120. Kevin Breuninger and Jacob Pramuk, "Trump Plays Campaign-Style Video in White House Coronavirus Briefing Touting His 'Decisive Action,'" *CNBC*, April 13, 2020, https://www.cnbc.com/2020/04/13/coronavirus-trump-plays-campaign-style-video-in-white-house-briefing.html.

121. Michael D. Shear and Sheila Kaplan, "A Debate over Masks Uncovers Deep White House Divisions," *New York Times*, April 3, 2020, https://www.nytimes.com/2020/04/03/us/politics/coronavirus-white-house-face-masks.html.

122. Katie Rogers, "Trump's Scientists Push Back on His Claim That Virus May Not Return This Fall," *New York Times*, April 22, 2020, https://www.nytimes.com/2020/04/22/us/politics/trump-coronavirus-fall.html.

123. Caroline Kelly, "Trump Disagrees with Fauci on US Testing Capacity," *CNN*, April 23, 2020, https://www.cnn.com/2020/04/23/politics/fauci-testing-capacity-not-overly-confident/index.html.

124. Jill Covin and Zeke Miller, "Trump Backs Off Total Authority Claim in Row with State Governors," *Yahoo*, April 15, 2020, https://news.yahoo.com/president-trump-moves-walk-back-052603212.html.

125. Kevin Liptak, "In Reversal, Trump Says Task Force Will Continue 'Indefinitely'—Eyes Vaccine Czar," *CNN*, May 6, 2020, https://www.cnn.com/2020/05/06/politics/trump-task-force-vaccine/index.html.

126. Stephen Collinson, "Trump's Rebuke of Fauci Encapsulates Rejection of Science in Virus Fight," *CNN*, May 14, 2020, https://www.cnn.com/2020/05/14/politics/donald-trump-anthony-fauci-science-coronavirus/index.html.

127. Jon Cohen, "'I'm Going to Keep Pushing': Anthony Fauci Tries to Make the White House Listen to Facts of the Pandemic," *Science*, March 22, 2020, https://www.sciencemag.org/news/2020/03/i-m-going-keep-pushing-anthony-fauci-tries-make-white-house-listen-facts-pandemic.

128. Gabriel Sherman, "Inside Donald Trump and Jared Kushner's Two Months of Magical Thinking," *Vanity Fair*, April 28, 2020, https://www.vanityfair.com/news/2020/04/donald-trump-jared-kushners-two-months-of-magical-thinking.

129. Joe Palca, "NIH Panel Recommends against Drug Combination Promoted by Trump for COVID-19," *NPR*, April 21, 2020, https://www.npr.org/sections/coronavirus-live-updates/2020/04/21/840341224/nih-panel-recommends-against-drug-combination-trump-has-promoted-for-covid-19.

130. Sheila Kaplan, "Stephen Hahn, F.D.A. Chief, Is Caught between Scientists and the President," *New York Times*, August 10, 2020, https://www.nytimes.com/2020/08/10/health/stephen-hahn-fda.html.

131. Charles Piller, "Former FDA Leaders Decry Emergency Authorization of Malaria Drugs for Coronavirus," *Science*, April 7, 2020, https://www.sciencemag.org/news/2020/04/former-fda-leaders-decry-emergency-authorization-malaria-drugs-coronavirus.

132. Palca, "NIH Panel Recommends against Drug Combination Promoted by Trump for COVID-19"; Jacqueline Howard, Arman Azad, and Maggie Fox, "FDA Revokes Authorization of Drug Trump Touted," *CNN*, June 15, 2020, https://www.cnn.com/2020/06/15/politics/fda-hydroxychloroquine-coronavirus/index.html.

133. Quint Forgey, "Trump Gets Stung from All Sides after Floating Injections of Disinfectants," *Politico*, April 24, 2020, https://www.politico.com/news/2020/04/24/lysol-maker-warns-against-injecting-disinfectants-trump-coronavirus-theory-206268.

134. Jonathan Martin and Maggie Haberman, "Nervous Republicans See Trump Sinking, and Taking Senate with Him," *New York Times*, April 25, 2020, https://www.nytimes.com/2020/04/25/us/politics/trump-election-briefings.html.

135. Jason Silverstein, "McConnell: 'Probably a Good Idea' for Coronavirus Briefings to Focus on Experts, Not Trump," *CBS News*, April 28, 2020, https://www.cbsnews.com/news/trump-coronavirus-briefings-health-experts-mcconnell/.

136. Ashley Parker and Philip Rucker, "Coronavirus Pushes Trump to Rely on Experts He Has Long Maligned," *Washington Post*, February 27, 2020, https://www.washingtonpost.com/politics/coronavirus-trump-experts/2020/02/27/71e8777c-5971-11ea-ab68-101ecfec2532_story.html.

137. Nancy Cook and Gabby Orr, "Trump's April Challenge: Leaning into the 'Deep State' to Quell a Raging Crisis," *Politico*, March 29, 2020, https://www.politico.com/news/2020/03/29/trump-april-challenge-deep-state-155059.

138. Eric Bradner and Gregory Krieg, "Biden Says Trump's Coronavirus Response Exposes Administration's 'Severe Shortcomings,'" *CNN*, March 12, 2020, https://www.cnn.com/2020/03/12/politics/biden-coronavirus-trump/index.html.

139. Robert Costa, Phillip Rucker, Yasmeen Abutaleb, and Josh Dawsey, "Trump's May Days: A Month of Distractions and Grievances as Nation Marks Bleak Coronavirus Milestone," *Washington Post,* May 31, 2020, https://www. washingtonpost.com/politics/trumps-may-days-a-month-of-distractions-and-grievances-as-nation-marks-bleak-coronavirus-milestone/2020/05/31/123e7e6a-a120-11ea-81bb-c2f70f01034b_story.html.

140. Yasmeen Abutaleb, Josh Dawsey, and Laurie McGinley, "Fauci Is Sidelined by the White House as He Steps Up Blunt Talk on Pandemic," *Washington Post,* July 11, 2020, https://www.washingtonpost.com/politics/2020/07/11/fauci-trump-coronavirus/.

141. At the time, Birx's credibility had been called into question by Speaker Nancy Pelosi (D-CA) because of her close relationship to Chief of Staff Mark Meadows's coronavirus working group. Max Cohen, "Trump Blasts Birx after She Warns Coronavirus Pandemic Is 'Extraordinarily Widespread'," *Politico,* August 3, 2020, https://www.politico.com/news/2020/08/03/trump-blasts-birx-after-coronavirus-claims-390881.

142. Lena H. Sun and Josh Dawsey, "CDC Feels Pressure from Trump as Rift Grows over Coronavirus Response," *Washington Post,* July 9, 2020, https://www.washingtonpost.com/health/trump-sidelines-public-health-advisers-in-growing-rift-over-coronavirus-response/2020/07/09/ad803218-c12a-11ea-9fdd-b7ac6b051dc8_story.html.

143. Savannah Behrmann, "'Science Should Not Stand in the Way' of Schools Reopening, White House Press Secretary Kayleigh McEnany Says," *USA Today,* July 16, 2020, https://www.usatoday.com/story/news/politics/2020/07/16/mcenany-science-should-not-stand-way-schools-reopening/5454168002/.

144. Ben Gittleson, Jordyn Phelps, and Libby Cathey, "Pandemic Probably Will 'Get Worse before It Gets Better': A Solo Trump Holds 1st Coronavirus Briefing in Months," *ABC News,* July 21, 2020, https://abcnews.go.com/Politics/trump-holds-briefing-focused-coronavirus-time-months/story?id=71905787; Elizabeth Thomas, "The New Doctor in Trump's Pandemic Response Briefings: Scott Atlas Agrees with Him on Masks, Opening Schools," *ABC News,* August 14, 2020, https://abcnews.go.com/Politics/doctor-trumps-pandemic-response-briefings-scott-atlas-agrees/story?id=72376728; Sheryl Gay Stolberg, "Top U.S. Officials Told C.D.C. to Soften Coronavirus Testing Guidelines," *New York Times,* August 26, 2020, https://www.nytimes.com/2020/08/26/us/politics/coronavirus-testing-trump-cdc.html; Katie Thomas and Sheri Fink, "F.D.A. 'Grossly Misrepresented' Blood Plasma Data, Scientists Say," *New*

York Times, August 24, 2020, https://www.nytimes.com/2020/08/24/health/fda-blood-plasma.html.

Chapter 8

1. J. David Alvis, Jeremy D. Bailey, and F. Flagg Taylor IV, *The Contested Removal Power: 1789–2010* (Lawrence: University Press of Kansas, 2013), ch. 1.
2. Kathyn Dunn Tenpas, "Tracking Turnover in the Trump Administration," Brookings Institution Report, April 2020, https://www.brookings.edu/research/tracking-turnover-in-the-trump-administration/.
3. Quoted in Andrew Rudalevige, *The New Imperial Presidency: Renewing Presidential Power after Watergate* (Ann Arbor: University of Michigan Press, 2005), 61.
4. Joel D. Aberbach and Bert A. Rockman, "Clashing Beliefs within the Executive Branch: The Nixon Administration Bureaucracy," *American Political Science Review* 70, no. 2 (June 1976): 456–468.
5. Terry M. Moe, "The Politicized Presidency," in *New Directions in American Politics*, eds. John E. Chubb and Paul E. Peterson (Washington, DC: Brookings Institution, 1985), 235–271; David E. Lewis, *The Politics of Presidential Appointments: Political Control and Bureaucratic Performance* (Princeton, NJ: Princeton University Press, 2008).
6. Toluse Olorunnipa, Ashley Parker, and Josh Dawsey, "Trump Embarks on Expansive Search for Disloyalty as Administration-Wide Purge Escalates," *Washington Post*, February 21, 2020, https://www.washingtonpost.com/politics/were-cleaning-it-out-trump-embarks-on-expansive-search-for-disloyalty-as-administration-wide-purge-escalates/2020/02/21/870e6c56-54c1-11ea-b119-4faabac6674f_story.html.
7. Jonathan Swan, "Scoop: Trump's Loyalty Cop Clashes with Agency Heads," *Axios*, June 14, 2020, https://www.axios.com/john-mcentee-white-house-trump-a799d519-aa2f-4e3d-b081-601f8193d75d.html.
8. Douglas T. Stuart, *Creating the National Security State: A History of the Law That Transformed America* (Princeton, NJ: Princeton University Press, 2008), 237.
9. 50 U.S.C. § 3021.
10. Stuart, *Creating the National Security State*, 130.
11. Amy B. Zegart, *Flawed by Design: The Evolution of the CIA, JCS, and NSC* (Stanford, CA: Stanford University Press, 1999), 10–11.

12. Harry S. Truman, *Memoirs*, Vol. 2: *Years of Trial and Hope* (Garden City, NY: Doubleday, 1956), 60.

13. Sidney W. Souers, "II. Policy Formulation for National Security," *American Political Science Review* 43, no. 3 (June 1949): 534–543, at 537.

14. Sean Gailmard and John Patty, *Learning While Governing: Expertise and Accountability in the Executive Branch* (Chicago: University of Chicago Press, 2013), 215–221.

15. Zegart, *Flawed by Design*, 94.

16. Stuart, *Creating*, 237.

17. Zegart, *Flawed by Design*, 79–81.

18. Robert Cutler, "The Development of the National Security Council," *Foreign Affairs* 34 (April 1956): 441–458, at 442.

19. Cutler, "Development of the National Security Council," 441, 455.

20. Greg Miller and Philip Rucker, "Michael Flynn Resigns as National Security Adviser," *Washington Post*, February 14, 2017, https://www.washingtonpost.com/world/national-security/michael-flynn-resigns-as-national-security-adviser/2017/02/13/0007c0a8-f26e-11e6-8d72-263470bf0401_story.html.

21. Bob Woodward, *Fear: Trump in the White House* (New York: Simon and Schuster, 2018), 89.

22. Alex Ward, "Trump's National Security Adviser, H. R. McMaster, Is Out. It Was a Long Time Coming," *Vox*, March 22, 2018, https://www.vox.com/2018/3/22/16065042/hr-mcmaster-trump-john-bolton-fired.

23. Philip Rucker and Carol Leonnig, *A Very Stable Genius: Donald J. Trump's Testing of America* (New York: Penguin Press, 2020), 165.

24. Woodward, *Fear*, 124–125.

25. Patrick Radden Keefe, "McMaster and Commander," *New Yorker*, April 23, 2018, https://www.newyorker.com/magazine/2018/04/30/mcmaster-and-commander.

26. Keefe, "McMaster and Commander"; Woodward, *Fear*, 126.

27. Keefe, "McMaster and Commander." Emphasis in original.

28. Ward, "Trump's National Security Adviser, H. R. McMaster, Is Out."

29. John Bolton, *The Room Where It Happened: A White House Memoir* (New York: Simon and Schuster, 2020), 34.

30. Jordyn Hermani, "Trump: I 'Temper' Bolton's Hawkish Instincts," *Politico*, May 9, 2019, https://www.politico.com/story/2019/05/09/donald-trump-john-bolton-1314722.

31. Eileen Sullivan, "Five Policy Clashes between John Bolton and President Trump," *New York Times*, September 10, 2019, https://www.nytimes.com/2019/09/10/us/politics/trump-bolton.html.

32. Peter Baker, Mujib Mashal, and Michael Crowley, "How Trump's Plan to Secretly Meet with the Taliban Came Together, and Fell Apart," *New York Times*, September 8, 2019, https://www.nytimes.com/2019/09/08/world/asia/afghanistan-trump-camp-david-taliban.html.

33. Peter Baker, "Trump Ousts John Bolton as National Security Adviser," *New York Times*, September 10, 2019, https://www.nytimes.com/2019/09/10/us/politics/john-bolton-national-security-adviser-trump.html.

34. Susan B. Glasser, "'It Won't End Well': Trump and His Obscure New National-Security Chief," *New Yorker*, September 19, 2019, https://www.newyorker.com/news/letter-from-trumps-washington/it-wont-end-well-trump-and-his-obscure-new-national-security-chief.

35. Michael Crowley, Peter Baker, and Maggie Haberman, "Robert O'Brien 'Looks the Part,' but Has Spent Little Time Playing It," *New York Times*, September 18, 2019, https://www.nytimes.com/2019/09/18/us/politics/national-security-adviser-robert-obrien.html.

36. Glasser, "'It Won't End Well.'"

37. Michael Crowley and David E. Sanger, "Under O'Brien, NSC Carries Out Trump's Policy, but Doesn't Develop It," *New York Times*, February 21, 2020, https://www.nytimes.com/2020/02/21/us/politics/national-security-council-trump-policy.html.

38. Robert C. O'Brien, "Robert C. O'Brien: Here's How I Will Streamline Trump's National Security Council," *Washington Post*, October 16, 2019, https://www.washingtonpost.com/opinions/robert-c-obrien-heres-how-i-will-streamline-trumps-national-security-council/2019/10/16/2b306360-f028-11e9-89eb-ec56cd414732_story.html.

39. President's Committee on Administrative Management, *Report of the Committee with Studies of Administrative Management in the Federal Government*, 74th Congress, 2nd Session (Washington, DC: US Government Printing Office, 1937), 5.

40. "'This Week' Transcript 1-12-20: House Speaker Nancy Pelosi, National Security Adviser Robert O'Brien," *ABC News*, January 12, 2020, https://abcnews.go.com/Politics/week-transcript-12-20-house-speaker-nancy-pelosi/story?id=68227362.

41. Jim Acosta, Zachary Cohen, Jake Tapper, and Jason Hoffman, "What National Security Adviser Robert O'Brien Is Saying about Russia Briefing 'Conflicts' with What Lawmakers Were Told," *CNN*, February 23, 2020, https://www.cnn.com/2020/02/22/politics/nsa-robert-obrien-intelligence-russia-help-sanders-trump/index.html.

42. Keefe, "McMaster and Commander"; Crowley and Sanger, "Under O'Brien, NSC Carries Out Trump's Policy, but Doesn't Develop It."

43. Lara Seligman, "Robert O'Brien Is the Anti-Bolton," *Foreign Policy*, January 27, 2020, https://foreignpolicy.com/2020/01/27/obrien-bolton-trump-impeachment/.

44. Crowley and Sanger, "Under O'Brien, NSC Carries Out Trump's Policy, but Doesn't Develop It."

45. Karen DeYoung, Dan Lamothe, Missy Ryan, and Kareem Fahim, "As Trump Withdraws US Forces from Northern Syria, His Administration Scrambles to Respond," *Washington Post*, October 13, 2019, https://www.washingtonpost.com/world/national-security/trump-orders-withdrawal-of-us-forces-from-northern-syria-days-after-pentagon-downplays-possibility/2019/10/13/83087baa-edbb-11e9-b2da-606ba1ef30e3_story.html.

46. Michael Crowley and Eric Schmitt, "White House Dismisses Reports of Bounties, But Is Silent on Russia," *New York Times*, July 1, 2020, https://www.nytimes.com/2020/07/01/us/politics/trump-russia-bounties-taliban.html.

47. Quoted in Noah Bierman, "White House Quietly Trims Dozens of National Security Experts," *Los Angeles Times*, February 12, 2020, https://www.latimes.com/politics/story/2020-02-12/white-house-quietly-trims-dozens-of-national-security-experts.

48. Seligman, "Robert O'Brien Is the Anti-Bolton"; Kathryn Dunn Tenpas, "Crippling the Capacity of the National Security Council," Brookings Institution, January 21, 2020, https://www.brookings.edu/blog/fixgov/2020/01/21/crippling-the-capacity-of-the-national-security-council/.

49. Kathryn Dunn Tenpas, "And Then There Were Ten: With 85% Turnover across President Trump's A Team, Who Remains?," Brookings Institution, April 13, 2020, https://www.brookings.edu/blog/fixgov/2020/04/13/and-then-there-were-ten-with-85-turnover-across-president-trumps-a-team-who-remains/.

50. Juliet Eilperin, Josh Dawsey, and Seung Min Kim, "'It's Way Too Many': As Vacancies Pile Up in Trump Administration, Senators Grow Concerned," *Washington Post*, February 4, 2019, https://www.washingtonpost.com/national/health-science/its-way-too-many-as-vacancies-pile-up-in-trump-administration-senators-grow-concerned/2019/02/03/c570eb94-24b2-11e9-ad53-824486280311_story.html.

51. Anne Joseph O'Connell, "Actings," *Columbia Law Review* 120, no. 3 (April 2020): 613–728.

52. Joel D. Aberbach and Bert A. Rockman, "The Appointments Process and the Administrative Presidency," *Presidential Studies Quarterly* 39, no. 1 (March 2009): 38–59.

53. Julie Hirschfeld Davis, Mark Mazzetti, and Maggie Haberman, "Firings and Discord Put Trump Transition Team in a State of Disarray," *New York Times*, November 15, 2016, https://www.nytimes.com/2016/11/16/us/politics/trump-transition.html.

54. David E. Lewis, "Deconstructing the Administrative State," *Journal of Politics* 81, no. 3 (July 2019): 767–789.

55. Robert P. Saldin and Steven M. Teles, *Never Trump: The Revolt of the Conservative Elites* (New York: Oxford University Press, 2020).

56. Christina M. Kinane, *Vacancy Politics: Presidential Appointments and the Strategic Evasion of Senate Consent*, Yale University, Book Manuscript.

57. Valerie C. Brannon, "The Vacancies Act: A Legal Overview," Report 44997, *Congressional Research Service*, July 20, 2018, 9–14.

58. Anonymous, *A Warning* (New York: Twelve, 2019), 49–50.

59. 50 U.S.C. § 3023(a)(1). Emphasis added.

60. Niels Lesniewski, "Former Senator Dan Coats Easily Confirmed as Intelligence Director," *Roll Call*, March 15, 2017, https://www.rollcall.com/2017/03/15/former-senator-dan-coats-easily-confirmed-as-intelligence-director/.

61. Jeremy Diamond, "Trump Sides with Putin over US Intelligence," *CNN*, July 16, 2018, https://www.cnn.com/2018/07/16/politics/donald-trump-putin-helsinki-summit/index.html.

62. Robert Draper, "Unwanted Truths: Inside Trump's Battles with US Intelligence Agencies," *New York Times Magazine*, August 8, 2020, https://www.nytimes.com/2020/08/08/magazine/us-russia-intelligence.html.

63. Maggie Haberman, Julian E. Barnes, and Peter Baker, "Dan Coats to Step Down as Intelligence Chief; Trump Picks Loyalist for Job," *New York Times*, July 28, 2019, https://www.nytimes.com/2019/07/28/us/politics/dan-coats-intelligence-chief-out.html.

64. Zachary Cohen, Pamela Brown, Allie Malloy, and Kaitlin Collins, "Trump Says Ratcliffe Is No Longer His Pick for Director of National Intelligence," *CNN*, August 2, 2019, https://www.cnn.com/2019/08/02/politics/trump-ratcliffe-dni/index.html.

65. Shane Harris and Ellen Nakashima, "Trump Announces Shakeup at Top of US Intelligence," *Washington Post*, August 8, 2019, https://www.washingtonpost.com/national-security/no-2-intelligence-official-

resigning-trump-announces/2019/08/08/9ed9d266-b54e-11e9-951e-de024209545d_story.html.

66. Draper, "Unwanted Truths."

67. Ellen Nakashima, Shane Harris, Josh Dawsey, and Anne Gearan, "Senior Intelligence Official Told Lawmakers That Russia Wants to See Trump Reelected," *Washington Post*, February 21, 2020, https://www. washingtonpost.com/national-security/after-a-congressional-briefing-on-election-threats-trump-soured-on-acting-spy-chief/2020/02/20/ 1ed2b4ec-53f1-11ea-b119-4faabac6674f_story.html.

68. Julian E. Barnes and Maggie Haberman, "Trump Names Richard Grenell as Acting Head of Intelligence," *New York Times*, February 19, 2020, https://www.nytimes.com/2020/02/19/us/politics/dni-national-intelligence-director-grenell.html.

69. Brooke Seipel, "Trump's New Intel Chief Makes Immediate Changes, Ousts Top Official," *The Hill*, February 21, 2020, https://thehill.com/ policy/national-security/484154-trumps-new-intel-chief-makes-immediate-changes-ousts-top-official.

70. Ratcliffe had subsequently served as part of Trump's defense team in his Senate impeachment trial.

71. Zachary Cohen and Jason Hoffman, "Trump Says He Will Nominate Rep. John Ratcliffe to Be Director of National Intelligence," *CNN*, February 28, 2020, https://www.cnn.com/2020/02/28/politics/john-ratcliffe-dni-nominate/index.html.

72. Nicholas Fandos and Julian E. Barnes, "Trump Ally Sees Easier Path to Intelligence Post in Second Attempt," *New York Times*, May 4, 2020, https://www.nytimes.com/2020/05/04/us/politics/ratcliffe-intelligence-director-confirmation.html.

73. Julian E. Barnes and Nicholas Fandos, "Republican Senate Panel Signals Support for John Ratcliffe as Intelligence Chief," *New York Times*, May 5, 2020, https://www.nytimes.com/2020/05/05/us/politics/john-ratcliffe-intelligence-director-confirmation-hearing.html.

74. Julian E. Barnes and Nicholas Fandos, "Senate Approves John Ratcliffe for Top Intelligene Job in Sharply Split Vote," *New York Times*, May 21, 2020, https://www.nytimes.com/2020/05/21/us/politics/john-ratcliffe-intelligence-director.html.

75. Alex Marquardt, Zachary Cohen, and Jeremy Herb, "Grenell Takes Parting Shot at Democrats as He Exits Top Intelligence Job," *CNN*, May 26, 2020, https://www.cnn.com/2020/05/26/politics/grenell-director-of-national-intelligence-final-days/index.html.

76. Julie Hirschfeld Davis and Michael D. Shear, *Border Wars: Inside Trump's Assault on Immigration* (New York: Simon and Schuster, 2019), 287.

77. Nick Miroff and Josh Dawsey, "Before Trump's Purge at DHS, Top Officials Challenged Plan for Mass Family Arrests," *Washington Post*, May 13, 2019, https://www.washingtonpost.com/immigration/before-trumps-purge-at-dhs-top-officials-challenged-plan-for-mass-family-arrests/2019/05/13/d7cb91ce-75af-11e9-bd25-c989555e7766_story.html.

78. Ted Hesson, "The Man behind Trump's 'Invisible Wall," *Politico Magazine*, September 20, 2018, https://www.politico.com/magazine/story/2018/09/20/uscis-director-lee-francis-cissna-profile-220141.

79. Ryan Devereaux, "US Citizenship and Immigration Services Will Remove 'Nation of Immigrants' from Mission Statement," *The Intercept*, February 22, 2018, https://theintercept.com/2018/02/22/u-s-citizenship-and-immigration-services-will-remove-nation-of-immigrants-from-mission-statement/.

80. Davis and Shear, *Border Wars*, 287, 376, 382, 388.

81. Nick Miroff, Josh Dawsey, and Maria Sacchetti, "Trump to Place Ken Cuccinelli at the Head of the Country's Legal Immigration System," *Washington Post*, May 24, 2019, https://www.washingtonpost.com/immigration/trump-to-place-ken-cuccinelli-at-the-head-of-the-countrys-legal-immigration-system/2019/05/24/143fdec8-7e64-11e9-a5b3-34f3edf1351e_story.html.

82. Ted Hesson, "Cuccinnelli Starts as Acting Immigration Official despite GOP Opposition," *Politico*, June 10, 2019, https://www.politico.com/story/2019/06/10/cuccinelli-acting-uscis-director-1520304.

83. Geneva Sands, "Ken Cuccinelli's Rise at the Department of Homeland Security," *CNN*, October 16, 2019, https://www.cnn.com/2019/10/16/politics/ken-cuccinelli-dhs/index.html.

84. The statement was made by Mark Krikorian, the executive director of the Center for Immigration Studies. Sands, "Ken Cuccinelli's Rise at the Department of Homeland Security."

85. Geneva Sands and Priscilla Alvarez, "Judge Says Ken Cuccinnelli Unlawfully Appointed to Lead US Immigration Agency," *CNN*, March 2, 2020, https://www.cnn.com/2020/03/01/politics/ken-cuccinelli-immigration-agency/index.html.

86. Kyle Cheney, "GAO Finds Chad Wolf, Ken Cuccinelli Are Ineligible to Serve in Their Top DHS Roles," *Politico*, August 14, 2020, https://www.politico.com/news/2020/08/14/gao-chad-wolf-ken-cuccinelli-ineligible-dhs-395222.

87. @HomelandKen, September 11, 2019, 7:46 PM, Twitter, https://twitter.com/HomelandKen/status/1171933152002093056.

88. @realDonaldTrump, November 25, 2017, 4:48 PM, Twitter,https://twitter.com/realdonaldtrump/status/934539256940417024.

89. David H. Carpenter, "The Consumer Financial Protection Bureau (CFPB): A Legal Analysis," Report 42572, *Congressional Research Service*, January 14, 2014, 9–12.

90. *NLRB v. Noel Canning*, 573 U.S. ___ (2014).

91. Manu Raju, Burgess Everett, and John Bresnahan, "Senate Deal Averts Nuclear Option," *Politico*, July 17, 2013, https://www.politico.com/story/2013/07/senate-nuclear-option-094259.

92. Jonnelle Marte, "Trump Administration Calls Structure of the Consumer Financial Protection Bureau Unconstitutional in Filing," *Washington Post*, March 17, 2017, https://www.washingtonpost.com/news/get-there/wp/2017/03/17/in-court-filing-trump-administration-calls-the-structure-of-the-cfpb-unconstitutional/.

93. Gillian B. White, "The Departing Consumer-Finance Director Moves to Thwart Trump," *The Atlantic*, November 24, 2017, https://www.theatlantic.com/business/archive/2017/11/cfpb-cordray-trump/546734/.

94. 12 U.S.C. § 5491(b); Nicholas Confessore, "Mick Mulvaney's Master Class in Destroying a Bureaucracy from Within," *New York Times Magazine*, April 16, 2019, https://www.nytimes.com/2019/04/16/magazine/consumer-financial-protection-bureau-trump.html.

95. Faith Karimi, "Confusion as Trump and Outgoing Director Pick Leaders for Consumer Agency," *CNN*, November 25, 2017, https://www.cnn.com/2017/11/25/politics/trump-consumer-agency-appointment/index.html.

96. Confessore, "Mick Mulvaney's Master Class in Destroying a Bureaucracy from Within."

97. Stephen A. Engel, Assistant Attorney General, "Designating an Acting Director of the Bureau of Consumer Financial Protection," Opinion of the Office of Legal Counsel, Department of Justice, November 25, 2017, 2, https://www.justice.gov/sites/default/files/opinions/attachments/2018/08/06/2017-11-25-acting-cfpb-dir.pdf.

98. Stacy Cowley, "Battle for Control of Consumer Agency Heads to Court," *New York Times*, November 26, 2017, https://www.nytimes.com/2017/11/26/business/trump-cfpb-consumer-agency.html.

99. Email from Leandra English to Zixta Martinez, Chris D'Angelo, David Silberman, Sartaj Alag, Mary McLeod, and Gail Hillebrand

re: "Delegations," November 27, 2017, 6:40 AM, Consumer Financial Protection Bureau. Published in "Records Show Richard Cordray Scrambled in Final Days to Name Successor, Thwart Trump's Nominee," Cause of Action Institute, January 31, 2018, https://causeofaction.org/records-show-richard-cordray-scrambled-final-days-name-successor-thwart-trumps-nominee/.

100. Katie Rogers, "2 Bosses Show Up to Lead the Consumer Financial Protection Bureau," *New York Times*, November 27, 2017, https://www.nytimes.com/2017/11/27/us/politics/cfpb-leandra-english-mulvaney.html.

101. Email from Mary E. McLeod, General Counsel, to the Senior Leadership Team, CFPB, re: "Acting Director of the CFPB," November 25, 2017, Consumer Financial Protection Bureau, 1, https://www.politico.com/f/?id=0000015f-fbe7-d90d-a37f-fff74f280000.

102. "Leandra English v. Donald Trump," *New York Times*, November 27, 2017, https://www.nytimes.com/interactive/2017/11/27/business/document-Leandra-English-vs-Donald-Trump.html.

103. Jesse Eisinger, "The CFPB's Declaration of Dependence," *ProPublica*, February 15, 2018, https://www.propublica.org/article/consumer-financial-protection-bureau-declaration-of-dependence.

104. Jessica Silver-Greenberg and Stacy Cowley, "Consumer Bureau's New Leader Steers a Sudden Reversal," *New York Times*, December 5, 2017, https://www.nytimes.com/2017/12/05/business/cfpb-mick-mulvaney.html.

105. Robert O'Harrow Jr., Shawn Boburg, and Renae Merle, "How Trump Appointees Curbed a Consumer Protection Agency Loathed by the GOP," *Washington Post*, December 4, 2018, https://www.washingtonpost.com/investigations/how-trump-appointees-curbed-a-consumer-protection-agency-loathed-by-the-gop/2018/12/04/3cb6cd56-de20-11e8-aa33-53bad9a881e8_story.html.

106. Yuka Hayashi and Lalita Clozel, "Donald Trump's Appointee Asserts Control over CFPB for Now," *Wall Street Journal*, November 27, 2017, https://www.wsj.com/articles/mick-mulvaney-arrives-to-assume-top-job-at-consumer-protection-bureau-1511795512.

107. Michael Grunwald, "Mulvaney Requests No Funding for Consumer Financial Protection Bureau," *Politico*, January 18, 2018, https://www.politico.com/story/2018/01/18/mulvaney-funding-consumer-bureau-cordray-345495; Glenn Thrush, "Mulvaney, Watchdog Bureau's Leader, Advises Bankers on Ways to Curtail Agency," *New York Times*, April 24,

2018, https://www.nytimes.com/2018/04/24/us/mulvaney-consumer-financial-protection-bureau.html.

108. O'Harrow, Boburg, and Merle, "How Trump Appointees Curbed a Consumer Protection Agency Loathed by the GOP."

109. Renae Merle, "Mulvaney Fires All 25 Members of Consumer Watchdog's Advisory Board," *Washington Post*, June 6, 2018, https://www.washingtonpost.com/news/business/wp/2018/06/06/mick-mulvaney-fires-members-of-cfpb-advisory-board/.

110. O'Harrow, Boburg, and Merle, "How Trump Appointees Curbed a Consumer Protection Agency Loathed by the GOP."

111. Confessore, "Mick Mulvaney's Master Class in Destroying a Bureaucracy from Within."

112. O'Harrow, Boburg, and Merle, "How Trump Appointees Curbed a Consumer Protection Agency Loathed by the GOP."

113. Confessore, "Mick Mulvaney's Master Class in Destroying a Bureaucracy from Within."

114. O'Harrow, Boburg, and Merle, "How Trump Appointees Curbed a Consumer Protection Agency Loathed by the GOP."

115. Confessore, "Mick Mulvaney's Master Class in Destroying a Bureaucracy from Within."

116. Eisinger, "CFPB's Declaration of Dependence."

117. Confessore, "Mick Mulvaney's Master Class in Destroying a Bureaucracy from Within."

118. O'Harrow, Boburg, and Merle, "How Trump Appointees Curbed a Consumer Protection Agency Loathed by the GOP."

119. O'Harrow, Boburg, and Merle, "How Trump Appointees Curbed a Consumer Protection Agency Loathed by the GOP"; Confessore, "Mick Mulvaney's Master Class in Destroying a Bureaucracy from Within."

120. Leandra English, "The Fight to Protect Consumers, at a Crossroads," *New York Daily News*, January 14, 2020, https://www.nydailynews.com/opinion/ny-oped-the-fight-to-protect-consumers-20200114-dd7juswygvgdxo4buwtqwvdf54-story.html.

121. *Seila Law LLC v. Consumer Financial Protection Bureau*, 591 U.S. ___ (2020) (slip op., 11, 22) (Roberts, C. J., opinion of the Court), https://www.supremecourt.gov/opinions/19pdf/19-7_n6io.pdf.

122. James Sherk, "Proposed Labor Reforms," Domestic Policy Council Memo, 2017, 12, available at https://assets.documentcloud.org/documents/6948593/Sherk-White-House-document.pdf; Erich Wagner, "White House Advisor Sought Legal Opinion to Allow Trump

to Fire Anyone in Government," *Government Executive*, June 25, 2020, https://www.govexec.com/management/2020/06/white-house-advisor-sought-legal-opinion-trump-can-fire-anyone-government/166445/.

123. Donald J. Trump, "Executive Order 13836—Developing Efficient, Effective, and Cost-Reducing Approaches to Federal Sector Collective Bargaining," May 25, 2018, *The American Presidency Project*, https://www.presidency.ucsb.edu/documents/executive-order-13836-developing-efficient-effective-and-cost-reducing-approaches-federal; Donald J. Trump, "Executive Order 13837—Ensuring Transparency, Accountability, and Efficiency in Taxpayer-Funded Union Time Use," May 25, 2018, *The American Presidency Project*, https://www.presidency.ucsb.edu/documents/executive-order-13837-ensuring-transparency-accountability-and-efficiency-taxpayer-funded; Donald J. Trump, "Executive Order 13839—Promoting Accountability and Streamlining Removal Procedures Consistent with Merit System Principles," May 25, 2018, *The American Presidency Project*, https://www.presidency.ucsb.edu/documents/executive-order-13839-promoting-accountability-and-streamlining-removal-procedures. (Note: After this book went to press, Trump went even further. Lisa Rein and Eric Yoder, "Trump Issues Sweeping Order for Tens of Thousands of Career Federal Employees to Lose Civil Service Protections," *Washington Post*, October 22, 2020, https://www.washingtonpost.com/politics/trump-order-federal-civil-service/2020/10/22/c73783f0-1481-11eb-bc10-40b25382f1be_story.html.)

124. Peter Baker, "Trump's Efforts to Remove the Disloyal Heightens Unease across His Administration," *New York Times*, February 22, 2020, https://www.nytimes.com/2020/02/22/us/politics/trump-disloyalty-turnover.html.

125. Donald J. Trump, "Executive Order 13842—Establishing an Exception to Competitive Examining Rules for Appointment to Certain Positions in the United States Marshals Service, Department of Justice," July 10, 2018, *The American Presidency Project*, https://www.presidency.ucsb.edu/documents/executive-order-13842-establishing-exception-competitive-examining-rules-for-appointment. The attorney general previously had authority to overrule immigration judge decisions, but the Trump DOJ issued an interim rule to delegate this responsibility to an unconfirmed political appointee in charge of the DOJ's Executive Office for Immigration Review. As Tabaddor saw it, "the immigration court has effectively been dismantled." Eric Katz, "Trump Administration Expands Political Power over Career Immigration Judges," *Government Executive*, August 26, 2019, https://www.govexec.com/management/

2019/08/trump-administration-expands-power-political-appointee-over-career-immigration-judges/159453/.

126. Steven M. Teles, *The Rise of the Conservative Legal Movement: The Battle for Control of the Law* (Princeton, NJ: Princeton University Press, 2008).

127. Chris Guthrie, Jeffrey J. Rachlinski, and Andrew J. Wistrich, "The 'Hidden Judiciary': An Empirical Examination of Executive Branch Justice," *Duke Law Journal* 58, no. 7 (April 2009): 1477–1530; Jack Beermann, "The Future of Administrative Law Judge Selection," *Regulatory Review*, October 29, 2019, https://www.theregreview.org/2019/10/29/beermann-administrative-law-judge-selection/.

128. Joanna L. Grisinger, *The Unwieldy American State: Administrative Politics since the New Deal* (New York: Cambridge University Press, 2012), 60; Joanna L. Grisinger, "The Hearing Examiners and the Administrative Procedure Act," *Journal of the National Association of Administrative Law Judiciary* 34, no. 1 (2014): 1–46; 5 U.S.C. § 556.

129. Bernard Schwartz, "Adjudication and the Administrative Procedure Act," *Tulsa Law Review* 32, no. 2 (Winter 1996): 203–219, at 210.

130. Margaret Newkirk and Greg Stohr, "Trump's War on 'Deep State' Judges," *Bloomberg Businessweek*, April 20, 2018, https://www.bloomberg.com/news/articles/2018-04-20/supreme-court-lucia-case-could-remove-agency-judge-protections.

131. Trevor Hunnicutt, "US SEC Fines, Bars 'Buckets of Money' Radio Host for Fraud," *Reuters*, July 9, 2013, https://www.reuters.com/article/radio-adviser-fined/u-s-sec-fines-bars-buckets-of-money-radio-host-for-fraud-idUSL1N0FF1QW20130709.

132. Andrew Chung, "US Supreme Court Takes Up Challenge to SEC In-House Judges," *Reuters*, January 12, 2018, https://www.reuters.com/article/us-usa-court-sec/u-s-supreme-court-takes-up-challenge-to-sec-in-house-judges-idUSKBN1F12JC.

133. Brief for Respondent, *Lucia, et al. v. Securities and Exchange Commission* (No. 17-130), 10–11, 14–15, 20, https://www.supremecourt.gov/DocketPDF/17/17-130/21998/20171129155714442_17-130%20Lucia.pdf.

134. *Lucia v. Securities and Exchange Commission*, 585 U.S. ___ (2018) (slip op., 1) (Kagan, J., opinion of the Court), https://www.supremecourt.gov/opinions/17pdf/17-130_4f14.pdf.

135. Interestingly, Kagan would later write the dissent in *Seila Law v. CFPB*. That, along with her narrow ruling here, suggests important but murky differences between her strong endorsement of "presidential

NOTES TO PAGES 156–159 287

administration" and the theory of the unitary executive. In *Seila,* Kagan took her stand with the "judgment of history," saying that Roberts's endorsement of the unitary theory "repudiates the lessons of American experience, from the 18th century to the present day." *Seila Law LLC v. Consumer Financial Protection Bureau,* 591 U.S. ___ (2020) (slip op., 3) (Kagan, J., dissenting), https://www.supremecourt.gov/opinions/19pdf/19-7_n6io.pdf.

136. Adam Liptak, "SEC Judges Were Appointed Unlawfully, Justices Rule," *New York Times,* June 21, 2018, https://www.nytimes.com/2018/06/21/us/politics/sec-judges-supreme-court.html.

137. *Lucia v. Securities and Exchange Commission,* 585 U.S. ___ (2018) (slip op., 2) (Thomas, J., concurring), https://www.supremecourt.gov/opinions/17pdf/17-130_4f14.pdf.

138. *Lucia v. Securities and Exchange Commission,* 585 U.S. ___ (2018) (slip op., 3, 6) (Breyer, J., concurring in part), https://www.supremecourt.gov/opinions/17pdf/17-130_4f14.pdf. Emphasis in original.

139. *Lucia v. Securities and Exchange Commission,* 585 U.S. ___ (2018) (slip op., 2-3) (Sotomayor, J., dissenting), https://www.supremecourt.gov/opinions/17pdf/17-130_4f14.pdf.

140. Donald J. Trump, "Executive Order 13843—Excepting Administrative Law Judges from the Competitive Service," July 10, 2018, *The American Presidency Project,* https://www.presidency.ucsb.edu/documents/executive-order-13843-excepting-administrative-law-judges-from-the-competitive-service.

141. Memorandum from Solicitor General to Agency General Counsels on "Guidance on Administrative Judges after *Lucia v. SEC* (S. Ct.)," Office of the Solicitor General, Department of Justice, undated [July 2018], 2–3, 9, https://static.reuters.com/resources/media/editorial/20180723/ALJ--SGMEMO.pdf; "Guidance on Administrative Law Judges after *Lucia v. SEC* (S. Ct.), July 2018," *Harvard Law Review* 132, no. 3 (January 2019): 1120–1127.

142. See, for example, Kent Barnett, "Raiding the OPM Den: The New Method of ALJ Hiring," *Notice & Comment,* July 11, 2018, https://www.yalejreg.com/nc/raiding-the-opm-den-the-new-method-of-alj-hiring-by-kent-barnett/.

143. Beermann, "The Future of Administrative Law Judge Selection."

144. E. Garrett West, "Clarifying the Employee-Officer Distinction in Appointments Clause Jurisprudence," *Yale Law Journal Forum* 127 (May 2017): 42–61.

145. Kent H. Barnett, "Resolving the ALJ Quandary," *Vanderbilt Law Review* 66, no. 3 (April 2013): 797–865.

146. Joel S. Nolette, "The ALJ Executive Order: A Modest Step towards Re-Integrating the Executive Branch," Federalist Society, July 24, 2018, https://fedsoc.org/commentary/fedsoc-blog/the-alj-executive-order-a-modest-step-towards-re-integrating-the-executive-branch.

147. Jessie Bur, "Administrative Law Judges Oppose Trump Executive Order," *Federal Times*, July 10, 2018, https://www.federaltimes.com/management/2018/07/10/trump-takes-federal-agency-judges-out-of-competitive-status/.

148. Jessie Bur, "Bipartisan Bill Would Counter Administrative Law Judge Executive Order," *Federal Times*, September 4, 2018, https://www.federaltimes.com/federal-oversight/congress/2018/09/04/bipartisan-bill-would-counter-administrative-law-judge-executive-order/.

149. *In Re: Aiken County*, No. 10-1050 (D.C. Cir. 2011) (Kavanaugh, Circuit Judge, concurring), 15, fn 5, https://www.cadc.uscourts.gov/internet/opinions.nsf/872039F019B626D7852578C00053956D/$file/10-1050-1316111.pdf.

150. Stephen Skowronek, "Franklin Roosevelt and the Modern Presidency," *Studies in American Political Development* 6, no. 2 (Fall 1992): 322–358.

151. The administration cited the Congressional Review Act's requirement that it should inform Congress whether a new regulation should be classified as a "major rule." Russell T. Vought, Memorandum for the Heads of Executive Departments re: "Guidance on Compliance with the Congressional Review Act," Office of Management and Budget, Executive Office of the President, April 11, 2019, https://www.whitehouse.gov/wp-content/uploads/2019/04/M-19-14.pdf; Cass R. Sunstein, "Trump White House Seeks New Power over Agencies," *Bloomberg Opinion*, April 23, 2019, https://www.bloomberg.com/opinion/articles/2019-04-23/trump-seeks-more-control-of-fed-sec-and-other-agencies.

152. Frederick A. Bradford, "The Banking Act of 1935," *American Economic Review* 25, no. 4 (December 1935): 661–672; Sarah Binder and Mark Spindel, *The Myth of Independence: How Congress Governs the Federal Reserve* (Princeton, NJ: Princeton University Press, 2017), ch. 4.

153. Donald F. Kettl, *Leadership at the Fed* (New Haven, CT: Yale University Press, 1986), 120–129; Lawrence R. Jacobs and Desmond King, *Fed Power: How Finance Wins* (New York: Oxford University Press, 2016), 78.

154. Jimmy Carter, "An Economic Position Paper for Now and Tomorrow," April 22, 1976, in *The Presidential Campaign 1976*, Vol. 1, Part 1: *Jimmy*

Carter (Washington, DC: Government Printing Office, 1978), 141–148, at 145.

155. Binder and Spindel, *Myth of Independence*, ch. 6.

156. Ana Swanson and Binyamin Appelbaum, "Trump Announces Jerome Powell as New Fed Chairman," *New York Times*, November 2, 2017, https://www.nytimes.com/2017/11/02/business/economy/jerome-powell-federal-reserve-trump.html.

157. Michael C. Bender, Rebecca Ballhaus, Peter Nicholas, and Alex Leary, "Trump Steps Up Attacks on Fed Chairman Jerome Powell," *Wall Street Journal*, October 23, 2018, https://www.wsj.com/articles/trump-steps-up-attacks-on-fed-chairman-jerome-powell-1540338090.

158. Philip Rucker, Josh Dawsey, and Damian Paletta, "Trump Slams Fed Chair, Questions Climate Change and Threatens to Cancel Putin Meeting in Wide-Ranging Interview with The Post," *Washington Post*, November 27, 2018, https://www.washingtonpost.com/politics/trump-slams-fed-chair-questions-climate-change-and-threatens-to-cancel-putin-meeting-in-wide-ranging-interview-with-the-post/2018/11/27/4362fae8-f26c-11e8-aeea-b85fd44449f5_story.html.

159. Peter Baker and Maggie Haberman, "For Trump, 'a War Every Day,' Waged Increasingly Alone," *New York Times*, December 22, 2018, https://www.nytimes.com/2018/12/22/us/politics/trump-two-years.html.

160. Matt Egan, "Why Jerome Powell's Quiet Show of Defiance against Trump and Wall Street Is So Important," *CNN Business*, December 20, 2018, https://www.cnn.com/2018/12/20/business/powell-fed-trump-markets/index.html.

161. "Full 60 Minutes Interview with Fed Chair Jerome Powell," *CBS News*, March 10, 2019, https://www.cbsnews.com/news/full-transcript-60-minutes-interview-with-fed-chair-jerome-powell/.

162. Jeanna Smialek, "How the Fed Chairman Is Shielding It from Trump," *New York Times*, January 28, 2020, https://www.nytimes.com/2020/01/28/business/economy/federal-reserve-jay-powell.html.

163. Bender, Ballhaus, Nicholas, and Leary, "Trump Steps Up Attacks on Fed Chairman Jerome Powell."

164. Justin Sink, Saleha Mohsin, Steven T. Dennis, and Jennifer Jacobs, "Trump's 0-for-4 Streak on Fed Choices Raises Concerns on Vetting," *Bloomberg*, May 2, 2019, https://www.bloomberg.com/news/articles/2019-05-02/trump-fed-vetting.

165. Smialek, "How the Fed Chairman Is Shielding It from Trump."

166. Egan, "Why Jerome Powell's Quiet Show of Defiance against Trump and Wall Street Is So Important."

167. Jeanna Smialek, "Trump Says He Could Demote Fed Chair Powell, Risking More Market Turmoil," *New York Times*, March 14, 2020, https://www.nytimes.com/2020/03/14/business/economy/trump-powell-fed-chair.html.

168. Peter Conti-Brown, "What Happens If Trump Tries to Fire Fed Chair Jerome Powell?," Brookings Institution, September 9, 2019, https://www.brookings.edu/blog/up-front/2019/09/09/what-happens-if-trump-tries-to-fire-fed-chair-jerome-powell/; Jeanna Smialek, "Trump Faces a Stubborn Opponent in Fed's Economic Experts," *New York Times*, August 25, 2019, https://www.nytimes.com/2019/08/25/business/trump-fed-opponent.html.

169. Nick Timiraos and Alex Leary, "Trump to Fed Chairman Powell: 'I Guess I'm Stuck with You,'" *Wall Street Journal*, April 2, 2019, https://www.wsj.com/articles/trump-to-fed-chairman-powell-i-guess-im-stuck-with-you-11554238931.

170. Bender, Ballhaus, Nicholas, and Leary, "Trump Steps Up Attacks on Fed Chairman Jerome Powell."

171. Victoria Guida, "Fed Breaks the Bank in Bid to Rescue Economy," *Politico*, March 24, 2020, https://www.politico.com/news/2020/03/24/federal-reserve-coronavirus-147342; Courtenay Brown, "Trump Says Fed Chairman Is Doing a 'Good Job' amid Coronavirus Crisis," *Axios*, March 24, 2020, https://www.axios.com/trump-jerome-powell-coronavirus-federal-reserve-4af50d30-23ff-4b01-9e72-7939034b505c.html.

Chapter 9

1. See, for example, David R. Mayhew, *Divided We Govern: Party Control, Lawmaking, and Investigations, 1946–2002*, 2nd ed. (New Haven, CT: Yale University Press, 2005); Douglas L. Kriner and Eric Schickler, *Investigating the President: Congressional Checks on Presidential Power* (Princeton, NJ: Princeton University Press, 2016).

2. Mathew D. McCubbins and Thomas Schwartz, "Congressional Oversight Overlooked: Police Patrols versus Fire Alarms," *American Journal of Political Science* 28, no. 1 (February 1984): 165–179.

3. David E. Kyvig, *The Age of Impeachment: American Constitutional Culture since 1960* (Lawrence: University Press of Kansas, 2008).

4. Carl Bernstein and Bob Woodward, *All the President's Men* (New York: Simon and Schuster, 1974).

5. Peter Baker, "Trump Pressed Ukraine's President to Investigate Democrats as 'a Favor,'" *New York Times*, September 25, 2019, https://www.nytimes.com/2019/09/25/us/politics/donald-trump-impeachment-probe.html; Josh Dawsey, Paul Sonne, Michael Kranish, and David L. Stern, "How Trump and Giuliani Pressured Ukraine to Investigate the President's Rivals," *Washington Post*, September 21, 2019, https://www.washingtonpost.com/politics/how-trump-and-giuliani-pressured-ukraine-to-investigate-the-presidents-rivals/2019/09/20/0955801c-dbb6-11e9-a688-303693fb4b0b_story.html.

6. Kenneth P. Vogel and Michael S. Schmidt, "Trump Envoys Pushed Ukraine to Commit to Investigations," *New York Times*, October 3, 2019, https://www.nytimes.com/2019/10/03/us/politics/trump-ukraine.html.

7. Caroline Kelly, "CNN Host Was Set to Interview Ukrainian President until Scandal Took Shape," *CNN*, November 7, 2019, https://www.cnn.com/2019/11/07/politics/volodymyr-zelensky-fareed-zakaria-ukraine-aid/index.html.

8. Eric Lipton, Maggie Haberman, and Mark Mazzetti, "Behind the Ukraine Aid Freeze: 84 Days of Conflict and Confusion," *New York Times*, December 29, 2019, https://www.nytimes.com/2019/12/29/us/politics/trump-ukraine-military-aid.html.

9. Michael S. Schmidt, Julian E. Barnes, and Maggie Haberman, "Trump Knew of Whistle-Blower Complaint When He Released Aid to Ukraine," *New York Times*, November 26, 2019, https://www.nytimes.com/2019/11/26/us/politics/trump-whistle-blower-complaint-ukraine.html.

10. *Legislation to Establish Offices of Inspector General—H.R. 8588*, Hearings before the Subcommittee on Governmental Efficiency and the District of Columbia of the Committee on Governmental Affairs, United States Senate, 95th Congress, 2nd Session (Washington, DC: Government Printing Office, 1978), 147, 20.

11. Whistleblower Complaint, August 12, 2019, 1. Available at "Document: Read the Whistle-Blower Complaint," *New York Times*, September 26, 2019, https://www.nytimes.com/interactive/2019/09/26/us/politics/whistle-blower-complaint.html.

12. Whistleblower Complaint, August 12, 2019, 3.

13. Letter from Office of the Inspector General of the Intelligence Community to Joseph Maguire, Director of National Intelligence (Acting), August 26, 2019, 5. Available at "Document: Read the Whistle-Blower Complaint,"

New York Times, September 26, 2019, https://www.nytimes.com/interactive/2019/09/26/us/politics/whistle-blower-complaint.html.

14. Adoree Kim, "The Partiality Norm: Systematic Deference in the Office of Legal Counsel," *Cornell Law Review* 103, no. 3 (March 2018): 757–816, at 778.

15. Schmidt, Barnes, and Haberman, "Trump Knew of Whistle-Blower Complaint When He Released Aid to Ukraine."

16. Bruce Ackerman, *The Decline and Fall of the American Republic* (Cambridge, MA: Belknap Press of Harvard University Press, 2010), 115.

17. Memorandum from Steven A. Engel, Assistant Attorney General, to Jason Klintenic, General Counsel of the Director of National Intelligence, Re: "'Urgent Concern' Determination by the Inspector General of the Intelligence Community," Opinion of the Office of Legal Counsel, Department of Justice, September 3, 2019, 1, 5, 7, https://www.justice.gov/olc/page/file/1205151/download.

18. Julian E. Barnes, Michael S. Schmidt, and Matthew Rosenberg, "Schiff, House Intel Chairman, Got Early Account of Whistle-Blower's Accusations," *New York Times*, October 2, 2019, https://www.nytimes.com/2019/10/02/us/politics/adam-schiff-whistleblower.html.

19. Natasha Bertrand and Daniel Lippman, "The Intelligence Watchdog at the Center of Ukraine Firestorm," *Politico*, September 23, 2019, https://www.politico.com/story/2019/09/23/atkinson-trump-ukraine-whistleblower-scandal-1508594.

20. "Chairman Schiff Issues Subpoena for Whistleblower Complaint Being Unlawfully Withheld by Acting DNI from Intelligence Committees," US House of Representatives, Permanent Select Committee on Intelligence, Press Releases, September 13, 2019, https://intelligence.house.gov/news/documentsingle.aspx?DocumentID=688.

21. Li Zhou, "Even Senate Republicans Want the White House to Share a Whistleblower Report on Trump with Congress," *Vox*, September 24, 2019, https://www.vox.com/policy-and-politics/2019/9/24/20882420/mitch-mconnell-chuck-schumer-senate-resolution-whistleblower-report.

22. Katherine Tully-McManus and Kellie Mejdrich, "Whistleblower Complaint Delivered to Intel Committees, House Still Votes for Its Release," *Roll Call*, September 25, 2019, https://www.rollcall.com/2019/09/25/whistleblower-complaint-delivered-to-intel-committees-house-still-votes-for-its-release/.

23. Michael S. Schmidt, Julian E. Barnes, and Maggie Haberman, "White House Seeks Deal for Whistle-Blower to Speak to Congress," *New York*

Times, September 24, 2019, https://www.nytimes.com/2019/09/24/us/politics/trump-whistleblower-congress.html.

24. Joan E. Greve and Max Benwell, "White House Accidentally Emails Trump-Ukraine Talking Points to Democrats," *Guardian*, September 25, 2019, https://www.theguardian.com/us-news/2019/sep/25/republican-ukraine-talking-points-email-accident-what-to-say.

25. Justin Baragona, "White House Adviser Stephen Miller: 'The President of the United States Is the Whistleblower,'" *Daily Beast*, September 29, 2019, https://www.thedailybeast.com/trump-advisor-stephen-miller-the-president-of-the-united-states-is-the-whistleblower.

26. Paul LeBlanc, "Trump Says He Wants to Meet Whistleblower: 'I Deserve to Meet My Accuser,'" *CNN*, September 30, 2019, https://www.cnn.com/2019/09/29/politics/trump-impeachment-inquiry-whistleblower-complaint-adam-schiff/index.html; Maggie Haberman and Katie Rogers, "Trump Attacks Whistle-Blower's Sources and Alludes to Punishment for Spies," *New York Times*, September 26, 2019, https://www.nytimes.com/2019/09/26/us/politics/trump-whistle-blower-spy.html.

27. @realDonaldTrump, October 14, 2019, 6:39 AM, Twitter, https://twitter.com/realDonaldTrump/status/1183693718500659200.

28. Salvador Rizzo, "Schiff's Claim That the Whistleblower Has a 'Statutory Right' to Anonymity," *Washington Post*, November 20, 2019, https://www.washingtonpost.com/politics/2019/11/20/schiffs-claim-that-whistleblower-has-statutory-right-anonymity/.

29. Barnes, Schmidt, and Rosenberg, "Schiff, House Intel Chairman, Got Early Account of Whistle-Blower's Accusations."

30. Maggie Haberman and Michael S. Schmidt, "Trump Has Considered Firing Intelligence Community Inspector General," *New York Times*, November 12, 2019, https://www.nytimes.com/2019/11/12/us/politics/trump-michael-atkinson-inspector-general.html.

31. "CIGIE Letter to the Office of Legal Counsel (OLC) in Response to OLC Opinion on a Whistleblower Disclosure," Council of the Inspectors General on Integrity and Efficiency, October 22, 2019, 4, 1, https://ignet.gov/sites/default/files/files/CIGIE_Letter_to_OLC_Whistleblower_Disclosure.pdf.

32. Ackerman, *Decline and Fall*, ch. 4.

33. "Nancy Pelosi's Statement on Impeachment: 'The President Must Be Held Accountable,'" *New York Times*, September 24, 2019, https://www.nytimes.com/2019/09/24/us/politics/nancy-pelosi-statement-impeachment.html.

34. "If that perfect phone call with the President of Ukraine Isn't considered appropriate, then no future President can EVER again speak to another foreign leader!"@realDonaldTrump, September 27, 2019, 11:24 AM, Twitter, https://twitter.com/realdonaldtrump/status/1177604833538392065.

35. Michael D. Shear and Katie Rogers, "Mulvaney Says, Then Denies, That Trump Held Back Ukraine Aid as Quid Pro Quo," *New York Times*, October 17, 2019, https://www.nytimes.com/2019/10/17/us/politics/mick-mulvaney-trump-ukraine.html.

36. Peter Baker, "Trump's Sweeping Case against Impeachment Is a Political Strategy," *New York Times*, October 9, 2019, https://www.nytimes.com/2019/10/09/us/politics/trump-case-against-impeachment.html.

37. @realDonaldTrump, October 1, 2019, 7:41 PM, Twitter, https://twitter.com/realDonaldTrump/status/1179179573541511176.

38. Nahal Toosi, "The Revenge of the State Department," *Politico*, October 20, 2019, https://www.politico.com/news/2019/10/20/state-department-trump-051564.

39. "Read the White House Letter in Response to the Impeachment Inquiry," *New York Times*, October 8, 2019, 5, 7, https://www.nytimes.com/interactive/2019/10/08/us/politics/white-house-letter-impeachment.html.

40. Jeremy Stahl, "DOJ: If Watergate Happened Today, We'd Block Evidence from Congress," *Slate*, October 8, 2019, https://slate.com/news-and-politics/2019/10/doj-blocks-watergate-impeachment-evidence-congress.html.

41. "Read Alexander Vindman's Prepared Opening Statement from the Impeachment Hearing," *New York Times*, November 19, 2019, https://www.nytimes.com/2019/11/19/us/politics/vindman-statement-testimony.html.

42. Toosi, "The Revenge of the State Department."

43. Jeffrey Gettleman, "State Dept. Dissent Cable on Trump's Ban Draws 1,000 Signatures," *New York Times*, January 31, 2017, https://www.nytimes.com/2017/01/31/world/americas/state-dept-dissent-cable-trump-immigration-order.html. This right to dissent is codified in the *Foreign Affairs Manual*. David T. Jones, "Advise and Dissent: The Diplomat as Protester," *Foreign Service Journal* (April 2000): 36–40.

44. Bill Chappell, "'I'm the Only One That Matters', Trump Says of State Dept. Job Vacancies," *NPR*, November 3, 2017, https://www.npr.org/sections/thetwo-way/2017/11/03/561797675/im-the-only-one-that-matters-trump-says-of-state-dept-job-vacancies.

45. Toosi, "The Revenge of the State Department."

46. "Read George Kent's Prepared Opening Statement from the Impeachment Hearing," *New York Times*, November 13, 2019, https://www.nytimes.com/2019/11/13/us/politics/george-kent-opening-statement-impeachment.html; Vanessa Friedman, "George Kent and the Bow Tie of History," *New York Times*, November 13, 2019, https://www.nytimes.com/2019/11/13/style/george-kent-bow-tie.html.

47. Sharon LaFraniere, Nicholas Fandos, and Andrew E. Kramer, "Ukraine Envoy Says She Was Told Trump Wanted Her Out over Lack of Trust," *New York Times*, October 11, 2019, https://www.nytimes.com/2019/10/11/us/politics/marie-yovanovitch-trump-impeachment.html.

48. Peter Baker, "Key Takeaways from Marie Yovanovitch's Hearing in the Impeachment Inquiry," *New York Times*, November 15, 2019, https://www.nytimes.com/2019/11/15/us/politics/impeachment-hearings.html.

49. Peter Baker, Lara Jakes, Julian E. Barnes, Sharon LaFraniere, and Edward Wong, "Trump's War on the 'Deep State' Turns against Him," *New York Times*, October 23, 2019, https://www.nytimes.com/2019/10/23/us/politics/trump-deep-state-impeachment.html; Toosi, "The Revenge of the State Department."

50. Nicholas Fandos and Michael S. Schmidt, "Gordon Sondland, EU Envoy, Testifies Trump Delegated Ukraine Policy to Giuliani," *New York Times*, October 17, 2019, https://www.nytimes.com/2019/10/17/us/politics/gordon-sondland-testimony.html.

51. Nicholas Fandoss and Michael S. Schmidt, "White House Signals It Won't Cooperate with Impeachment Inquiry," *New York Times*, October 8, 2019, https://www.nytimes.com/2019/10/08/us/politics/sondland-trump-ukraine-impeach.html.

52. Michael S. Schmidt, "Sondland Updates Impeachment Testimony, Describing Ukraine Quid pro Quo," *New York Times*, November 5, 2019, https://www.nytimes.com/2019/11/05/us/politics/impeachment-trump.html.

53. "Read Gordon Sondland's Opening Statement," *New York Times*, November 20, 2019, 14, 4, https://www.nytimes.com/interactive/2019/11/20/us/politics/gordon-sondland-opening-statement-ukraine.html.

54. "Read the Ukraine Envoy's Statement to Impeachment Inquiry," *New York Times*, October 22, 2019, 4, 12, https://www.nytimes.com/interactive/2019/10/22/us/politics/william-taylor-ukraine-testimony.html.

55. Julia Arciga, "White House: Bill Taylor Testimony Part of a 'Coordinated Smear Campaign' by 'Radical Unelected Bureaucrats,'" *Daily Beast*, October 22, 2019, https://www.thedailybeast.com/

white-house-bill-taylor-testimony-part-of-a-coordinated-smear-campaign-by-radical-unelected-bureaucrats.

56. *Congressional Record*, 116th Congress, 2nd Session (January 21, 2020), S320.

57. James Madison, "The Federalist No. 51" [February 6, 1788], in *The Federalist*, ed. Terence Ball (New York: Cambridge University Press, 2003), 252.

58. *Congressional Record*, 116th Congress, 2nd Session (January 21, 2020), S378.

59. *Congressional Record*, 116th Congress, 2nd Session (January 21, 2020), S291.

60. *Congressional Record*, 116th Congress, 2nd Session (January 21, 2020), S317.

61. *Congressional Record*, 116th Congress, 2nd Session (January 21, 2020), S385.

62. *Congressional Record*, 116th Congress, 2nd Session (January 29, 2020), S650.

63. Kelsey Snell, "McConnell: 'I'm Not Impartial' about Impeachment," *NPR*, December 17, 2019, https://www.npr.org/2019/12/17/788924966/mcconnell-i-m-not-impartial-about-impeachment.

64. Emily Cochrane: "Republicans' Emerging Defense: Trump's Actions Were Bad, but Not Impeachable," *New York Times*, February 2, 2020, https://www.nytimes.com/2020/02/02/us/politics/trump-impeachment-republicans.html.

65. "Remarks by President Trump to the Nation," White House, February 6, 2020, https://www.whitehouse.gov/briefings-statements/remarks-president-trump-nation/.

66. James Politi and Kadhim Shubber, "Donald Trump Emboldened to Seek Vengeance after Acquittal," *Financial Times*, February 13, 2020, https://www.ft.com/content/8ac4aeba-4dea-11ea-95a0-43d18ec715f5.

67. Sean D. Naylor, "'We're Not Some Banana Republic': National Security Adviser Defends Removal of Trump Impeachment Witness from White House Job," *Yahoo News*, February 11, 2020, https://news.yahoo.com/national-security-advisor-defends-removal-of-trump-impeachment-witness-white-house-jobs-022643587.html.

68. Alexander S. Vindman, "Alexander Vindman: Coming Forward Ended My Career. I Still Believe Doing What's Right Matters." *Washington Post*, August 1, 2020, https://www.washingtonpost.com/opinions/2020/08/01/alexander-vindman-retiring-oped/; Eric Schmitt and Helene Cooper,

"Army Officer Who Clashed with Trump over Impeachment Is Set to Retire," *New York Times*, July 8, 2020, https://www.nytimes.com/2020/07/08/us/politics/vindman-trump-ukraine-impeachment.html.

69. Helene Cooper, "John Rood, Top Defense Official, Latest to Be Ousted after Impeachment Saga," *New York Times*, February 19, 2020, https://www.nytimes.com/2020/02/19/us/politics/john-rood-trump.html.

70. Natasha Bertrand and Andrew Desiderio, "Trump Fires Intelligence Community Watchdog Who Defied Him on Whistleblower Complaint," *Politico*, April 3, 2020, https://www.politico.com/news/2020/04/03/trump-fires-intelligence-community-inspector-general-164287.

71. Matt Zapotosky, "Barr Says He Supports Trump's Ouster of Intelligence Watchdog Who Received Whistleblower Complaint That Helped Spark Impeachment," *Washington Post*, April 10, 2020, https://www.washingtonpost.com/national-security/barr-says-he-supports-trumps-ouster-of-intelligence-watchdog-who-received-whistleblower-complaint-that-helped-spark-impeachment/2020/04/10/8064386a-7aa8-11ea-9bee-c5bf9d2e3288_story.html.

72. Ed Pilkington, "Ousted US Intelligence Inspector General Urges Whistleblowers Not to Be 'Silenced' by Trump," *Guardian*, April 6, 2020, https://www.theguardian.com/us-news/2020/apr/06/ousted-us-intelligence-inspector-general-urges-others-to-speak-out-and-defend-whistleblowers.

73. Bertrand and Desiderio, "Trump Fires Intelligence Community Watchdog Who Defied Him on Whistleblower Complaint."

74. Andrew Desiderio, "Trump Defends Firing 'Terrible' Intel Community Watchdog as Republicans Question Sacking," *Politico*, April 4, 2020, https://www.politico.com/news/2020/04/04/chuck-grassley-intel-community-watchdog-firing-164831.

75. Rebecca Falconer, "Bipartisan Group of Senators Demands Explanation from Trump on IG Firing," *Axios*, April 9, 2020, https://www.axios.com/chuck-grassley-bipartisan-letter-trump-ig-firing-603f2b09-99fe-4117-baf3-dd8a9d89bf93.html.

76. Melissa Quinn, "Ousted State Department IG Tells Congress Top Officials Knew of Probes into Pompeo," *CBS News*, June 4, 2020, https://www.cbsnews.com/news/state-department-inspector-general-steve-linick-pompeo-conduct-top-officials/.

77. Kyle Cheney, "Trump's Drive against Watchdogs Faces Constitutional Reckoning," *Politico*, May 24, 2020, https://www.politico.com/news/2020/05/24/trump-inspectors-general-constitution-275359.

78. Jeff Stein and Devlin Barrett: "Trump Takes Immediate Step to Try to Curb New Inspector General's Autonomy, as Battle over Stimulus Oversight Begins," *Washington Post*, March 28, 2020, https://www.washingtonpost.com/business/2020/03/27/trump-coronavirus-inspector-general/.

79. Ben Kesling, Andrew Restuccia, and Dustin Volz, "Trump Removes Watchdog Who Heads Panel Overseeing Pandemic Stimulus Spending," *Wall Street Journal*, April 7, 2020, https://www.wsj.com/articles/trump-removes-acting-defense-department-inspector-general-11586277895.

80. Peter Baker, "Trump Moves to Replace Watchdog Who Identified Critical Medical Shortages," *New York Times*, May 1, 2020, https://www.nytimes.com/2020/05/01/us/politics/trump-health-department-watchdog.html; Christi A. Grimm, Principal Deputy Inspector General, *Hospital Experiences Responding to the COVID-19 Pandemic: Results of a National Pulse Survey March 23–27, 2020*, Report OEI-06-20-00300, Office of Inspector General, US Department of Health and Human Services, April 2020, https://oig.hhs.gov/oei/reports/oei-06-20-00300.pdf.

81. Sheryl Gay Stolberg and Nicholas Fandos, "From Afar, Congress Moves to Oversee Trump Coronavirus Response," *New York Times*, April 2, 2020, https://www.nytimes.com/2020/04/02/us/politics/coronavirus-congress-oversight-trump.html.

Chapter 10

1. Bruce Miroff, *Presidents on Political Ground: Leaders in Action and What They Face* (Lawrence: University Press of Kansas, 2016), ch. 1.

2. Jon D. Michaels, *Constitutional Coup: Privatization's Threat to the American Republic* (Cambridge, MA: Harvard University Press, 2017); Michael Lewis, *The Fifth Risk* (New York: W. W. Norton, 2018).

3. William P. Barr, "Attorney General William P. Barr Delivers the 19th Annual Barbara K. Olson Memorial Lecture at the Federalist Society's 2019 National Lawyers Convention," November 15, 2019, Office of Public Affairs, Department of Justice, https://www.justice.gov/opa/speech/attorney-general-william-p-barr-delivers-19th-annual-barbara-k-olson-memorial-lecture.

4. Charlie Savage, *Takeover: The Return of the Imperial Presidency and the Subversion of American Democracy* (Boston: Little, Brown, 2007); Suzanne Mettler and Robert C. Lieberman, *Four Threats: The Recurring Crises of American Democracy* (New York: St. Martin's Press, 2020).

5. Anonymous, *A Warning* (New York: Twelve, 2019), 19, 120.

6. Susan Hennessy and Benjamin Wittes, "The Disintegration of the American Presidency," *The Atlantic*, January 21, 2020, https://www.theatlantic.com/ideas/archive/2020/01/trump-myth-unitary-executive/605062/.

7. @realDonaldTrump, March 9, 2020, 7:39 AM, Twitter, https://twitter.com/realdonaldtrump/status/1236979946175725568.

8. Peter M. Shane, *Madison's Nightmare: How Executive Power Threatens American Democracy* (Chicago: University of Chicago Press, 2009).

9. For Max Weber's discussion of the "ethic of responsibility," see "Politics as a Vocation" [1918], in *From Max Weber: Essays in Sociology*, eds. H. H. Gerth and C. Wright Mills (New York: Oxford University Press, 1946), 77–128.

10. Eric A. Posner and Adrian Vermeule, *The Executive Unbound: After the Madisonian Republic* (New York: Oxford University Press, 2010).

11. Desmond King, "Forceful Federalism against American Racial Inequality," *Government and Opposition* 52, no. 2 (April 2017): 356–382; Stephen Skowronek and Karen Orren, "The Adaptability Paradox: Constitutional Resilience and Principles of Good Government in Twenty-First Century America," *Perspectives on Politics* 18, no. 2 (June 2020): 354–369.

12. James L. Sundquist, *The Decline and Resurgence of Congress* (Washington, DC: Brookings Institution, 1981).

13. Jeffrey Mervis, "Scientific Integrity Bill Advances in US House with Bipartisan Support," *Science*, October 17, 2019, https://www.sciencemag.org/news/2019/10/scientific-integrity-bill-advances-us-house-bipartisan-support.

14. Paul Kane, "Democrats Seek to Rein In the Contact between White House, Justice Department on Probes," *Washington Post*, June 19, 2019, https://www.washingtonpost.com/powerpost/democrats-seek-to-rein-in-the-contact-between-white-house-justice-department-on-probes/2019/06/19/4b38bf86-92b8-11e9-b58a-a6a9afaa0e3e_story.html.

15. James A. Gagliano, "It's Not Just Barr—We Need a New Way to Keep Attorneys General Nonpartisan," *CNN*, November 4, 2019, https://www.cnn.com/2019/11/04/opinions/barr-new-way-keep-attorneys-general-nonpartisan-gagliano/index.html.

16. Kyle Cheney, "Democrats Seek Protections for Inspectors General after Trump Attacks," *Politico*, April 10, 2020, https://www.politico.com/news/2020/04/10/democrats-seek-protections-for-inspectors-general-after-trump-attacks-178785; Kyle Cheney, "A Watchdog out of Trump's Grasp Unleashes Wave of Coronavirus Audits," *Politico*, April 20, 2020, https://www.politico.com/news/2020/04/20/watchdog-trump-coronavirus-audits-192272.

17. Cass R. Sunstein, "Imagine That Donald Trump Has Almost No Control over Justice," *New York Times*, February 20, 2020, https://www.nytimes.com/2020/02/20/opinion/sunday/trump-barr-justice-department.html. On measures to make DOJ more independent, see also Melissa Mortazavi, "Institutional Independence: Lawyers and the Administrative State," *Fordham Law Review* 87, no. 5 (April 2019): 1937–1964; Jed Handelsman Shugerman, "Professionals, Politicos, and Crony Attorneys General: A Historical Sketch of the US Attorney General as a Case for Structural Independence," *Fordham Law Review* 87, no. 5 (April 2019): 1965–1994; Andrew Kent, "Congress and the Independence of Federal Law Enforcement," *UC Davis Law Review* 52, no. 4 (April 2019): 1927–1997.

18. Thomas E. Mann and Norman J. Ornstein, *The Broken Branch: How Congress Is Failing America and How to Get It Back on Track* (New York: Oxford University Press, 2006).

19. *Seila Law LLC v. Consumer Financial Protection Bureau*, 591 U.S. ___ (2020).

20. John Quincy Adams called it "the most complicated government on the face of the globe." *A Discourse on the Constitution of the United States* (New York: Berford, 1848), 115.

21. Nathan Persily, ed., *Solutions to Political Polarization in America* (New York: Cambridge University Press, 2015); Frances McCall Rosenbluth and Ian Shapiro, *Responsible Parties: Saving Democracy from Itself* (New Haven, CT: Yale University Press, 2018); Daniel Schlozman and Sam Rosenfeld, "The Hollow Parties," in *Can America Govern Itself?*, eds. Frances E. Lee and Nolan McCarty (New York: Cambridge University Press, 2019), 120–152.

22. Dwight Waldo, *The Administrative State: A Study of the Political Theory of American Public Administration* (New York: Ronald Press, 1948); Christopher Hood, "A Public Management for All Seasons?," *Public Administration* 69, no. 1 (March 1991): 3–19.

23. For a proposal for constitutional reform which is attuned to the political problem we are raising, see Brian J. Cook, *The Fourth Branch: Reconstructing the Administrative State for the Commercial Republic* (Lawrence: University Press of Kansas, 2021).

24. Richard P. Nathan, *The Plot That Failed: Nixon and the Administrative Presidency* (New York: Wiley, 1975).

Afterword

1. Lisa Rein, "The Federal Government Puts Out a 'Help Wanted' Notice as Biden Seeks to Undo Trump Cuts," *Washington Post*, May 21, 2021, https://www.washingtonpost.com/politics/2021/05/21/biden-trump-government-rebuilding/.

2. Rudy Mehrbani, "Biden Inherited a Broken Government. Attracting a New Generation of Civil Servants Won't Be Easy," Monkey Cage, *Washington Post*, October 25, 2021, https://www.washingtonpost.com/politics/2021/10/25/biden-inherited-broken-government-attracting-new-generation-civil-servants-wont-be-easy/. On the conditions under which federal employees are more likely to leave their jobs, see Mark D. Richardson, "Politicization and Expertise: Exit, Effort, and Investment," *Journal of Politics* 81, no. 3 (July 2019): 878–891.

3. Joe Davidson, "Top Civil Servants Leaving Trump Administration at a Quick Clip," *Washington Post*, September 9, 2018, https://www.washingtonpost.com/politics/2018/09/10/top-civil-servants-leaving-trump-administration-quick-clip/.

4. Rein, "The Federal Government Puts Out a 'Help Wanted' Notice as Biden Seeks to Undo Trump Cuts"; Eric Kratz, "The Number of Top Career Execs Leaving Government Nearly Doubled in Trump's First Year," *Government Executive*, September 5, 2018, https://www.govexec.com/management/2018/09/number-top-career-execs-leaving-government-nearly-doubled-trumps-first-year/151033/; Kathleen M. Doherty, David E. Lewis, and Scott Limbocker, "Executive Control and Turnover in the Senior Executive Service," *Journal of Public Administration Research and Theory* 29, no. 2 (April 2019): 159–174. On agency ideologies, see Joshua D. Clinton, Anthony Bertelli, Christian R. Grose, David E. Lewis, and David C. Nixon, "Separated Powers in the United States: The Ideology of Agencies, Presidents, and Congress," *American Journal of Political Science* 56, no. 2 (April 2012): 341–354.

5. Jody Freeman and Sharon Jacobs, "Structural Deregulation," *Harvard Law Review* 135, no. 2 (December 2021): 585–665.

6. Rein, "The Federal Government Puts Out a 'Help Wanted' Notice as Biden Seeks to Undo Trump Cuts."

7. Glenn Thrush, "Biden's First Task at Housing Agency: Rebuilding Trump-Depleted Ranks," *New York Times*, June 18, 2021, https://www.nytimes.com/2021/06/18/us/politics/biden-housing-agency-trump.html.

8. David Lazarus, "Column: $1 Fines from Consumer Agency were Common under Trump. That's about to Change," *Los Angeles Times*, January 11, 2021, https://www.latimes.com/business/story/2021-01-11/column-cfpb-biden.

9. Kathryn Dunn Tenpas, quoted in Megan Cassella and Alice Miranda Ollstein, "Biden Confronts Staffing Crisis at Federal Agencies," *Politico*, November 12, 2020, https://www.politico.com/news/2020/11/12/shrinking-workforce-can-hurt-biden-436164.

10. Mehrbani, "Biden Inherited a Broken Government. Attracting a New Generation of Civil Servants Won't Be Easy."

11. Rein, "The Federal Government Puts Out a 'Help Wanted' Notice as Biden Seeks to Undo Trump Cuts."

12. *Bureau of Land Management: Better Workforce Planning and Data Would Help Mitigate the Effects of Recent Staff Vacancies*, U.S. Government Accountability Office, Report GAO-22-104247, November 2021, 15, https://www.gao.gov/assets/gao-22-104247.pdf. Joshua Partlow, "Bureau of Land Management Headquarters to Return to D.C., Reversing Trump Decision," *Washington Post*, September 17, 2021, https://www.washingtonpost.com/climate-environment/2021/09/17/bureau-land-management-headquarters-return-dc-reversing-trump-decision/; Joshua Partlow, "After Trump, An Agency Key to Biden's Climate Agenda Tries to Rebuild," *Washington Post*, October 29, 2021, https://www.washingtonpost.com/climate-environment/2021/10/29/bureau-land-management-grand-junction/.

13. Coral Davenport, Lisa Friedman, and Christopher Flavelle, "Biden's Climate Plans are Stunted after Dejected Experts Fled Trump," *New York Times*, August 1, 2021, https://www.nytimes.com/2021/08/01/climate/biden-scientists-shortage-climate.html.

14. Rebecca Hamlin, "Trump's Immigration Legacy," *The Forum* 19, no. 1 (2021): 97–116.

15. Reade Levinson, Kristina Cooke, and Mica Rosenberg, "Special Report: How Trump Administration Left Indelible Mark on U.S. Immigration Courts," *Reuters*, March 8, 2021, https://www.reuters.com/article/us-usa-immigration-trump-court-special-r/special-report-how-trump-administration-left-indelible-mark-on-u-s-immigration-courts-idUSKBN2B0179.

16. IJs can be removed for cause by the attorney general without a hearing; they are subject to an initial two-year probationary period during which they can be removed without cause; and they can be reassigned by the Executive Office of Immigration Review. Amit Jain, "Bureaucrats in Robes: Immigration Judges and the Trappings of Courts," *Georgetown Immigration Law Journal* 33, no. 2 (Winter 2019): 261–326, at 275–276.

17. Josh Gerstein and Sabrina Rodriguez, "Biden Administration Replaces Top Immigration Court Official," *Politico*, January 27, 2021, https://

www.politico.com/news/2021/01/27/biden-replaces-immigration-court-463053; Erich Wagner, "Biden Admin. Suspends Immigration Judge Quotas, Prompting Similar Requests Elsewhere," *Government Executive*, October 26, 2021, https://www.govexec.com/workforce/2021/10/biden-admin-suspends-immigration-judge-quotas-prompting-similar-requests-elsewhere/186396/.

18. Eric Katz, "Biden Proposes Dramatic Hiring Surge in Asylum Workforce as Part of Immigration Overhaul," *Government Executive*, August 18, 2021, https://www.govexec.com/workforce/2021/08/biden-proposes-dramatic-hiring-surge-asylum-workforce-part-immigration-overhaul/184647/.

19. In December 2021 Trump took credit for the vaccine and its efficacy, but by then vaccine resistance had become a staple of Trumpism. Philip Bump, "Trump's Message on Vaccines Isn't as Powerful as Trumpism's Message," *Washington Post*, December 21, 2021, https://www.washingtonpost.com/politics/2021/12/21/trumps-message-vaccines-isnt-powerful-trumpisms-message/; Sam Dorman, "DeSantis Says Florida 'Chose Freedom over Fauci-ism,' Urges Conservatives to Have a 'Backbone,'" *Fox News*, July 15, 2021, https://www.foxnews.com/politics/ron-desantis-fauci-freedom-speech.

20. Philip Bump, "The Two Halves of the Pandemic," *Washington Post*, December 2, 2021, https://www.washingtonpost.com/politics/2021/12/01/two-halves-pandemic/; Daniel Wood and Geoff Brumfiel, "Pro-Trump Counties Now Have Far Higher COVID Death Rates. Misinformation is to Blame," *NPR*, December 5, 2021, https://www.npr.org/sections/health-shots/2021/12/05/1059828993/data-vaccine-misinformation-trump-counties-covid-death-rate. The pandemic also had a disproportionate impact on communities of color, especially during Wave One. Gerda Hooijer and Desmond King, "The Racialized Pandemic: Wave One of COVID-19 and the Reproduction of Global North Inequalities," *Perspectives on Politics* 20, no. 2 (June 2022), https://doi.org/10.1017/S153759272100195X.

21. Stephen Skowronek, *Presidential Leadership in Political Time: Reprise and Reappraisal*, 3rd ed. (Lawrence, KS: University Press of Kansas, 2020), ch. 7.

22. Jacob Finkel, "Trump's Power Won't Peak for Another 20 years," *The Atlantic*, April 10, 2021, https://www.theatlantic.com/ideas/archive/2021/04/trump-circuit-court-judges/618533/; Amanda Hollis-Brusky and Celia Parry, "'In the Mold of Justice Scalia': The Contours & Consequences of the Trump Judiciary," *The Forum* 19, no. 1 (2021): 117–142.

23. Micah Schwartzman and David Fontana, "Trump Picked the Youngest Judges to Sit on the Federal Bench. Your Move, Biden," *Washington Post*, February 16, 2021, https://www.washingtonpost.com/outlook/2021/02/16/court-appointments-age-biden-trump-judges-age/.

24. Benjamin Swasey and Connie Hanzhang Jin, "Narrow Wins in These Key States Powered Biden to the Presidency," *NPR*, December 2, 2020, https://www.npr.org/2020/12/02/940689086/narrow-wins-in-these-key-states-powered-biden-to-the-presidency.

25. The transparency rule was an example of a "meta rule" which "may weaken or eliminate an agency's ability to carry out statutory mandates." David L. Noll, "Administrative Sabotage," *Michigan Law Review,* forthcoming, 37.

26. Rachel Frazin, "Court Tosses Trump EPA's 'Secret Science' Rule," *The Hill*, February 1, 2021, https://thehill.com/policy/energy-environment/536787-court-tosses-trump-epas-secret-science-rule.

27. Zachary Cohen and Jeremy Herb, "Intelligence Report Contradicts Claims by Trump and His Team on China Election Interference," *CNN*, March 17, 2021, https://www.cnn.com/2021/03/17/politics/us-intel-report-trump-china-election-interference-claims/index.html; Alan Feuer, "A Retired Colonel's Unlikely Role in Pushing Baseless Election Claims," *New York Times*, December 21, 2021, https://www.nytimes.com/2021/12/21/us/politics/phil-waldron-jan-6.html.

28. Zachary Cohen, "Whistle blower Trump Appointees of Downplaying Russian Interference and White Supremacist Threat," *CNN*, September 9, 2020, https://www.cnn.com/2020/09/09/politics/dhs-whistleblower-white-supremacist-threat/index.html.

29. Jonathan Swan and Alayna Treene, "Scoop: Trump's Post-Election Execution List," *Axios*, October 25, 2020, https://www.axios.com/trump-firing-wray-haspel-esper-088cbd70-3524-4625-91f1-dbc985767c71.html.

30. Michael Wines, "At the Census Bureau, a Technical Memo Raises Alarms Over Politics," *New York Times*, August 6, 2020, https://www.nytimes.com/2020/08/06/us/2020-census-undocumented-immigrants.html.

31. Emily Bazelon and Michael Wines, "How the Census Bureau Stood Up to Donald Trump's Meddling," *New York Times*, August 12, 2021, https://www.nytimes.com/2021/08/12/sunday-review/census-redistricting-trump-immigrants.html; Adam Liptak, "Justices Put Off Ruling on Trump Plan for Unauthorized Immigrants and Census," *New York Times*, December 18, 2020, https://www.nytimes.com/2020/12/18/us/supreme-court-census.html; Joseph R. Biden, "Executive Order 13986—Ensuring

a Lawful and Accurate Enumeration and Apportionment Pursuant to the Decennial Census," January 20, 2021, *The American Presidency Project*, https://www.presidency.ucsb.edu/documents/executive-order-13986-ensuring-lawful-and-accurate-enumeration-and-apportionment-pursuant.

32. Jacob Bogage, "Postal Service Workers Quietly Resist DeJoy's Changes with Eye on Election," *Washington Post*, September 29, 2020, https://www.washingtonpost.com/business/2020/09/29/usps-workers-election-mail/.

33. Emily Cochrane, Hailey Fuchs, Kenneth P. Vogel, and Jessica Silver-Greenberg, "Decision to Halt Postal Changes Does Little to Quell Election Concerns," *New York Times*, August 19, 2020, https://www.nytimes.com/2020/08/19/business/economy/postal-service-changes-dejoy.html; Jacob Bogage and Christopher Ingraham, "USPS Processed 150,000 Ballots After Election Day, Jeopardizing Thousands of Votes," *Washington Post*, November 6, 2020, https://www.washingtonpost.com/business/2020/11/05/usps-late-ballots-election/.

34. Aaron Mak and Mark Joseph Stern, "Why Biden Can't Fire Postmaster General Louis DeJoy," *Slate*, February 8, 2021, https://slate.com/news-and-politics/2021/02/biden-cannot-fire-usps-louis-dejoy.html.

35. Donald P. Moynihan, "Public Management for Populists: Trump's Schedule F Executive Order and the Future of the Civil Service," *Public Administration Review*, 82, no. 1 (January/February 2022): 174–178, at 174.

36. Lisa Rein, "Trump's 11th-Hour Assault on the Civil Service By Stripping Job Protections Runs Out of Time," *Washington Post*, January 18, 2021, https://www.washingtonpost.com/politics/trump-civil-service-biden/2021/01/18/5daf34c4-59b3-11eb-b8bd-ee36b1cd18bf_story.html.

37. Erich Wagner, "The Fine Print of Biden's Directive Rescinding Trump-Era Workforce Orders," *Government Executive*, January 25, 2021, https://www.govexec.com/management/2021/01/fine-print-bidens-directive-rescinding-trump-era-workforce-orders/171620/.

38. Moynihan, "Public Management for Populists," 174, 177.

39. Bethany A. Davis Noll, "'Tired of Winning': Judicial Review of Regulatory Policy in the Trump Era," *Administrative Law Review* 73, no. 2 (2021): 353–419; "Roundup: Trump-Era Agency Policy in the Courts," Institute for Policy Integrity, New York University School of Law, https://policyintegrity.org/trump-court-roundup.

40. Bethany Davis Noll, "Trump's Regulatory 'Whack-a-Mole,'" *Politico*, April 10, 2019, https://www.politico.com/agenda/story/2019/04/10/trump-federal-regulations-000890/. See also Sharece Thrower, "Policy

Disruption Through Regulatory Delay in the Trump Administration," *Presidential Studies Quarterly* 48, no. 3 (September 2018): 517–536.

41. Charlie Savage and Adam Goldman, "Trump-Era Special Counsel Secures Indictment of Lawyer for Firm With Democratic Ties," *New York Times*, September 16, 2021, https://www.nytimes.com/2021/09/16/us/politics/michael-sussmann-indictment-durham-investigation.html.

42. Zachary Cohen, Evan Perez, and Katelyn Polantz, "Russian Analyst Who Was Source for Steele Dossier Charged with Lying to FBI," *CNN*, November 4, 2021, https://www.cnn.com/2021/11/04/politics/igor-danchenko-arrested/index.html.

43. "All the People President Trump Pardoned on His Way Out of Office," *Washington Post*, January 20, 2021, https://www.washingtonpost.com/politics/2020/12/23/trump-pardons-list/.

44. Katelyn Polantz and Caroline Kelly, "Barr Says Voting by Mail is 'Playing with Fire," *CNN*, September 2, 2020, https://www.cnn.com/2020/09/02/politics/barr-mail-in-voting-playing-with-fire-situation-room/index.html.

45. Jonathan D. Karl, "Inside William Barr's Breakup With Trump," *The Atlantic*, June 27, 2021, https://www.theatlantic.com/politics/archive/2021/06/william-barrs-trump-administration-attorney-general/619298/; Dartunorro Clark and Ken Dilanian, "Justice Department's Election Crimes Chief Resigns after Barr Allows Prosecutors to Investigate Voter Fraud Claims," *NBC News*, November 9, 2020, https://www.nbcnews.com/politics/2020-election/doj-s-election-crimes-chief-resigns-after-barr-directs-prosecutors-n1247220. On the lack of evidence for claims of election fraud, see Andrew C. Eggers, Haritz Garro, and Justin Grimmer, "No Evidence for Systematic Voter Fraud: A Guide to Statistical Claims about the 2020 Election," *Proceedings of the National Academy of Sciences* 118, no. 45 (2021): e2103619118.

46. Carol Leonnig and Philip Rucker, "'I'm Getting the Word Out': Inside the Feverish Mind of Donald Trump Two Months After Leaving the White House," *Vanity Fair*, July 19, 2021, https://www.vanityfair.com/news/2021/07/the-feverish-mind-of-trump-after-leaving-the-white-house.

47. Katie Benner, "Trump Pressed Official to Wield Dept. to Back Election Claims," *New York Times*, June 15, 2021, https://www.nytimes.com/2021/06/15/us/politics/trump-justice-department-election.html.

48. Andrew Desiderio, "Trump Pressured DOJ to Call Election 'Corrupt,' Ex-Official Wrote," *Politico*, July 30, 2021, https://www.politico.com/news/2021/07/30/trump-doj-corrupt-election-501775.

49. Devlin Barrett, "Senate Report Gives New Details of Trump Efforts to Use Justice Dept. to Overturn Election," *Washington Post*, October 7, 2021, https://www.washingtonpost.com/national-security/durbin-report-trump-pressure-justice/2021/10/07/b51712d4-2769-11ec-8d53-67cfb452aa60_story.html.

50. Barrett, "Senate Report Gives New Details of Trump Efforts to Use Justice Dept. to Overturn Election."

51. Nick Niedzwiadek, "Jordan Tears into DOJ Officials for Hostility to Meadows' Election Fraud Inquiries," *Politico*, June 15, 2021, https://www.politico.com/news/2021/06/15/jordan-doj-meadows-election-fraud-494697.

52. Bob Woodward and Robert Costa, *Peril* (New York: Simon and Schuster, 2021), 101–102.

53. Robert Burns and Lolita C. Baldor, "Trump Fires Esper as Pentagon Chief after Election Defeat," *Associated Press*, November 9, 2020, https://apnews.com/article/election-2020-donald-trump-ap-top-news-elections-mark-esper-58adf1d272afe333562c54daba541e84.

54. Bruce Ackerman, *The Decline and Fall of the American Republic* (Cambridge, MA: Belknap Press of Harvard University Press, 2010), 49–50.

55. Woodward and Costa, *Peril*, 106–107.

56. Woodward and Costa, *Peril*, 152, xix–xxiv.

57. Dominick Mastrangelo, "Vindman Calls for Milley's Resignation: 'He Usurped Civilian Authority,'" *The Hill*, September 15, 2021, https://thehill.com/policy/defense/572330-vindman-calls-for-milleys-resignation-he-usurped-civilian-authority.

58. Nicholas Fandos, "Trump Impeached for Inciting Insurrection," *New York Times*, January 13, 2021, https://www.nytimes.com/2021/01/13/us/politics/trump-impeached.html.

59. Alayna Treene, "The Senate Acquits Trump," *Axios*, February 13, 2021, https://www.axios.com/the-senate-acquits-trump-1d4f4a6d-4d20-4af7-abfb-470a8048bceb.html.

60. Nick Niedzwiadek, "Watchdog: 13 Trump Officials Violated Hatch Act During 2020 Campaign," *Politico*, November 9, 2021, https://www.politico.com/news/2021/11/09/trump-officials-hatch-act-violated-520420.

61. Jesse R. Binnall, "Memorandum in Support of Donald J. Trump's and Donald Trump Jr.'s Motion to Dismiss," *Washington Post*, May 26, 2021, 9, 12, 10, https://www.washingtonpost.com/context/memorandum-in-

support-of-donald-j-trump-and-donald-trump-jr-motion-to-dismiss/332ff059-24c9-4f7b-a53a-4404333ffb68/.

62. Ashley Parker, Nick Miroff, Sean Sullivan, and Tyler Page, "'No End in Sight': Inside the Biden Administration's Failure to Contain the Border Surge," *Washington Post*, March 20, 2021, https://www.washingtonpost.com/politics/biden-border-surge/2021/03/20/21824e94-8818-11eb-8a8b-5cf82c3dffe4_story.html.

63. Tamara Keith, "With 28 Executive Orders Signed, President Biden Is Off to a Record Start," *NPR*, February 3, 2021, https://www.npr.org/2021/02/03/963380189/with-28-executive-orders-signed-president-biden-is-off-to-a-record-start.

64. Adam Andrzejewski, "Biden's Bloated White House Payroll Is Most Expensive in American History," *Forbes*, July 1, 2021, https://www.forbes.com/sites/adamandrzejewski/2021/07/01/bidens-white-house-payroll-is-most-expensive-in-american-history/?sh=190ea9561f7f.

65. Joseph R. Biden, "Memorandum on Modernizing Regulatory Review," January 20, 2021, *The American Presidency Project*, https://www.presidency.ucsb.edu/documents/memorandum-modernizing-regulatory-review.

66. Rebecca Beitsch, "Biden Faces Calls to Implement Day 1 Promise of Regulatory Reforms," *The Hill*, November 17, 2021, https://thehill.com/regulation/pending-regs/581958-biden-faces-calls-to-implement-day-1-promise-of-regulatory-reforms.

67. David Montgomery, "Merrick Garland Will Not Deliver Your Catharsis," *Washington Post Magazine*, July 19, 2021, https://www.washingtonpost.com/magazine/2021/07/19/merrick-garland-justice-department-catharsis/; C. Ryan Barber, "Democrats Reveal Their Criticisms and Frustrations with Biden's Attorney General Merrick Garland," *Business Insider*, November 17, 2021, https://www.businessinsider.com/merrick-garland-leadership-justice-department-frustrate-democrats-biden-white-house-2021-11; Harper Neidig and Rebecca Beitsch, "Garland Sparks Anger with Willingness to Side with Trump," *The Hill*, June 12, 2021, https://thehill.com/homenews/administration/558071-garland-sparks-anger-with-willingness-to-side-with-trump.

68. Victoria Guida, "Biden Renames Powell to Lead Fed, Risking the Left's Wrath," *Politico*, November 22, 2021, https://www.politico.com/news/2021/11/22/biden-renames-powell-to-lead-fed-risking-the-lefts-wrath-523177.

69. Scott Wong, "Progressive Leader Calls on Biden to Unilaterally Act on Agenda," *The Hill*, December 20, 2021, https://thehill.com/homenews/house/586639-progressive-leader-calls-on-biden-to-unilaterally-act-on-agenda.

70. Sarah Owermohle, "Biden's Top-Down Booster Plan Sparks Anger at FDA," *Politico*, August 31, 2021, https://www.politico.com/news/2021/08/31/biden-booster-plan-fda-508149. The FDA advisory committee member quoted is Paul Offit, a University of Pennsylvania infectious disease expert.

71. Lauren Gardner, "Departing FDA Regulators Pan Covid Boosters in Paper," *Politico*, September 13, 2021, https://www.politico.com/news/2021/09/13/fda-covid-vaccine-boosters-research-paper-511638.

72. Sara G. Miller, Reynolds Lewis, and Erika Edwards, "FDA Advisory Group Rejects Covid Boosters for Most, Limits to High-Risk Groups," *NBC News*, September 17, 2021, https://www.nbcnews.com/health/health-news/fda-advisory-group-rejects-covid-boosters-limits-high-risk-groups-rcna2074.

73. Caitlin Owens, "Booster Snafu: Shots Lagged Data by Months," *Axios*, November 23, 2021, https://www.axios.com/covid-vaccine-boosters-thanksgiving-5851be4a-79a7-423a-93bb-390d1eb7d4d3.html; Philip R. Krause and Luciana Borio, "The Biden Administration Has Been Sidelining Vaccine Experts," *Washington Post*, December 16, 2021, https://www.washingtonpost.com/outlook/2021/12/16/vaccines-fda-cdc-boosters-expert-panel/.

74. Alex Thompson and Tina Sfondeles, "Biden v. the Pentagon," *Politico*, August 30, 2021, https://www.politico.com/newsletters/west-wing-playbook/2021/08/30/biden-v-the-pentagon-494176.

75. Sarah Kolinovsky and Conor Finnegan, "Biden Says Military Withdrawal from Afghanistan Will Conclude Aug. 31," *ABC News*, July 8, 2021, https://abcnews.go.com/Politics/biden-military-withdrawal-afghanistan-conclude-aug-31/story?id=78729387.

76. Tara Copp, "Austin, Milley Say White House Was Advised to Keep Troops in Afghanistan," *Defense One*, September 28, 2021, https://www.defenseone.com/policy/2021/09/austin-milley-insist-no-one-foresaw-kabuls-quick-fall-some-senators-are-dubious/185667/; Robin Givhan, "The Limits of the Military's Best Advice," *Washington Post*, September 28, 2021, https://www.washingtonpost.com/nation/2021/09/28/limits-militarys-best-advice/.

77. Matt Viser, "Biden's Promise to Restore Competence to the Presidency Is Undercut By Chaos in Afghanistan," *Washington Post*, August 16, 2021, https://www.washingtonpost.com/politics/bidens-promise-to-restore-competence-to-the-presidency-undercut-by-chaos-in-afghanistan/2021/08/16/4feaaebc-feaf-11eb-ba7e-2cf966e88e93_story.html.

78. Tunku Varadarajan, "David Petraeus Reflects on the Afghan Debacle," *Wall Street Journal*, August 20, 2021, https://www.wsj.com/articles/biden-trump-petraeus-taliban-afghanistan-withdrawal-war-nation-building-jihadist-terrorist-11629488184.

79 Richard Haas, "The Age of America First," *Foreign Affairs*, November/December 2021, https://www.foreignaffairs.com/articles/united-states/2021-09-29/biden-trump-age-america-first.

80 Sarah Lyall, "For Some, Afghanistan Outcome Affirms a Warning: Beware the Blob," *New York Times*, September 16, 2021, https://www.nytimes.com/2021/09/16/us/politics/blob-afghanistan-withdrawal-biden.html.

81. Charlie Savage, "Proponents of Post-Trump Curbs on Executive Power Prepare New Push," *New York Times*, September 9, 2021, https://www.nytimes.com/2021/09/09/us/politics/executive-orders-trump.html.

82. Savage, "Proponents of Post-Trump Curbs on Executive Power Prepare New Push."

83. Statement of Administration Policy, H.R. 5314—Protecting Our Democracy Act, Office of Management and Budget, Executive Office of the President, December 9, 2021, https://www.whitehouse.gov/wp-content/uploads/2021/12/SAP-on-H.R.-5314-Protecting-Our-Democracy-Act.pdf.

84. *U.S. v. Anthrex*, 594 U.S. ___ (2021) (slip op., 14, 23) (Roberts, C.J., opinion of the Court), https://www.supremecourt.gov/opinions/20pdf/19-1434_ancf.pdf.

85. *Collins v. Yellen*, 594 U.S. ___ (2021) (slip op., 26) (Alito, J., opinion of the Court), https://www.supremecourt.gov/opinions/20pdf/19-422_k537.pdf.

86. *Collins v. Yellen*, 594 U.S. ___ (2021) (slip op., 32, fn 21) (Alito, J., opinion of the Court), https://www.supremecourt.gov/opinions/20pdf/19-422_k537.pdf.

87. Evan Weinberger, "CFPB Director Kraninger Resigns at Biden's Request," *Bloomberg Law*, January 20, 2021, https://www.bloomberglaw.com/bloomberglawnews/banking-law/X5QNH8SC000000.

88 Katy O'Donnell, "Biden Removes FHFA Director after Supreme Court Ruling," *Politico*, June 23, 2021, https://www.politico.com/news/2021/06/23/supreme-court-biden-fannie-mae-freddie-mac-housing-495673.

89. Lisa Rein and Anne Gearan, "Biden is Firing Some Top Trump Holdovers, But in Some Cases, His Hands May Be Tied," *Washington Post*, January 24, 2021, https://www.washingtonpost.com/politics/biden-trump-burrowing-federal/2021/01/24/a495ae76-5c02-11eb-b8bd-ee36b1cd18bf_story.html.

90. Eric Katz, "Biden Employs Aggressive Strategy to Sideline Top Career Officials at Consumer Protection Bureau," *Government Executive*, June 14, 2021, https://www.govexec.com/management/2021/06/biden-employs-aggressive-strategy-sideline-top-career-officials-consumer-protection-bureau/174711/.

91. "Trump's Spy Chiefs to Be Members of Cabinet: White House," *Reuters*, February 8, 2017, https://www.reuters.com/article/us-usa-trump-cabinet-spies/trumps-spy-chiefs-to-be-members-of-cabinet-white-house-idUSKBN15N28M; Kevin Xiao, "Independence in Intelligence: National Security Reform after 9/11," Yale University, working paper, December 2021.

92. Joe Davidson, "For Judges, Biden's Actions Are a Split Decision," *Washington Post*, July 4, 2021, https://www.washingtonpost.com/politics/for-judges-bidens-actions-are-a-split-decision/2021/07/04/3233f122-dce9-11eb-a501-0e69b5d012e5_story.html.

93. Erich Wagner, "House Panel Advances Bill to Undo Trump Order on Administrative Law Judges," *Government Executive*, July 23, 2021, https://www.govexec.com/workforce/2021/07/house-panel-advances-bill-undo-trump-order-administrative-law-judges/184002/.

94. Lisa Rein, "Biden Fires Head of Social Security Administration, a Trump Holdover Who Drew the Ire of Democrats," *Washington Post*, July 11, 2021, https://www.nytimes.com/2021/06/18/us/politics/biden-housing-agency-trump.html.

95. "Constitutionality of the Commissioner of Social Security's Tenure Protection," Slip Opinion, Office of Legal Counsel, Department of Justice, July 8, 2021, 1, 5, https://www.justice.gov/olc/file/1410736/download.

96. "Constitutionality of the Commissioner of Social Security's Tenure Protection," 15.

97. At a gathering of former Trump political appointees, Trump's former chief strategist, Steve Bannon, focused on how to ensure a next Republican president could seize control more effectively: "If you're going to take over the administrative state and deconstruct it, then you have to have shock troops prepared to take it over immediately." Jonathan Allen, "Bannon Fires Up 'Shock Troops' for Next GOP White House," *NBC News*, October 2, 2021, https://www.nbcnews.com/politics/politics-news/bannon-fires-shock-troops-next-gop-white-house-n1280591/.

98. David M. Driesen, *The Specter of Dictatorship: Judicial Enabling of Presidential Power* (Stanford, CA: Stanford University Press, 2021).

99. *Seila Law LLC v. Consumer Financial Protection Bureau*, 591 U.S. ___ (2020) (slip op., 2, 1) (Kagan, J., dissenting), https://www.supremecourt. gov/opinions/19pdf/19-7_n6io.pdf.

100. David E. Lewis, *The Politics of Presidential Appointments: Political Control and Bureaucratic Performance* (Princeton, NJ: Princeton University Press, 2008), 212–216.

101. Kent H. Barnett, "Resolving the ALJ Quandary," *Vanderbilt Law Review* 66, no. 3 (April 2013): 797–865.

102. Philip Wallach and Kevin R. Kosar, "The Case for a Congressional Regulation Office," *National Affairs*, Fall 2016, https://www.nationalaffairs. com/publications/detail/the-case-for-a-congressional-regulation-office.

103. Theodore J. Lowi, *The Personal President: Power Invested, Promise Unfulfilled* (Ithaca, NY: Cornell University Press, 1985).

104. Julia Azari, "Is the U.S. the Exception to Presidential Perils?" *Democracy and Autocracy* 19, no. 1 (April 2021): 12–16, at 15, https://connect. apsanet.org/wp-content/uploads/sites/26/2021/04/Democracy-and-Autocracy_April-2021_Constraining-Presidents.pdf.

105. Frances McCall Rosenbluth and Ian Shapiro, *Responsible Parties: Saving Democracy from Itself* (New Haven, CT: Yale University Press, 2018).

106. Along these lines, the House passed the For the People Act in March 2021, but its prospects in the Senate seem remote. Dartunorro Clark, "House Passes Sweeping Voting Rights, Ethics Bill," *NBC News*, March 3, 2021, https://www.nbcnews.com/politics/congress/house-pass

Index

This is an index to the original text. Other relevant material will be found in the Foreword and Afterword.

For the benefit of digital users, indexed terms that span two pages (e.g., 52–53) may, on occasion, appear on only one of those pages.

Tables are indicated by an italic *t* following the page number.